CO-AKC-052

The
MCSE™ Windows® 2000 Directory Services Design Cram Sheet

This Cram Sheet contains the distilled, key facts about MCSE Windows 2000 Directory Services Design. Review this information last thing before you enter the test room, paying special attention to those areas where you feel you need the most review. You can transfer any of these facts onto a blank sheet of paper before beginning the exam.

BUSINESS ANALYSIS AND REQUIREMENTS

1. Consider the following points when assessing the business:
   - Scope of the rollout
   - Organizational model
     - Centralized
     - Decentralized
     - Centralized-decentralized
   - Business priorities
   - Client computing requirements
   - LAN/WAN connectivity
     - Speed
     - Available bandwidth
   - Server and workstation distribution
   - Security requirements
   - Performance requirements

ACTIVE DIRECTORY DESIGN ELEMENTS

Forests

2. In its most basic form, a *forest* is a single domain but can contain multiple domains depending on the requirements of the business.

3. The first domain installed becomes the *forest root domain*. This domain cannot be renamed without reinstalling Active Directory.

4. Each domain added to the forest inherits a portion of its namespace from its parent domain.

5. All domains within a single forest share the following items:
   - Schema
   - Schema Admin
   - Configuration Container
   - Enterprise Admin
   - Global Catalog

6. When you're planning a forest structure, a single-forest environment is recommended. However, here are some of the business requirements that may require the creation of multiple forests:
   - Limited trusts with subsidiaries
   - Separate Global Catalogs
   - Separate schema

7. Two-way transitive trusts are automatically established between all parent and child domains within the same forest.

8. An explicit one-way trust must be defined between two forests.

Trees

9. Domains within the same tree share a contiguous namespace (that is, a child domain will inherit a portion of its namespace from its parent domain).

10. Domains requiring a unique namespace can be established as a new tree within a forest.

11. Subsidiaries within a business requiring their own Internet presence can be established as a new tree within the forest; this will allow them to still have access to forest-wide resources and information.

12. Two-way transitive trusts are automatically established between any new trees established within the forest and the forest root domain; this creates a trust path throughout the forest, making resources available forest wide.

Domains

13. Domains have the following characteristics:

    - Domains determine both the security and administrative boundaries within Active Directory.
    - Domain controllers within a domain use the multi-master replication model.
    - Domains can be nested within one another (parent–child relationship).
    - Two-way transitive trusts can be established between parent domains and child domains within the same tree.

14. When at all possible a single domain structure is recommended, but any business having any of the following requirements may result in a multiple domain structure.

    - Decentralized administration
    - Distinct administrative boundaries
    - Separate security policies
    - Separate and distinct namespaces
    - Slow physical links

15. Table 1 summarizes the security groups available in Windows 2000.

Table 1   Windows 2000 security groups.

Group Type	Membership	Scope
Local	Can contain user accounts on the local computer.	Local groups are used to assign user permissions on a local computer.
Global	Can contain user accounts from the local domain.	Global groups are used to assign user permissions to resources throughout the forest.
Domain local	Can contain user accounts and global groups from any domain within the forest.	Domain local groups are used to assign permissions to resources within the domain where the group is created.
Universal	Can contain other universal groups, global groups, or user accounts from any domain in the forest.	Universal groups are used to assign permissions to resources throughout the forest.

Organizational Units

16. Organizational Units (OUs) are container objects used to organize objects within a domain.

17. The OU structure that's designed should be based on the business' current administrative model. This way, the business can continue to delegate authority in such a way that meets its needs.

Sites

18. Sites are created within Active Directory to optimize replication.

19. Sites are groups of IP subnets connected by high-speed reliable links; a thorough assessment of the physical network will determine which IP subnets should be grouped together.

20. Sites are used to control the following traffic-generating events:

    - User authentication
    - Controlled replication
    - Site-aware applications

21. Keep the following points in mind when planning site boundaries:

    - Create a site for each group of subnets connected by a fast, reliable link.
    - A single site is usually recommended for a single-LAN environment.
    - Create separate sites for those IP subnets connected by slow, unreliable, heavily used links.

22. Site links are created between sites. The site links are transitive by default; therefore, if a site link is defined between sites A and B as well as between sites B and C, it is assumed that sites A and C can communicate.

23. For those networks that are not fully routable, the transitiveness of site links can be turned off and site link bridges can be created to establish a replication path.

24. Several configurable options are available for site links. Table 2 summarizes the options used to control replication.

Table 2   Replication control.

Option	Description
Transport	This is the method for transferring data between two sites. RPC or SMTP can be used.
Schedule	This specifies the time when replication can occur over the link.
Cost	This is the value assigned to the link. When multiple links exist, the link with the lowest cost is tried first.
Interval	This specifies how often during the scheduled times a site link can be used to check for updates within another site.

25. When planning sites, you'll need to select an intersite transport. Keep in mind the points shown in Tables 3 and 4 when selecting an intersite transport. These tables summarize the advantages and disadvantages of RPC and SMTP.

26. All intrasite replication is done using RPC.

27. Replication within a site occurs among all domain controllers. Between sites, connections are established among dedicated computers called *bridgehead servers*.

28. Bridgehead servers are responsible for receiving updates from other sites; once the bridgehead receives updates from another bridgehead in another site, the

MCSE™
Windows® 2000
Directory
Services Design

Dennis Scheil
Diana Bartley

MCSE™ Windows® 2000 Directory Services Design Exam Cram

Limits of Liability and Disclaimer of Warranty

The author and publisher of this book have used their best efforts in preparing the book and the programs contained in it. These efforts include the development, research, and testing of the theories and programs to determine their effectiveness. The author and publisher make no warranty of any kind, expressed or implied, with regard to these programs or the documentation contained in this book.

The author and publisher shall not be liable in the event of incidental or consequential damages in connection with, or arising out of, the furnishing, performance, or use of the programs, associated instructions, and/or claims of productivity gains.

Trademarks

Trademarked names appear throughout this book. Rather than list the names and entities that own the trademarks or insert a trademark symbol with each mention of the trademarked name, the publisher states that it is using the names for editorial purposes only and to the benefit of the trademark owner, with no intention of infringing upon that trademark.

The Coriolis Group, LLC
14455 N. Hayden Road
Suite 220
Scottsdale, Arizona 85260

(480)483-0192
FAX (480)483-0193
www.coriolis.com

Library of Congress Cataloging-in-Publication Data
Scheil, Dennis.
    MCSE Windows 2000 Directory Services Design exam cram/by
Dennis Scheil and Diana Bartley.
        p.   cm.
    Includes index.
    ISBN 1-57610-714-0
    1. Electronic data processing personnel--Certification.   2. Microsoft
software--Examinations--Study guides.   3. Directory Services (Computer
network technology)--Examinations--Study guides.   I. Bartley,
Diana.   II. Title.
QA76.3.S34   2000
005.4'769--dc21   00-058927
                                                            CIP

Printed in the United States of America
10 9 8 7 6 5 4 3 2 1

President and CEO
Keith Weiskamp

Publisher
Steve Sayre

Acquisitions Editor
Shari Jo Hehr

Marketing Specialist
Brett Woolley

Project Editor
Tom Lamoureux

Technical Reviewer
Eugenio Reis

Production Coordinator
Wendy Littley

Cover Designer
Jesse Dunn

Layout Designer
April Nielsen

The Coriolis Group, LLC • 14455 North Hayden Road, Suite 220 • Scottsdale, Arizona 85260

ExamCram.com Connects You to the Ultimate Study Center!

Our goal has always been to provide you with the best study tools on the planet to help you achieve your certification in record time. Time is so valuable these days that none of us can afford to waste a second of it, especially when it comes to exam preparation.

Over the past few years, we've created an extensive line of *Exam Cram* and *Exam Prep* study guides, practice exams, and interactive training. To help you study even better, we have now created an e-learning and certification destination called **ExamCram.com**. (You can access the site at **www.examcram.com**.) Now, with every study product you purchase from us, you'll be connected to a large community of people like yourself who are actively studying for their certifications, developing their careers, seeking advice, and sharing their insights and stories.

I believe that the future is all about collaborative learning. Our **ExamCram.com** destination is our approach to creating a highly interactive, easily accessible collaborative environment, where you can take practice exams and discuss your experiences with others, sign up for features like "Questions of the Day," plan your certifications using our interactive planners, create your own personal study pages, and keep up with all of the latest study tips and techniques.

I hope that whatever study products you purchase from us—*Exam Cram* or *Exam Prep* study guides, *Personal Trainers*, *Personal Test Centers*, or one of our interactive Web courses—will make your studying fun and productive. Our commitment is to build the kind of learning tools that will allow you to study the way you want to, whenever you want to.

Visit ExamCram.com now to enhance your study program.

Help us continue to provide the very best certification study materials possible. Write us or email us at **learn@examcram.com** and let us know how our study products have helped you study. Tell us about new features that you'd like us to add. Send us a story about how we've helped you. We're listening!

Good luck with your certification exam and your career. Thank you for allowing us to help you achieve your goals.

Keith Weiskamp
President and CEO

Look for these other products from The Coriolis Group:

**MCSE Windows 2000 Accelerated
Exam Prep**
By Lance Cockcroft, Erik Eckel,
and Ron Kauffman

MCSE Windows 2000 Server Exam Prep
By David Johnson and Dawn Rader

**MCSE Windows 2000 Professional
Exam Prep**
By Michael D. Stewart, James Bloomingdale,
and Neall Alcott

MCSE Windows 2000 Network Exam Prep
By Tammy Smith and Sandra Smeeton

**MCSE Windows 2000 Directory Services
Exam Prep**
By David V. Watts, Will Willis, and Tillman
Strahan

**MCSE Windows 2000 Security Design
Exam Prep**
By Richard Alan McMahon and Glen Bicking

**MCSE Windows 2000 Network Design
Exam Prep**
By Geoffrey Alexander, Anoop Jalan,
and Joseph Alexander

**MCSE Migrating from NT 4
to Windows 2000
Exam Prep**
By Glen Bergen, Graham Leach,
and David Baldwin

**MCSE Windows 2000
Directory Services Design
Exam Prep**
By J. Peter Bruzzese and Wayne Dipchan

**MCSE Windows 2000 Core Four
Exam Prep Pack**

**MCSE Windows 2000 Server
Exam Cram**
By Natasha Knight

**MCSE Windows 2000 Professional
Exam Cram**
By Dan Balter, Dan Holme, Todd Logan,
and Laurie Salmon

**MCSE Windows 2000 Network
Exam Cram**
By Hank Carbeck, Derek Melber,
and Richard Taylor

**MCSE Windows 2000 Directory Services
Exam Cram**
By Will Willis, David V. Watts,
and J. Peter Bruzzese

**MCSE Windows 2000 Security Design
Exam Cram**
By Phillip G. Schein

**MCSE Windows 2000 Network Design
Exam Cram**
By Kim Simmons, Jarret W. Buse,
and Todd Halpin

**MCSE Windows 2000 Core Four
Exam Cram Pack**

and...
MCSE Windows 2000 Foundations
By James Michael Stewart and Lee Scales

This book is dedicated, with love, to my son Mike.
—Dennis Scheil
❧

To my mom who is my source of inspiration,
and to my dad for his never-ending support.
—Diana Bartley
❧

About the Authors

. . . .

Dennis Scheil is Chief Technologist and a partner in Delta Corporate Services, a full-service consulting firm he helped start in 1991. He has over twenty years of technical, project management, and teaching experience on a wide range of hardware, software, and applications. Dennis has worked with numerous clients to develop cost-effective, well-designed, and user-friendly business systems. As an instructor and lecturer, Dennis uses his consulting background to help his audience understand complex technical issues in a business context, and provides real-world scenarios to help illustrate the technical issues involved. Despite all of this, he has still maintained a sense of humor.

Dennis is a graduate of Syracuse University and holds a graduate degree from Princeton University in Germanic literature. He is a Microsoft Certified Systems Engineer + Internet (MCSE+I), a Microsoft Certified Trainer (MCT), a Certified Technical Trainer (CTT), a Certified NetWare Engineer (CNE), a LAN Server Engineer (LSE), Certified OS/2 Engineer, a Certified Network Professional (CNP), and an Accomplished Toastmaster (ATM). He has just been awarded the prestigious CAC (Certified Acronym Collector) designation as well.

In his few moments of spare time, Dennis can be found biking, boardsailing, woodworking, horseback riding, or brewing up a batch of homemade ale.

Diana Bartley holds a Bachelor of Education degree from the University of Manitoba and over the past few years has earned several industry certifications including her MCSE, MCT, and MCP+I. Diana has been actively involved in IT training for several years and currently works for the Entrepreneur Technology and Education Centers (ETEC) where she oversees the engineering program and pursues her passion for continued technical training and development, with a focus on Windows NT 4.0 and Windows 2000 training.

Acknowledgments

There are so many people who have helped me, directly and indirectly, in the preparation of this book. I know I will miss someone, so my apologies in advance if I have forgotten to mention you.

First, a big "Thank you!" to Tom Lamoureux, Bart Reed, and Eugenio Reis at Coriolis, for their patience and understanding in dealing with a first-time author. Their thoughtful editing suggestions were invaluable, and I often found myself wondering how they managed to decipher some particularly tortured bit of my English syntax, so that they could suggest more understandable sentence structure. Thanks to Wendy Littley, the production coordinator, April Nielsen, the interior designer, Jesse Dunn, the cover designer, and Marcos Uzueta for drawing some really great line art.

Words cannot express my gratitude to my co-author, Diana Bartley, who really is responsible for making this book happen. She always was willing to take on a little more, and somehow always managed to get everything done by the deadline. No one has ever done more to earn a dinner and Broadway show! Thanks, Diana!

There are certain people who have helped me over the past twenty years who deserve more than just a mention here, but if I wrote about everyone, and everything they have done to help and guide me, these acknowledgements would be become Chapter 12. So, hoping not to offend at such a brief mention, thanks (chronologically) to Jimmy Cryer, Joel Sobo, Dean Livingston, Ray Warrick, Walt Kapica, Lowell Higgins, Mike Iovino, and Tom Prisk. Yes, there are many more, but the rest of you will get your turn with the next book.

I really need to thank my "sanity crew." Without their help, friendship and support, I would have self-destructed long ago. The ESG bunch, Alison, Cindy, and Jenn, have kept me relatively sane in the office for years. Thanks for absolutely, positively everything to Chris and crew, and Marie et al.! And, I would not be writing these acknowledgements at all if it weren't for Carol Small-McGrath, whose words of encouragement came at just the right time.

Finally, any mention of people who have helped my career would be incomplete without a thank-you to my parents, who taught me that anything is possible.

—*Dennis Scheil*

Thanks to my talented co-author, Dennis Scheil, whose brilliant mind and vast experience has made this book possible. His suggestions and kindly criticisms were much appreciated. I'd like to thank several of my coworkers: Jonathon Elcomb, for helping me to get started and keeping me on track; Ryan Johanneson and Brad Hryhoruk for being a source of knowledge (and laughter); Martial Marcoux and Marielle Dyck for being a source of encouragement. Finally, thanks to all those who offered me their support during the past few months, you are all greatly appreciated!

—*Diana Bartley*

Contents at a Glance

Table of Contents

Introduction

Welcome to *MCSE Windows 2000 Directory Design Exam Cram*! Whether this is your first or your fifteenth *Exam Cram* book, you'll find information here and in Chapter 1 that will help ensure your success as you pursue knowledge, experience, and certification. This book aims to help you get ready to take—and pass—the Microsoft certification Exam 70-219, titled "Designing a Microsoft Windows 2000 Directory Services Infrastructure." This Introduction explains Microsoft's certification programs in general and talks about how the *Exam Cram* series can help you prepare for Microsoft's Windows 2000 certification exams.

Exam Cram books help you understand and appreciate the subjects and materials you need to pass Microsoft certification exams. *Exam Cram* books are aimed strictly at test preparation and review. They do not teach you everything you need to know about a topic. Instead, we (the authors) present and dissect the questions and problems we've found that you're likely to encounter on a test. We've worked to bring together as much information as possible about Microsoft certification exams.

Nevertheless, to completely prepare yourself for any Microsoft test, we recommend that you begin by taking the Self-Assessment included in this book immediately following this Introduction. This tool will help you evaluate your knowledge base against the requirements for an MCSE under both ideal and real circumstances.

Based on what you learn from that exercise, you might decide to begin your studies with some classroom training or some background reading. On the other hand, you might decide to pick up and read one of the many study guides available from Microsoft or third-party vendors on certain topics, including The Coriolis Group's *Exam Prep* series. We also recommend that you supplement your study program with visits to **ExamCram.com** to receive additional practice questions, get advice, and track the Windows 2000 MCSE program.

We also strongly recommend that you install, configure, and fool around with the software that you'll be tested on, because nothing beats hands-on experience and familiarity when it comes to understanding the questions you're likely to encounter on a certification test. Book learning is essential, but hands-on experience is the best teacher of all!

The Microsoft Certified Professional (MCP) Program

The MCP Program currently includes the following separate tracks, each of which boasts its own special acronym (as a certification candidate, you need to have a high tolerance for alphabet soup of all kinds):

➤ *MCP (Microsoft Certified Professional)*—This is the least prestigious of all the certification tracks from Microsoft. Passing one of the major Microsoft exams qualifies an individual for the MCP credential. Individuals can demonstrate proficiency with additional Microsoft products by passing additional certification exams.

➤ *MCP+SB (Microsoft Certified Professional + Site Building)*—This certification program is designed for individuals who are planning, building, managing, and maintaining Web sites. Individuals with the MCP+SB credential will have demonstrated the ability to develop Web sites that include multimedia and searchable content and Web sites that connect to and communicate with a back-end database. It requires one MCP exam, plus two of these three exams: "70-055: Designing and Implementing Web Sites with Microsoft FrontPage 98," "70-057: Designing and Implementing Commerce Solutions with Microsoft Site Server 3.0, Commerce Edition," and "70-152: Designing and Implementing Web Solutions with Microsoft Visual InterDev 6.0."

➤ *MCSE (Microsoft Certified Systems Engineer)*—Anyone who has a current MCSE is warranted to possess a high level of networking expertise with Microsoft operating systems and products. This credential is designed to prepare individuals to plan, implement, maintain, and support information systems, networks, and internetworks built around Microsoft Windows 2000 and its BackOffice Server 2000 family of products.

To obtain an MCSE, an individual must pass four core operating system exams, one optional core exam, and two elective exams. The operating system exams require individuals to prove their competence with desktop and server operating systems and networking/internetworking components.

For Windows NT 4 MCSEs, the Accelerated exam, "70-240: Microsoft Windows 2000 Accelerated Exam for MCPs Certified on Microsoft Windows NT 4.0," is an option. This free exam covers all of the material tested in the Core Four exams. The hitch in this plan is that you can take the test only once. If you fail, you must take all four core exams to recertify. The Core Four exams are: "70-210: Installing, Configuring and Administering Microsoft Windows 2000 Professional," "70-215: Installing, Configuring and Administering Microsoft

Windows 2000 Server," "70-216: Implementing and Administering a Microsoft Windows 2000 Network Infrastructure," and "70-217: Implementing and Administering a Microsoft Windows 2000 Directory Services Infrastructure."

To fulfill the fifth core exam requirement, you can choose from three design exams: "70-219: Designing a Microsoft Windows 2000 Directory Services Infrastructure," "70-220: Designing Security for a Microsoft Windows 2000 Network," or "70-221: Designing a Microsoft Windows 2000 Network Infrastructure." You are also required to take two elective exams. An elective exam can fall in any number of subject or product areas, primarily BackOffice Server 2000 components. The two design exams that you don't select as your fifth core exam also qualify as electives. If you are on your way to becoming an MCSE and have already taken some exams, visit **www.microsoft.com/trainingandservices/** for information about how to complete your MCSE certification.

In September 1999, Microsoft announced its Windows 2000 track for MCSE and also announced retirement of Windows NT 4.0 MCSE core exams on 12/31/2000. Individuals who wish to remain certified MCSEs after 12/31/2001 must "upgrade" their certifications on or before 12/31/2001. For more detailed information than is included here, visit **www.microsoft.com/trainingandservices/**.

New MCSE candidates must pass seven tests to meet the MCSE requirements. It's not uncommon for the entire process to take a year or so, and many individuals find that they must take a test more than once to pass. The primary goal of the *Exam Prep* and *Exam Cram* test preparation books is to make it possible, given proper study and preparation, to pass all Microsoft certification tests on the first try. Table 1 shows the required and elective exams for the Windows 2000 MCSE certification.

➤ *MCSD (Microsoft Certified Solution Developer)*—The MCSD credential reflects the skills required to create multitier, distributed, and COM-based solutions, in addition to desktop and Internet applications, using new technologies. To obtain an MCSD, an individual must demonstrate the ability to analyze and interpret user requirements; select and integrate products, platforms, tools, and technologies; design and implement code, and customize applications; and perform necessary software tests and quality assurance operations.

To become an MCSD, you must pass a total of four exams: three core exams and one elective exam. Each candidate must choose one of these three desktop application exams — "70-016: Designing and Implementing Desktop Applications with Microsoft Visual C++ 6.0," "70-156: Designing and Implementing Desktop Applications with Microsoft Visual FoxPro 6.0," or "70-176: Designing and Implementing Desktop Applications with Microsoft

Table 1   MCSE Windows 2000 Requirements

Core

If you have not passed these 3 Windows NT 4 exams	
Exam 70-067	Implementing and Supporting Microsoft Windows NT Server 4.0
Exam 70-068	Implementing and Supporting Microsoft Windows NT Server 4.0 in the Enterprise
Exam 70-073	Microsoft Windows NT Workstation 4.0
then you must take these 4 exams	
Exam 70-210	Installing, Configuring and Administering Microsoft Windows 2000 Professional
Exam 70-215	Installing, Configuring and Administering Microsoft Windows 2000 Server
Exam 70-216	Implementing and Administering a Microsoft Windows 2000 Network Infrastructure
Exam 70-217	Implementing and Administering a Microsoft Windows 2000 Directory Services Infrastructure
If you have already passed exams 70-067, 70-068, and 70-073, you may take this exam	
Exam 70-240	Microsoft Windows 2000 Accelerated Exam for MCPs Certified on Microsoft Windows NT 4.0

5th Core Option

Choose 1 from this group	
Exam 70-219*	Designing a Microsoft Windows 2000 Directory Services Infrastructure
Exam 70-220*	Designing Security for a Microsoft Windows 2000 Network
Exam 70-221*	Designing a Microsoft Windows 2000 Network Infrastructure

Elective

Choose 2 from this group	
Exam 70-019	Designing and Implementing Data Warehouse with Microsoft SQL Server 7.0
Exam 70-219*	Designing a Microsoft Windows 2000 Directory Services Infrastructure
Exam 70-220*	Designing Security for a Microsoft Windows 2000 Network
Exam 70-221*	Designing a Microsoft Windows 2000 Network Infrastructure
Exam 70-222	Migrating from Microsoft Windows NT 4.0 to Microsoft Windows 2000
Exam 70-028	Administering Microsoft SQL Server 7.0
Exam 70-029	Designing and Implementing Databases on Microsoft SQL Server 7.0
Exam 70-080	Implementing and Supporting Microsoft Internet Explorer 5.0 by Using the Internet Explorer Administration Kit
Exam 70-081	Implementing and Supporting Microsoft Exchange Server 5.5
Exam 70-085	Implementing and Supporting Microsoft SNA Server 4.0
Exam 70-086	Implementing and Supporting Microsoft Systems Management Server 2.0
Exam 70-088	Implementing and Supporting Microsoft Proxy Server 2.0

This is not a complete listing—you can still be tested on some earlier versions of these products. However, we have included mainly the most recent versions so that you may test on these versions and thus be certified longer. We have not included any tests that are scheduled to be retired.

* The 5th Core Option exam does not double as an elective.

Visual Basic 6.0"—*plus* one of these three distributed application exams—"70-015: Designing and Implementing Distributed Applications with Microsoft Visual C++ 6.0," "70-155: Designing and Implementing Distributed Applications with Microsoft Visual FoxPro 6.0," or "70-175: Designing and Implementing Distributed Applications with Microsoft Visual Basic 6.0." The third core exam is "70-100: Analyzing Requirements and Defining Solution Architectures." Elective exams cover specific Microsoft applications and languages, including Visual Basic, C++, the Microsoft Foundation Classes, Access, SQL Server, Excel, and more.

➤ *MCDBA (Microsoft Certified Database Administrator)*—The MCDBA credential reflects the skills required to implement and administer Microsoft SQL Server databases. To obtain an MCDBA, an individual must demonstrate the ability to derive physical database designs, develop logical data models, create physical databases, create data services by using Transact-SQL, manage and maintain databases, configure and manage security, monitor and optimize databases, and install and configure Microsoft SQL Server.

To become an MCDBA, you must pass a total of three core exams and one elective exam. The required core exams are "70-028: Administering Microsoft SQL Server 7.0," "70-029: Designing and Implementing Databases with Microsoft SQL Server 7.0," and "70-215: Installing, Configuring and Administering Microsoft Windows 2000 Server."

The elective exams that you can choose from cover specific uses of SQL Server and include "70-015: Designing and Implementing Distributed Applications with Microsoft Visual C++ 6.0," "70-019: Designing and Implementing Data Warehouses with Microsoft SQL Server 7.0," "70-155: Designing and Implementing Distributed Applications with Microsoft Visual FoxPro 6.0," "70-175: Designing and Implementing Distributed Applications with Microsoft Visual Basic 6.0," and two exams that relate to Windows 2000: "70-216: Implementing and Administering a Microsoft Windows 2000 Network Infrastructure," and "70-087: Implementing and Supporting Microsoft Internet Information Server 4.0."

If you have taken the three core Windows NT 4 exams on your path to becoming an MCSE, you qualify for the Accelerated exam (it replaces the Network Infrastructure exam requirement). The Accelerated exam covers the objectives of all four of the Windows 2000 core exams. In addition to taking the Accelerated exam, you must take only the two SQL exams—Administering and Database Design.

> ➤ *MCT (Microsoft Certified Trainer)*—Microsoft Certified Trainers are deemed able to deliver elements of the official Microsoft curriculum, based on technical knowledge and instructional ability. Thus, it is necessary for an individual seeking MCT credentials (which are granted on a course-by-course basis) to pass the related certification exam for a course and complete the official Microsoft training in the subject area, and to demonstrate an ability to teach.
>
> This teaching skill criterion may be satisfied by proving that one has already attained training certification from Novell, Banyan, Lotus, the Santa Cruz Operation, or Cisco, or by taking a Microsoft-sanctioned workshop on instruction. Microsoft makes it clear that MCTs are important cogs in the Microsoft training channels. Instructors must be MCTs before Microsoft will allow them to teach in any of its official training channels, including Microsoft's affiliated Certified Technical Education Centers (CTECs) and its online training partner network. As of January 1, 2001, MCT candidates must also possess a current MCSE.

Microsoft has announced that the MCP+I and MCSE+I credentials will not be continued when the MCSE exams for Windows 2000 are in full swing because the skill set for the Internet portion of the program has been included in the new MCSE program. Therefore, details on these tracks are not provided here; go to **www.microsoft.com/trainingandservices/** if you need more information.

Once a Microsoft product becomes obsolete, MCPs typically have to recertify on current versions (if individuals do not recertify, their certifications become invalid). Because technology keeps changing and new products continually supplant old ones, this should come as no surprise. This explains why Microsoft has announced that MCSEs have 12 months past the scheduled retirement date for the Windows NT 4 exams to recertify on Windows 2000 topics. (Note that this means taking at least two exams, if not more.)

The best place to keep tabs on the MCP program and its related certifications is on the Web. The URL for the MCP program is **www.microsoft.com/trainingandservices/**. But Microsoft's Web site changes often, so if this URL doesn't work, try using the Search tool on Microsoft's site with either "MCP" or the quoted phrase "Microsoft Certified Professional" as a search string. This will help you find the latest and most accurate information about Microsoft's certification programs.

Taking a Certification Exam

Once you've prepared for your exam, you need to register with a testing center. Each computer-based MCP exam costs $100, and if you don't pass, you may retest for $100 for each additional try. In the United States and Canada, tests are administered by Prometric and by Virtual University Enterprises (VUE). Here's how you can contact them:

➤ *Prometric*—You can sign up for a test through the company's Web site at **www.prometric.com**. Or, you can register by phone at 800-755-3926 (within the United States or Canada) or at 410-843-8000 (outside the United States and Canada).

➤ *Virtual University Enterprises*—You can sign up for a test or get the phone numbers for local testing centers through the Web page at **www.vue.com/ms/**.

To sign up for a test, you must possess a valid credit card, or contact either company for mailing instructions to send them a check (in the U.S.). Only when payment is verified, or a check has cleared, can you actually register for a test.

To schedule an exam, call the number or visit either of the Web pages at least one day in advance. To cancel or reschedule an exam, you must call before 7 P.M. pacific standard time the day before the scheduled test time (or you may be charged, even if you don't appear to take the test). When you want to schedule a test, have the following information ready:

➤ Your name, organization, and mailing address.

➤ Your Microsoft Test ID. (Inside the United States, this means your Social Security number; citizens of other nations should call ahead to find out what type of identification number is required to register for a test.)

➤ The name and number of the exam you wish to take.

➤ A method of payment. (As we've already mentioned, a credit card is the most convenient method, but alternate means can be arranged in advance, if necessary).

Once you sign up for a test, you'll be informed as to when and where the test is scheduled. Try to arrive at least 15 minutes early. You must supply two forms of identification—one of which must be a photo ID—to be admitted into the testing room.

All exams are completely closed-book. In fact, you will not be permitted to take anything with you into the testing area, but you will be furnished with a blank sheet of paper and a pen or, in some cases, an erasable plastic sheet and an erasable pen. We suggest that you immediately write down on that sheet of paper all the information you've memorized for the test. In *Exam Cram* books, this information appears on a tear-out sheet inside the front cover of each book. You will have some time to compose yourself, record this information, and take a sample orientation exam before you begin the real thing. We suggest you take the orientation test before taking your first exam, but because they're all more or less identical in layout, behavior and controls, you probably won't need to do this more than once.

When you complete a Microsoft certification exam, the software will tell you whether you've passed or failed. If you need to retake an exam, you'll have to schedule a new test with Prometric or VUE and pay another $100.

 The first time you fail a test, you can retake the test the next day. However, if you fail a second time, you must wait 14 days before retaking that test. The 14-day waiting period remains in effect for all retakes after the second failure.

Tracking MCP Status

As soon as you pass any Microsoft exam (except Networking Essentials), you'll attain Microsoft Certified Professional (MCP) status. Microsoft also generates transcripts that indicate which exams you have passed. You can view a copy of your transcript at any time by going to the MCP secured site and selecting Transcript Tool. This tool will allow you to print a copy of your current transcript and confirm your certification status.

Once you pass the necessary set of exams, you'll be certified. Official certification normally takes anywhere from six to eight weeks, so don't expect to get your credentials overnight. When the package for a qualified certification arrives, it includes a Welcome Kit that contains a number of elements (see Microsoft's Web site for other benefits of specific certifications):

➤ A certificate suitable for framing, along with a wallet card and lapel pin.

➤ A license to use the MCP logo, thereby allowing you to use the logo in advertisements, promotions, and documents, and on letterhead, business cards, and so on. Along with the license comes an MCP logo sheet, which includes camera-ready artwork. (Note: Before using any of the artwork, individuals must sign and return a licensing agreement that indicates they'll abide by its terms and conditions.)

➤ A subscription to *Microsoft Certified Professional Magazine*, which provides ongoing data about testing and certification activities, requirements, and changes to the program.

Many people believe that the benefits of MCP certification go well beyond the perks that Microsoft provides to newly anointed members of this elite group.

We're starting to see more job listings that request or require applicants to have an MCP, MCSE, and so on, and many individuals who complete the program can qualify for increases in pay and/or responsibility. As an official recognition of hard work and broad knowledge, one of the MCP credentials is a badge of honor in many IT organizations.

How to Prepare for an Exam

Preparing for any Windows 2000 Server-related test (including "Designing a Microsoft Windows 2000 Directory Services Infrastructure") requires that you obtain and study materials designed to provide comprehensive information about the product and its capabilities that will appear on the specific exam for which you are preparing. The following list of materials will help you study and prepare:

➤ The Windows 2000 Server product CD includes comprehensive online documentation and related materials; it should be a primary resource when you are preparing for the test.

➤ The exam preparation materials, practice tests, and self-assessment exams on the Microsoft Training & Services page at **www.microsoft.com/ trainingandservices/default.asp?PageID=mcp**. The Testing Innovations link offers samples of the new question types found on the Windows 2000 MCSE exams. Find the materials, download them, and use them!

➤ The exam preparation advice, practice tests, questions of the day, and discussion groups on the **ExamCram.com** e-learning and certification destination Web site (**www.examcram.com**).

In addition, you'll probably find any or all of the following materials useful in your quest for Directory Services Design expertise:

➤ *Microsoft training kits*—Microsoft Press offers training kits that specifically target Exam Windows 2000 exams. For more information, visit: **http://mspress.microsoft. com/findabook/list/series_ak.htm**.

➤ *Microsoft TechNet CD*—This monthly CD-based publication delivers numerous electronic titles that include coverage of Directory Services Design and related topics on the Technical Information (TechNet) CD. Its offerings include product facts, technical notes, tools and utilities, and information on how to access the Seminars Online training materials for Directory Services Design. A subscription to TechNet costs $299 per year, but it is well worth the price. Visit **www.microsoft.com/technet/** and check out the information under the "TechNet Subscription" menu entry for more details.

➤ *Study guides*—Several publishers—including The Coriolis Group—offer Windows 2000 titles. The Coriolis Group series includes the following:

➤ *The Exam Cram series*—These books give you information about the material you need to know to pass the tests.

➤ *The Exam Prep series*—These books provide a greater level of detail than the *Exam Cram* books and are designed to teach you everything you need to know from an exam perspective. Each book comes with a CD that contains interactive practice exams in a variety of testing formats.

Together, the two series make a perfect pair.

➤ *Multimedia*—These Coriolis Group materials are designed to support learners of all types—whether you learn best by reading or doing:

➤ *The Exam Cram Personal Trainer*—Offers a unique, personalized self-paced training course based on the exam.

➤ *The Exam Cram Personal Test Center*—Features multiple test options that simulate the actual exam, including Fixed-Length, Random, Review, and Test All. Explanations of correct and incorrect answers reinforce concepts learned.

➤ *Classroom training*—CTECs, online partners, and third-party training companies (like Wave Technologies, Learning Tree, Data-Tech, and others) all offer classroom training on Windows 2000. These companies aim to help you prepare to pass Exam 70-219. Although such training runs upwards of $350 per day in class, most of the individuals lucky enough to partake find it to be quite worthwhile.

➤ *Other publications*—There's no shortage of materials available about Directory Services Design. The resource sections at the end of each chapter should give you an idea of where we think you should look for further discussion.

By far, this set of required and recommended materials represents a nonpareil collection of sources and resources for Directory Services Design and related topics. We anticipate that you'll find that this book belongs in this company

About this Book

Each topical *Exam Cram* chapter follows a regular structure, along with graphical cues about important or useful information. Here's the structure of a typical chapter:

➤ *Opening hotlists*—Each chapter begins with a list of the terms, tools, and techniques that you must learn and understand before you can be fully conversant with that chapter's subject matter. We follow the hotlists with one or two introductory paragraphs to set the stage for the rest of the chapter.

➤ *Topical coverage*—After the opening hotlists, each chapter covers a series of topics related to the chapter's subject title. Throughout this section, we highlight topics or concepts likely to appear on a test using a special Exam Alert layout, like this:

 This is what an Exam Alert looks like. Normally, an Exam Alert stresses concepts, terms, software, or activities that are likely to relate to one or more certification test questions. For that reason, we think any information found offset in Exam Alert format is worthy of unusual attentiveness on your part. Indeed, most of the information that appears on The Cram Sheet appears as Exam Alerts within the text.

Pay close attention to material flagged as an Exam Alert; although all the information in this book pertains to what you need to know to pass the exam, we flag certain items that are really important. You'll find what appears in the meat of each chapter to be worth knowing, too, when preparing for the test. Because this book's material is very condensed, we recommend that you use this book along with other resources to achieve the maximum benefit.

In addition to the Exam Alerts, we have provided tips that will help you build a better foundation for Directory Services Design knowledge. Although the information may not be on the exam, it is certainly related and will help you become a better test-taker.

 This is how tips are formatted. Keep your eyes open for these, and you'll become a Directory Services guru in no time!

➤ *Practice questions*—Although we talk about test questions and topics throughout the book, a section at the end of each chapter presents a series of mock test questions and explanations of both correct and incorrect answers.

➤ *Details and resources*—Every chapter ends with a section titled "Need to Know More?". This section provides direct pointers to Microsoft and third-party resources offering more details on the chapter's subject. In addition, this section tries to rank or at least rate the quality and thoroughness of the topic's coverage by each resource. If you find a resource you like in this collection, use it, but don't feel compelled to use all the resources. On the other hand, we recommend only resources we use on a regular basis, so none of our recommendations will be a waste of your time or money (but purchasing them all at once probably represents an expense that many network administrators and would-be MCPs and MCSEs might find hard to justify).

The bulk of the book follows this chapter structure slavishly, but there are a few other elements that we'd like to point out. Chapter 10 includes a sample test that provides a good review of the material presented throughout the book to ensure you're ready for the exam. Chapter 11 is an answer key to the sample test that appears in Chapter 10. In addition, you'll find a handy glossary and an index.

Finally, the tear-out Cram Sheet attached next to the inside front cover of this *Exam Cram* book represents a condensed and compiled collection of facts and tips that we think you should memorize before taking the test. Because you can dump this information out of your head onto a piece of paper before taking the exam, you can master this information by brute force—you need to remember it only long enough to write it down when you walk into the test room. You might even want to look at it in the car or in the lobby of the testing center just before you walk in to take the test.

How to Use this Book

We've structured the topics in this book to build on one another. Therefore, some topics in later chapters make more sense after you've read earlier chapters. That's why we suggest you read this book from front to back for your initial test preparation. If you need to brush up on a topic or you have to bone up for a second try, use the index or table of contents to go straight to the topics and questions that you need to study. Beyond helping you prepare for the test, we think you'll find this book useful as a tightly focused reference to some of the most important aspects of Directory Services.

Given all the book's elements and its specialized focus, we've tried to create a tool that will help you prepare for—and pass—Microsoft Exam 70-219. Please share your feedback on the book with us, especially if you have ideas about how we can improve it for future test-takers. We'll consider everything you say carefully, and we'll respond to all suggestions.

Send your questions or comments to us at **learn@examcram.com**. Please remember to include the title of the book in your message; otherwise, we'll be forced to guess which book you're writing about. And we don't like to guess—we want to *know*! Also, be sure to check out the Web pages at **www.examcram.com**, where you'll find information updates, commentary, and certification information.

Thanks, and enjoy the book!

Self-Assessment

The reason we included a Self-Assessment in this *Exam Prep* book is to help you evaluate your readiness to tackle MCSE certification. It should also help you understand what you need to know to master the topic of this book—namely, Exam 70-219, "Designing a Microsoft Windows 2000 Directory Services Infrastructure." But before you tackle this Self-Assessment, let's talk about concerns you may face when pursuing an MCSE for Windows 2000, and what an ideal MCSE candidate might look like.

MCSEs in the Real World

In the next section, we describe an ideal MCSE candidate, knowing full well that only a few real candidates will meet this ideal. In fact, our description of that ideal candidate might seem downright scary, especially with the changes that have been made to the program to support Windows 2000. But take heart: Although the requirements to obtain an MCSE may seem formidable, they are by no means impossible to meet. However, be keenly aware that it does take time, involves some expense, and requires real effort to get through the process.

Increasing numbers of people are attaining Microsoft certifications, so the goal is within reach. You can get all the real-world motivation you need from knowing that many others have gone before, so you will be able to follow in their footsteps. If you're willing to tackle the process seriously and do what it takes to obtain the necessary experience and knowledge, you can take—and pass—all the certification tests involved in obtaining an MCSE. In fact, we've designed *Exam Preps*, the companion *Exam Crams*, *Exam Cram Personal Trainers*, and *Exam Cram Personal Test Centers* to make it as easy on you as possible to prepare for these exams. We've also greatly expanded our Web site, **www.examcram.com**, to provide a host of resources to help you prepare for the complexities of Windows 2000.

Besides MCSE, other Microsoft certifications include:

➤ MCSD, which is aimed at software developers and requires one specific exam, two more exams on client and distributed topics, plus a fourth elective exam drawn from a different, but limited, pool of options.

➤ Other Microsoft certifications, whose requirements range from one test (MCP) to several tests (MCP+SB, MCDBA).

The Ideal Windows 2000 MCSE Candidate

Just to give you some idea of what an ideal MCSE candidate is like, here are some relevant statistics about the background and experience such an individual might have. Don't worry if you don't meet these qualifications, or don't come that close—this is a far from ideal world, and where you fall short is simply where you'll have more work to do.

➤ Academic or professional training in network theory, concepts, and operations. This includes everything from networking media and transmission techniques through network operating systems, services, and applications.

➤ Three-plus years of professional networking experience, including experience with Ethernet, token ring, modems, and other networking media. This must include installation, configuration, upgrade, and troubleshooting experience.

Note: The Windows 2000 MCSE program is much more rigorous than the previous NT MCSE program; therefore, you'll really need some hands-on experience. Some of the exams require you to solve real-world case studies and network design issues, so the more hands-on experience you have, the better.

➤ Two-plus years in a networked environment that includes hands-on experience with Windows 2000 Server, Windows 2000 Professional, Windows NT Server, Windows NT Workstation, and Windows 95 or Windows 98. A solid understanding of each system's architecture, installation, configuration, maintenance, and troubleshooting is also essential.

➤ Knowledge of the various methods for installing Windows 2000, including manual and unattended installations.

➤ A thorough understanding of key networking protocols, addressing, and name resolution, including TCP/IP, IPX/SPX, and NetBEUI.

➤ A thorough understanding of NetBIOS naming, browsing, and file and print services.

➤ Familiarity with key Windows 2000-based TCP/IP-based services, including HTTP (Web servers), DHCP, WINS, DNS, plus familiarity with one or more of the following: Internet Information Server (IIS), Index Server, and Proxy Server.

➤ An understanding of how to implement security for key network data in a Windows 2000 environment.

➤ Working knowledge of NetWare 3.x and 4.x, including IPX/SPX frame formats, NetWare file, print, and directory services, and both Novell and Microsoft client software. Working knowledge of Microsoft's Client Service For NetWare (CSNW), Gateway Service For NetWare (GSNW), the NetWare Migration Tool (NWCONV), and the NetWare Client For Windows (NT, 95, and 98) is important, but not essential.

➤ A good working understanding of Active Directory. The more you work with Windows 2000, the more you'll realize that this new operating system is quite different than Windows NT. New technologies like Active Directory have really changed the way that Windows is configured and used. We recommend that you find out as much as you can about Active Directory and acquire as much experience using this technology as possible. The time you take learning about Active Directory will be time very well spent!

Fundamentally, this boils down to a bachelor's degree in computer science, plus three years of experience working in a position involving network design, installation, configuration, and maintenance. We believe that well under half of all certification candidates meet these requirements, and that, in fact, most meet less than half of these requirements—at least, when they begin the certification process. But because all the people who already have been certified have survived this ordeal, you can survive it too—especially if you heed what our Self-Assessment can tell you about what you already know and what you need to learn.

Put Yourself to the Test

The following series of questions and observations is designed to help you figure out how much work you must do to pursue Microsoft certification and what kinds of resources you may consult on your quest. Be absolutely honest in your answers, or you'll end up wasting money on exams you're not yet ready to take. There are no right or wrong answers, only steps along the path to certification. Only you can decide where you really belong in the broad spectrum of aspiring candidates.

Two things should be clear from the outset, however:

➤ Even a modest background in computer science will be helpful.

➤ Hands-on experience with Microsoft products and technologies is an essential ingredient to certification success.

Educational Background

1. Have you ever taken any computer-related classes? [Yes or No]

   If Yes, proceed to question 2; if No, proceed to question 4.

2. Have you taken any classes on computer operating systems? [Yes or No]

   If Yes, you will probably be able to handle Microsoft's architecture and system component discussions. If you're rusty, brush up on basic operating system concepts, especially virtual memory, multitasking regimes, user mode versus kernel mode operation, and general computer security topics.

   If No, consider some basic reading in this area. We strongly recommend a good general operating systems book, such as *Operating System Concepts, 5th Edition*, by Abraham Silberschatz and Peter Baer Galvin (John Wiley & Sons, 1998, ISBN 0-471-36414-2). If this title doesn't appeal to you, check out reviews for other, similar titles at your favorite online bookstore.

3. Have you taken any networking concepts or technologies classes? [Yes or No]

   If Yes, you will probably be able to handle Microsoft's networking terminology, concepts, and technologies (brace yourself for frequent departures from normal usage). If you're rusty, brush up on basic networking concepts and terminology, especially networking media, transmission types, the OSI Reference Model, and networking technologies such as Ethernet, token ring, FDDI, and WAN links.

   If No, you might want to read one or two books in this topic area. The two best books that we know of are *Computer Networks, 3rd Edition*, by Andrew S. Tanenbaum (Prentice-Hall, 1996, ISBN 0-13-349945-6) and *Computer Networks and Internets, 2nd Edition*, by Douglas E. Comer (Prentice-Hall, 1998, ISBN 0-130-83617-6).

   Skip to the next section, "Hands-on Experience."

4. Have you done any reading on operating systems or networks? [Yes or No]

   If Yes, review the requirements stated in the first paragraphs after questions 2 and 3. If you meet those requirements, move on to the next section. If No, consult the recommended reading for both topics. A strong background will help you prepare for the Microsoft exams better than just about anything else.

Hands-on Experience

The most important key to success on all of the Microsoft tests is hands-on experience, especially with Windows 2000 Server and Professional, plus the many add-on services and BackOffice components around which so many of the Microsoft certification exams revolve. If we leave you with only one realization after taking this Self-Assessment, it should be that there's no substitute for time spent installing, configuring, and using the various Microsoft products upon which you'll be tested repeatedly and in depth.

5. Have you installed, configured, and worked with:

➤ Windows 2000 Server? [Yes or No]

If Yes, make sure you understand basic concepts as covered in Exam 70-215. You should also study the TCP/IP interfaces, utilities, and services for Exam 70-216, plus implementing security features for Exam 70-220. You will also need to be very comfortable with Active Directory in order to properly prepare for Exam 70-219.

 You can download objectives, practice exams, and other data about Microsoft exams from the Training and Certification page at **www.microsoft.com/trainingandservices/default.asp?PageID=mcp/**. Use the "Exams" link to obtain specific exam information.

If you haven't worked with Windows 2000 Server, you must obtain one or two machines and a copy of Windows 2000 Server. Then, learn the operating system and whatever other software components on which you'll also be tested.

In fact, we recommend that you obtain two computers, each with a network interface, and set up a two-node network on which to practice. With decent Windows 2000-capable computers selling for about $500 to $600 apiece these days, this shouldn't be too much of a financial hardship. You may have to scrounge to come up with the necessary software, but if you scour the Microsoft Web site you can usually find low-cost options to obtain evaluation copies of most of the software that you'll need.

➤ Windows 2000 Professional? [Yes or No]

If Yes, make sure you understand the concepts covered in Exam 70-210.

If No, you will want to obtain a copy of Windows 2000 Professional and learn how to install, configure, and maintain it. You can use *MCSE Windows 2000 Professional Exam Cram* to guide your activities and studies, or work straight from Microsoft's test objectives if you prefer.

For any and all of these Microsoft exams, the Resource Kits for the topics involved are a good study resource. You can purchase softcover Resource Kits from Microsoft Press (search for them at **http://mspress.microsoft.com/**), but they also appear on the TechNet CDs (**www.microsoft.com/technet**). Along with *Exam Crams* and *Exam Preps*, we believe that Resource Kits are among the best tools you can use to prepare for Microsoft exams.

6. For any specific Microsoft product that is not itself an operating system (for example, SQL Server), have you installed, configured, used, and upgraded this software? [Yes or No]

If the answer is Yes, skip to the next section. If it's No, you must get some experience. Read on for suggestions on how to do this.

Experience is a must with any Microsoft product exam, be it something as simple as FrontPage 2000 or as challenging as SQL Server 7.0. For trial copies of other software, search Microsoft's Web site using the name of the product as your search term. Also, search for bundles like "BackOffice" or "Small Business Server."

If you have the funds, or your employer will pay your way, consider taking a class at a Certified Training and Education Center (CTEC) or at an Authorized Academic Training Partner (AATP). In addition to classroom exposure to the topic of your choice, you get a copy of the software that is the focus of your course, along with a trial version of whatever operating system it needs, with the training materials for that class.

Before you even think about taking any Microsoft exam, make sure you've spent enough time with the related software to understand how it may be installed and configured, how to maintain such an installation, and how to troubleshoot that software when things go wrong. This will help you in the exam, and in real life!

Testing Your Exam-Readiness

Whether you attend a formal class on a specific topic to get ready for an exam or use written materials to study on your own, some preparation for the Microsoft certification exams is essential. At $100 a try, pass or fail, you want to do everything you can to pass on your first try. That's where studying comes in.

We have included a practice exam in this book, so if you don't score that well on the test, you can study more and then tackle the test again. We also have exams that you can take online through the **ExamCram.com** Web site at **www.examcram.com**. If you still don't hit a score of at least 80 percent after these tests, you'll want to investigate the other practice test resources we mention in this section.

For any given subject, consider taking a class if you've tackled self-study materials, taken the test, and failed anyway. The opportunity to interact with an instructor and fellow students can make all the difference in the world, if you can afford that privilege. For information about Microsoft classes, visit the Training and Certification page at **www.microsoft.com/education/partners/ctec.asp** for Microsoft Certified Education Centers or **www.microsoft.com/aatp/default.htm** for Microsoft Authorized Training Providers.

If you can't afford to take a class, visit the Training and Certification page anyway, because it also includes pointers to free practice exams and to Microsoft Certified Professional Approved Study Guides and other self-study tools. And even if you can't afford to spend much at all, you should still invest in some low-cost practice exams from commercial vendors.

7. Have you taken a practice exam on your chosen test subject? [Yes or No]

If Yes, and you scored 80 percent or better, you're probably ready to tackle the real thing. If your score isn't above that threshold, keep at it until you break that barrier.

If No, obtain all the free and low-budget practice tests you can find and get to work. Keep at it until you can break the passing threshold comfortably.

When it comes to assessing your test readiness, there is no better way than to take a good-quality practice exam and pass with a score of 70 percent or better. When we're preparing ourselves, we shoot for 80-plus percent, just to leave room for the "weirdness factor" that sometimes shows up on Microsoft exams.

Assessing Readiness for Exam 70-219

In addition to the general exam-readiness information in the previous section, there are several things you can do to prepare for the Designing a Microsoft Windows 2000 Directory Services Infrastructure exam. As you're getting ready for Exam 70-219, visit the Exam Cram Windows 2000 Resource Center at **www.examcram.com/studyresource/w2kresource/**. Another valuable resource is the Exam Cram Insider newsletter. Sign up at **www.examcram.com** or send a blank email message to **subscribe-ec@mars.coriolis.com**. We also suggest that you join an active MCSE mailing list. One of the better ones is managed by Sunbelt Software. Sign up at **www.sunbelt-software.com** (look for the Subscribe button).

You can also cruise the Web looking for "braindumps" (recollections of test topics and experiences recorded by others) to help you anticipate topics you're likely to encounter on the test. The MCSE mailing list is a good place to ask where the useful braindumps are, or you can check Shawn Gamble's list at **www.commandcentral.com**.

 You can't be sure that a braindump's author can provide correct answers. Thus, use the questions to guide your studies, but don't rely on the answers in a braindump to lead you to the truth. Double-check everything you find in any braindump.

Microsoft exam mavens also recommend checking the Microsoft Knowledge Base (available on its own CD as part of the TechNet collection, or on the Microsoft Web site at **http://support.microsoft.com/support/**) for "meaningful technical support issues" that relate to your exam's topics. Although we're not sure exactly what the quoted phrase means, we have also noticed some overlap between technical support questions on particular products and troubleshooting questions on the exams for those products.

Onward, through the Fog!

Once you've assessed your readiness, undertaken the right background studies, obtained the hands-on experience that will help you understand the products and technologies at work, and reviewed the many sources of information to help you prepare for a test, you'll be ready to take a round of practice tests. When your scores come back positive enough to get you through the exam, you're ready to go after the real thing. If you follow our assessment regime, you'll not only know what you need to study, but when you're ready to make a test date at Prometric or VUE. Good luck!

Microsoft
Certification Exams

. . . .

Terms you'll need to understand:

✓ Case study

✓ Multiple-choice question formats

✓ Build-list-and-reorder question format

✓ Create-a-tree question format

✓ Drag-and-connect question format

✓ Select-and-place question format

✓ Fixed-length tests

✓ Simulations

✓ Adaptive tests

✓ Short-form tests

Techniques you'll need to master:

✓ Assessing your exam-readiness

✓ Answering Microsoft's varying question types

✓ Altering your test strategy depending on the exam format

✓ Practicing (to make perfect)

✓ Making the best use of the testing software

✓ Budgeting your time

✓ Guessing (as a last resort)

Exam taking is not something that most people anticipate eagerly, no matter how well prepared they may be. In most cases, familiarity helps offset test anxiety. In plain English, this means you probably won't be as nervous when you take your fourth or fifth Microsoft certification exam as you'll be when you take your first one.

Whether it's your first exam or your tenth, understanding the details of taking the new exams (how much time to spend on questions, the environment you'll be in, and so on) and the new exam software will help you concentrate on the material rather than on the setting. Likewise, mastering a few basic exam-taking skills should help you recognize—and perhaps even outfox—some of the tricks and snares you're bound to find in some exam questions.

This chapter, besides explaining the exam environment and software, describes some proven exam-taking strategies that you should be able to use to your advantage.

Assessing Exam-Readiness

We strongly recommend that you read through and take the Self-Assessment included with this book (it appears just before this chapter, in fact). This will help you compare your knowledge base to the requirements for obtaining an MCSE, and it will also help you identify parts of your background or experience that may be in need of improvement, enhancement, or further learning. If you get the right set of basics under your belt, obtaining Microsoft certification will be that much easier.

Once you've gone through the Self-Assessment, you can remedy those topical areas where your background or experience may not measure up to an ideal certification candidate. But you can also tackle subject matter for individual tests at the same time, so you can continue making progress while you're catching up in some areas.

Once you've worked through an *Exam Cram*, have read the supplementary materials, and have taken the practice test, you'll have a pretty clear idea of when you should be ready to take the real exam. Although we strongly recommend that you keep practicing until your scores top the 75 percent mark, 80 percent would be a good goal to give yourself some margin for error in a real exam situation (where stress will play more of a role than when you practice). Once you hit that point, you should be ready to go. But if you get through the practice exam in this book without attaining that score, you should keep taking practice tests and studying the materials until you get there. You'll find more pointers on how to study and prepare in the Self-Assessment. But now, on to the exam itself!

The Exam Situation

When you arrive at the testing center where you scheduled your exam, you'll need to sign in with an exam coordinator. He or she will ask you to show two forms of identification, one of which must be a photo ID. After you've signed in and your time slot arrives, you'll be asked to deposit any books, bags, or other items you brought with you. Then, you'll be escorted into a closed room.

All exams are completely closed book. In fact, you will not be permitted to take anything with you into the testing area, but you will be furnished with a blank sheet of paper and a pen or, in some cases, an erasable plastic sheet and an erasable pen. Before the exam, you should memorize as much of the important material as you can, so you can write that information on the blank sheet as soon as you are seated in front of the computer. You can refer to this piece of paper anytime you like during the test, but you'll have to surrender the sheet when you leave the room.

You will have some time to compose yourself, to record this information, and to take a sample orientation exam before you begin the real thing. We suggest you take the orientation test before taking your first exam, but because they're all more or less identical in layout, behavior, and controls, you probably won't need to do this more than once.

Typically, the room will be furnished with anywhere from one to half a dozen computers, and each workstation will be separated from the others by dividers designed to keep you from seeing what's happening on someone else's computer. Most test rooms feature a wall with a large picture window. This permits the exam coordinator to monitor the room, to prevent exam-takers from talking to one another, and to observe anything out of the ordinary that might go on. The exam coordinator will have preloaded the appropriate Microsoft certification exam—for this book, that's Exam 70-219—and you'll be permitted to start as soon as you're seated in front of the computer.

All Microsoft certification exams allow a certain maximum amount of time in which to complete your work (this time is indicated on the exam by an on-screen counter/clock, so you can check the time remaining whenever you like). All Microsoft certification exams are computer generated. In addition to multiple choice, you'll encounter select and place (drag and drop), create a tree (categorization and prioritization), drag and connect, and build list and reorder (list prioritization) on most exams. Although this may sound quite simple, the questions are constructed not only to check your mastery of basic facts and figures about Directory Services Design, but they also require you to evaluate one or more sets of circumstances or requirements. Often, you'll be asked to give more than one answer to a question. Likewise, you might be asked to select the best or most effective solution to a problem from a range of choices, all of which technically are correct. Taking the exam is quite an adventure, and it involves real thinking. This book shows you what to expect and how to deal with the potential problems, puzzles, and predicaments.

In the next section, you'll learn more about how Microsoft test questions look and how they must be answered.

Exam Layout and Design: New Case Study Format

The format of Microsoft's Windows 2000 exams is different from that of its previous exams. For the design exams (70-219, 70-220, 70-221), each exam consists entirely of a series of case studies, and the questions can be of six types. For the Core Four exams (70-210, 70-215, 70-216, 70-217), the same six types of questions can appear, but you are not likely to encounter complex multiquestion case studies.

For design exams, each case study or "testlet" presents a detailed problem that you must read and analyze. Figure 1.1 shows an example of what a case study looks like. You must select the different tabs in the case study to view the entire case.

Following each case study is a set of questions related to the case study; these questions can be one of six types (which are discussed next). Careful attention to details provided in the case study is the key to success. Be prepared to toggle frequently between the case study and the questions as you work. Some of the case studies also include diagrams, which are called *exhibits*, that you'll need to examine closely to understand how to answer the questions.

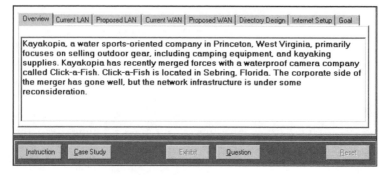

Figure 1.1   This is how case studies appear.

Once you complete a case study, you can review all the questions and your answers. However, once you move on to the next case study, you may not be able to return to the previous case study and make any changes.

The six types of question formats are:

➤ Multiple choice, single answer

➤ Multiple choice, multiple answers

➤ Build list and reorder (list prioritization)

➤ Create a tree

➤ Drag and connect

➤ Select and place (drag and drop)

Note: Exam formats may vary by test center location. Although most design exams consist entirely of a series of case studies or testlets, a test-taker may occasionally encounter a strictly multiple-choice test. You may want to call the test center or visit ExamCram.com to see if you can find out which type of test you'll encounter.

Multiple-Choice Question Format

Some exam questions require you to select a single answer, whereas others ask you to select multiple correct answers. The following multiple-choice question requires you to select a single correct answer. Following the question is a brief summary of each potential answer and why it is either right or wrong.

Question 1

You have three domains connected to an empty root domain under one contiguous domain name: tutu.com. This organization is formed into a forest arrangement with a secondary domain called frog.com. How many Schema Masters exist for this arrangement?

○ a. 1

○ b. 2

○ c. 3

○ d. 4

The correct answer is a because only one Schema Master is necessary for a forest arrangement. The other answers (b, c, d) are misleading because they try to make you believe that Schema Masters might be in each domain, or perhaps that you should have one for each contiguous namespaced domain.

This sample question format corresponds closely to the Microsoft certification exam format—the only difference on the exam is that questions are not followed by answer keys. To select an answer, you would position the cursor over the radio button next to the answer. Then, click the mouse button to select the answer.

Let's examine a question where one or more answers are possible. This type of question provides checkboxes rather than radio buttons for marking all appropriate selections.

Question 2

> How can you seize FSMO roles? [Check all correct answers]
>
> ❑ a. The ntdsutil.exe utility
>
> ❑ b. The Replication Monitor
>
> ❑ c. The secedit.exe utility
>
> ❑ d. Active Directory Domains and FSMOs

Answers a and b are correct. You can seize roles from a server that is still running through the Replication Monitor or, in the case of a server failure, you can seize roles with the ntdsutil.exe utility. The secedit utility is used to force group policies into play; therefore, answer c is incorrect. Active Directory Domains and Trusts are a combination of truth and fiction; therefore, answer d is incorrect.

For this particular question, two answers are required. Microsoft sometimes gives partial credit for partially correct answers. For Question 2, you have to check the boxes next to items a and b to obtain credit for a correct answer. Notice that picking the right answers also means knowing why the other answers are wrong!

Build-List-and-Reorder Question Format

Questions in the build-list-and-reorder format present two lists of items—one on the left and one on the right. To answer the question, you must move items from the list on the right to the list on the left. The final list must then be reordered into a specific order.

These questions can best be characterized as "From the following list of choices, pick the choices that answer the question. Arrange the list in a certain order." To give you practice with this type of question, some questions of this type are included in this study guide. Here's an example of how they appear in this book; for a sample of how they appear on the test, see Figure 1.2.

Question 3

> From the following list of famous people, pick those that have been elected President of the United States. Arrange the list in the order that they served.
>
> Thomas Jefferson
>
> Ben Franklin
>
> Abe Lincoln
>
> George Washington
>
> Andrew Jackson
>
> Paul Revere

The correct answer is:

George Washington

Thomas Jefferson

Andrew Jackson

Abe Lincoln

On an actual exam, the entire list of famous people would initially appear in the list on the right. You would move the four correct answers to the list on the left, and then reorder the list on the left. Notice that the answer to the question did not include all items from the initial list. However, this may not always be the case.

To move an item from the right list to the left list, first select the item by clicking on it, and then click on the Add button (left arrow). Once you move an item from one list to the other, you can move the item back by first selecting the item and then clicking on the appropriate button (either the Add button or the Remove button). Once items have been moved to the left list, you can reorder an item by selecting the item and clicking on the up or down button.

Create-a-Tree Question Format

Questions in the create-a-tree format also present two lists—one on the left side of the screen and one on the right side of the screen. The list on the right consists of individual items, and the list on the left consists of nodes in a tree. To answer the question, you must move items from the list on the right to the appropriate node in the tree.

These questions can best be characterized as simply a matching exercise. Items from the list on the right are placed under the appropriate category in the list on the left. Here's an example of how they appear in this book; for a sample of how they appear on the test, see Figure 1.3.

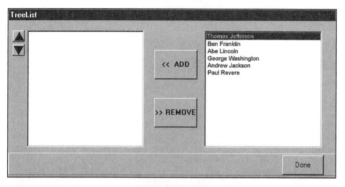

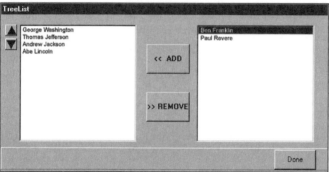

Figure 1.2   This is how build-list-and-reorder questions appear.

Question 4

> The calendar year is divided into four seasons:
>
> > Winter
> >
> > Spring
> >
> > Summer
> >
> > Fall
>
> Identify the season when each of the following holidays occurs:
>
> > Christmas
> >
> > Fourth of July
> >
> > Labor Day
> >
> > Flag Day
> >
> > Memorial Day
> >
> > Washington's Birthday
> >
> > Thanksgiving
> >
> > Easter

The correct answer is:

Winter

Christmas

Washington's Birthday

Spring

Flag Day

Memorial Day

Easter

Summer

Fourth of July

Labor Day

Fall

Thanksgiving

In this case, all the items in the list were used. However, this may not always be the case.

To move an item from the right list to its appropriate location in the tree, you must first select the appropriate tree node by clicking on it. Then, you select the item to be moved and click on the Add button. If one or more items have been added to a tree node, the node will be displayed with a "+" icon to the left of the node name. You can click on this icon to expand the node and view the item(s) that have been added. If any item has been added to the wrong tree node, you can remove it by selecting it and clicking on the Remove button.

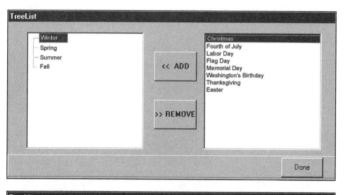

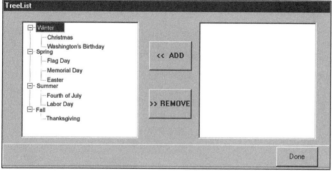

Figure 1.3   This is how create-a-tree questions appear.

Drag-and-Connect Question Format

Questions in the drag-and-connect format present a group of objects and a list of "connections." To answer the question, you must move the appropriate connections between the objects.

This type of question is best described using graphics. Here's an example.

Question 5

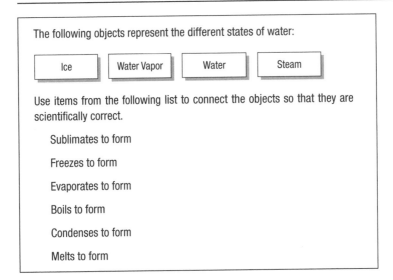

The following objects represent the different states of water:

| Ice | Water Vapor | Water | Steam |

Use items from the following list to connect the objects so that they are scientifically correct.

Sublimates to form

Freezes to form

Evaporates to form

Boils to form

Condenses to form

Melts to form

The correct answer is:

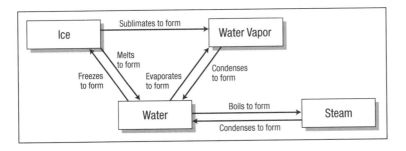

For this type of question, it's not necessary to use every object, and each connection can be used multiple times.

Select-and-Place Question Format

Questions in the select-and-place (drag-and-drop) format present a diagram with blank boxes, and a list of labels that need to be dragged to correctly fill in the blank boxes. To answer the question, you must move the labels to their appropriate positions on the diagram.

This type of question is best described using graphics. Here's an example.

Question 6

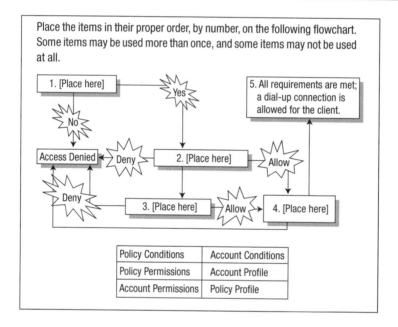

The correct answer is:

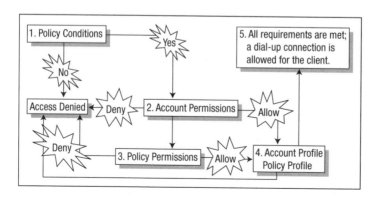

Microsoft's Testing Formats

Currently, Microsoft uses four different testing formats:

➤ Case study

➤ Fixed length

➤ Adaptive

➤ Short form

As we mentioned earlier, the case study approach is used with Microsoft's design exams, such as the one covered by this book. These exams consist of a set of case studies that you must analyze to enable you to answer questions related to the case studies. Such exams include one or more case studies (tabbed topic areas), each of which is followed by 4 to 10 questions. The question types for design exams and for Core Four Windows 2000 exams are multiple choice, build list and reorder, create a tree, drag and connect, and select and place. Depending on the test topic, some exams are totally case-based, whereas others are not.

Other Microsoft exams employ advanced testing capabilities that might not be immediately apparent. Although the questions that appear are primarily multiple choice, the logic that drives them is more complex than older Microsoft tests, which use a fixed sequence of questions, called a *fixed-length test*. Some questions employ a sophisticated user interface, which Microsoft calls a *simulation*, to test your knowledge of the software and systems under consideration in a more or less "live" environment that behaves just like the original. The Testing Innovations link at **www.microsoft.com/trainingandservices/default.asp?PageID=mcp** includes a downloadable practice simulation.

For some exams, Microsoft has turned to a well-known technique, called *adaptive testing*, to establish a test-taker's level of knowledge and product competence. Adaptive exams look the same as fixed-length exams, but they discover the level of difficulty at which an individual test-taker can correctly answer questions. Test-takers with differing levels of knowledge or ability therefore see different sets of questions; individuals with high levels of knowledge or ability are presented with a smaller set of more difficult questions, whereas individuals with lower levels of knowledge are presented with a larger set of easier questions. Two individuals may answer the same percentage of questions correctly, but the test-taker with a higher knowledge or ability level will score higher because his or her questions are worth more.

Also, the lower-level test-taker will probably answer more questions than his or her more-knowledgeable colleague. This explains why adaptive tests use ranges of values to define the number of questions and the amount of time it takes to complete the test.

Adaptive tests work by evaluating the test-taker's most recent answer. A correct answer leads to a more difficult question (and the test software's estimate of the test-taker's knowledge and ability level is raised). An incorrect answer leads to a less difficult question (and the test software's estimate of the test-taker's knowledge and ability level is lowered). This process continues until the test targets the test-taker's true ability level. The exam ends when the test-taker's level of accuracy meets a statistically acceptable value (in other words, when his or her performance demonstrates an acceptable level of knowledge and ability), or when the maximum number of items has been presented (in which case, the test-taker is almost certain to fail).

Microsoft also introduced a short-form test for its most popular tests. This test delivers 25 to 30 questions to its takers, giving them exactly 60 minutes to complete the exam. This type of exam is similar to a fixed-length test, in that it allows readers to jump ahead or return to earlier questions, and to cycle through the questions until the test is done. Microsoft does not use adaptive logic in this test, but claims that statistical analysis of the question pool is such that the 25 to 30 questions delivered during a short-form exam conclusively measure a test-taker's knowledge of the subject matter in much the same way as an adaptive test. You can think of the short-form test as a kind of "greatest hits exam" (that is, the most important questions are covered) version of an adaptive exam on the same topic.

Note: Some of the Microsoft exams can contain a combination of adaptive and fixed-length questions.

Microsoft tests can come in any one of these forms. Whatever you encounter, you must take the test in whichever form it appears; you can't choose one form over another. If anything, it pays more to prepare thoroughly for an adaptive exam than for a fixed-length or a short-form exam: The penalties for answering incorrectly are built into the test itself on an adaptive exam, whereas the layout remains the same for a fixed-length or short-form test, no matter how many questions you answer incorrectly.

The biggest difference between an adaptive test and a fixed-length or short-form test is that on a fixed-length or short-form test, you can revisit questions after you've read them over one or more times. On an adaptive test, you must answer the question when it's presented and will have no opportunities to revisit that question thereafter.

Strategies for Different Testing Formats

Before you choose a test-taking strategy, you must know if your test is case study based, fixed length, short form, or adaptive. When you begin your exam, you'll know right away if the test is based on case studies. The interface will consist of a tabbed window that allows you to easily navigate through the sections of the case.

If you are taking a test that is not based on case studies, the software will tell you that the test is adaptive, if in fact the version you're taking is an adaptive test. If your introductory materials fail to mention this, you're probably taking a fixed-length test (50 to 70 questions). If the total number of questions involved is 25 to 30, you're taking a short-form test. Some tests announce themselves by indicating that they will start with a set of adaptive questions, followed by fixed-length questions.

 You'll be able to tell for sure if you are taking an adaptive, fixed-length, or short-form test by the first question. If it includes a checkbox that lets you mark the question for later review, you're taking a fixed-length or short-form test. If the total number of questions is 25 to 30, it's a short-form test; if more than 30, it's a fixed-length test. Adaptive test questions can be visited (and answered) only once, and they include no such checkbox.

The Case Study Exam Strategy

Most test-takers find that the case study type of test used for the design exams (70-219, 70-220, and 70-221) is the most difficult to master. When it comes to studying for a case study test, your best bet is to approach each case study as a standalone test. The biggest challenge you'll encounter is that you'll feel that you won't have enough time to get through all of the cases that are presented.

 Each case provides a lot of material that you'll need to read and study before you can effectively answer the questions that follow. The trick to taking a case study exam is to first scan the case study to get the highlights. Make sure you read the overview section of the case so that you understand the context of the problem at hand. Then, quickly move on and scan the questions.

As you are scanning the questions, make mental notes to yourself so that you'll remember which sections of the case study you should focus on. Some case studies may provide a fair amount of extra information that you don't really need to answer the questions. The goal with our scanning approach is to avoid having to study and analyze material that is not completely relevant.

When studying a case, carefully read the tabbed information. It is important to answer each and every question. You will be able to toggle back and forth from case to questions, and from question to question within a case testlet. However, once you leave the case and move on, you may not be able to return to it. You may want to take notes while reading useful information so you can refer to them when you tackle the test questions. It's hard to go wrong with this strategy when taking any kind of Microsoft certification test.

The Fixed-Length and Short-Form Exam Strategy

A well-known principle when taking fixed-length or short-form exams is to first read over the entire exam from start to finish while answering only those questions you feel absolutely sure of. On subsequent passes, you can dive into more complex questions more deeply, knowing how many such questions you have left.

Fortunately, the Microsoft exam software for fixed-length and short-form tests makes the multiple-visit approach easy to implement. At the top-left corner of each question is a checkbox that permits you to mark that question for a later visit.

Note: Marking questions makes review easier, but you can return to any question by clicking the Forward or Back button repeatedly.

As you read each question, if you answer only those you're sure of and mark for review those that you're not sure of, you can keep working through a decreasing list of questions as you answer the trickier ones in order.

 There's at least one potential benefit to reading the exam over completely before answering the trickier questions: Sometimes, information supplied in later questions sheds more light on earlier questions. At other times, information you read in later questions might jog your memory about Directory Services Design facts, figures, or behavior that helps you answer earlier questions. Either way, you'll come out ahead if you defer those questions about which you're not absolutely sure.

Here are some question-handling strategies that apply to fixed-length and short-form tests. Use them if you have the chance:

➤ When returning to a question after your initial read-through, read every word again—otherwise, your mind can fall quickly into a rut. Sometimes, revisiting a question after turning your attention elsewhere lets you see something you missed, but the strong tendency is to see what you've seen before. Try to avoid that tendency at all costs.

➤ If you return to a question more than twice, try to articulate to yourself what you don't understand about the question, why answers don't appear to make sense, or what appears to be missing. If you chew on the subject awhile, your subconscious might provide the details you lack, or you might notice a "trick" that points to the right answer.

As you work your way through the exam, another counter that Microsoft provides will come in handy—the number of questions completed and questions outstanding. For fixed-length and short-form tests, it's wise to budget your time by making sure that you've completed one-quarter of the questions one-quarter of the way through the exam period, and three-quarters of the questions three-quarters of the way through.

If you're not finished when only five minutes remain, use that time to guess your way through any remaining questions. Remember, guessing is potentially more valuable than not answering, because blank answers are always wrong, but a guess may turn out to be right. If you don't have a clue about any of the remaining questions, pick answers at random, or choose all a's, b's, and so on. The important thing is to submit an exam for scoring that has an answer for every question.

 At the very end of your exam period, you're better off guessing than leaving questions unanswered.

The Adaptive Exam Strategy

If there's one principle that applies to taking an adaptive test, it could be summed up as "Get it right the first time." You cannot elect to skip a question and move on to the next one when taking an adaptive test, because the testing software uses your answer to the current question to select whatever question it plans to present next. Nor can you return to a question once you've moved on, because the software gives you only one chance to answer the question. You can, however, take notes, because sometimes information supplied in earlier questions will shed more light on later questions.

Also, when you answer a question correctly, you are presented with a more difficult question next, to help the software gauge your level of skill and ability. When you answer a question incorrectly, you are presented with a less difficult question, and the software lowers its current estimate of your skill and ability. This continues until the program settles into a reasonably accurate estimate of what you know and can do, and takes you on average through somewhere between 15 and 30 questions as you complete the test.

The good news is that if you know your stuff, you'll probably finish most adaptive tests in 30 minutes or so. The bad news is that you must really, really know your stuff to do your best on an adaptive test. That's because some questions are so convoluted, complex, or hard to follow that you're bound to miss one or two, at a minimum, even if you do know your stuff. So the more you know, the better you'll do on an adaptive test, even accounting for the occasionally weird or unfathomable questions that appear on these exams.

 Because you can't always tell in advance if a test is fixed length, short form, or adaptive, you will be best served by preparing for the exam as if it were adaptive. That way, you should be prepared to pass no matter what kind of test you take. But if you do take a fixed-length or short-form test, remember our tips from the preceding section. They should help you improve on what you could do on an adaptive test.

If you encounter a question on an adaptive test that you can't answer, you must guess an answer immediately. Because of how the software works, you may suffer for your guess on the next question if you guess right, because you'll get a more difficult question next!

Question-Handling Strategies

For those questions that take only a single answer, usually two or three of the answers will be obviously incorrect, and two of the answers will be plausible—of course, only one can be correct. Unless the answer leaps out at you (if it does, reread the question to look for a trick; sometimes those are the ones you're most likely to get wrong), begin the process of answering by eliminating those answers that are most obviously wrong.

Almost always, at least one answer out of the possible choices for a question can be eliminated immediately because it matches one of these conditions:

➤ The answer does not apply to the situation.

➤ The answer describes a nonexistent issue, an invalid option, or an imaginary state.

After you eliminate all answers that are obviously wrong, you can apply your retained knowledge to eliminate further answers. Look for items that sound correct but refer to actions, commands, or features that are not present or not available in the situation that the question describes.

If you're still faced with a blind guess among two or more potentially correct answers, reread the question. Try to picture how each of the possible remaining answers would alter the situation. Be especially sensitive to terminology; some-times the choice of words ("remove" instead of "disable") can make the difference between a right answer and a wrong one.

Only when you've exhausted your ability to eliminate answers, but remain un-clear about which of the remaining possibilities is correct, should you guess at an answer. An unanswered question offers you no points, but guessing gives you at least some chance of getting a question right; just don't be too hasty when mak-ing a blind guess.

Note: If you're taking a fixed-length or a short-form test, you can wait until the last round of reviewing marked questions (just as you're about to run out of time, or out of unanswered questions) before you start making guesses. You will have the same option within each case study testlet (but once you leave a testlet, you may not be allowed to return to it). If you're taking an adaptive test, you'll have to guess to move on to the next question if you can't figure out an answer some other way. Either way, guessing should be your technique of last resort!

Numerous questions assume that the default behavior of a particular utility is in effect. If you know the defaults and understand what they mean, this knowledge will help you cut through many Gordian knots.

Mastering the Inner Game

In the final analysis, knowledge breeds confidence, and confidence breeds suc-cess. If you study the materials in this book carefully and review all the practice questions at the end of each chapter, you should become aware of those areas where additional learning and study are required.

After you've worked your way through the book, take the practice exam in the back of the book. Taking this test will provide a reality check and help you iden-tify areas to study further. Make sure you follow up and review materials related to the questions you miss on the practice exam before scheduling a real exam. Only when you've covered that ground and feel comfortable with the whole scope of the practice exam should you set an exam appointment. Only if you score 80 percent or better should you proceed to the real thing (otherwise, obtain some additional practice tests so you can keep trying until you hit this magic number).

If you take a practice exam and don't score at least 80 to 85 percent correct, you'll want to practice further. Microsoft provides links to prac-tice exam providers and also offers self-assessment exams at **www.microsoft.com/trainingandservices/**. You should also check out **ExamCram.com** for downloadable practice questions.

Armed with the information in this book and with the determination to augment your knowledge, you should be able to pass the certification exam. However, you need to work at it, or you'll spend the exam fee more than once before you finally pass. If you prepare seriously, you should do well. We are confident that you can do it!

The next section covers other sources you can use to prepare for the Microsoft certification exams.

Additional Resources

A good source of information about Microsoft certification exams comes from Microsoft itself. Because its products and technologies—and the exams that go with them—change frequently, the best place to go for exam-related information is online.

If you haven't already visited the Microsoft Certified Professional site, do so right now. The MCP home page resides at **www.microsoft.com/trainingandservices** (see Figure 1.4).

Note: This page might not be there by the time you read this, or may be replaced by something new and different, because things change regularly on the Microsoft site. Should this happen, please read the sidebar titled "Coping with Change on the Web."

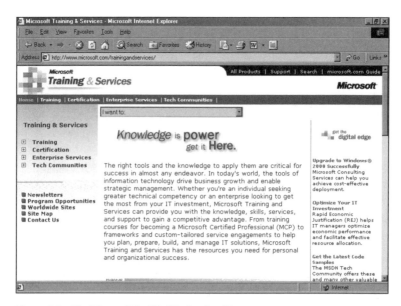

Figure 1.4 The Microsoft Certified Professional home page.

Coping with Change on the Web

Sooner or later, all the information we've shared with you about the Microsoft Certified Professional pages and the other Web-based resources mentioned throughout the rest of this book will go stale or be replaced by newer information. In some cases, the URLs you find here might lead you to their replacements; in other cases, the URLs will go nowhere, leaving you with the dreaded "404 File not found" error message. When that happens, don't give up.

There's always a way to find what you want on the Web if you're willing to invest some time and energy. Most large or complex Web sites—and Microsoft's qualifies on both counts—offer a search engine. On all of Microsoft's Web pages, a Search button appears along the top edge of the page. As long as you can get to Microsoft's site (it should stay at **www.microsoft.com** for a long time), use this tool to help you find what you need.

The more focused you can make a search request, the more likely the results will include information you can use. For example, you can search for the string

```
"training and certification"
```

to produce a lot of data about the subject in general, but if you're looking for the preparation guide for Exam 70-219, "Designing a Microsoft Windows 2000 Directory Services Infrastructure," you'll be more likely to get there quickly if you use a search string similar to the following:

```
"Exam 70-219" AND "preparation guide"
```

Likewise, if you want to find the Training and Certification downloads, try a search string such as this:

```
"training and certification" AND "download page"
```

Finally, feel free to use general search tools—such as **www.search.com**, **www.altavista.com**, and **www.excite.com**—to look for related information. Although Microsoft offers great information about its certification exams online, there are plenty of third-party sources of information and assistance that need not follow Microsoft's party line. Therefore, if you can't find something where the book says it lives, intensify your search.

Overview of Active
Directory Design Elements

Terms you'll need to understand:

✓ Contiguous namespace

✓ Disjoint namespace

✓ Domain

✓ Forest

✓ Global Catalog Server

✓ Organizational Unit (OU)

✓ Site

✓ Tree

✓ Schema

✓ Global Catalog

Techniques you'll need to master:

✓ Using the design elements that make up Active Directory hierarchy

✓ Understanding the function of each design element within Active Directory

✓ Selecting a naming scheme to be implemented in an Active Directory design

✓ Identifying the two types of namespaces available in Active Directory: contiguous and disjoint

Active Directory is a relatively new technology, yet it is the core of a Windows 2000 network, as Microsoft explains:

Active Directory is an essential and inseparable part of the Windows 2000 network architecture that improves on the domain architecture of the Windows NT 4.0 operating system to provide a directory service designed for distributed networking environments. Active Directory lets organizations efficiently share and manage information about network resources and users. In addition, Active Directory acts as the central authority for network security, letting the operating system readily verify a user's identity and control his or her access to network resources. Equally important, Active Directory acts as an integration point for bringing systems together and consolidating management tasks (Microsoft Corporation, 2000).

In order for experts to properly implement an Active Directory infrastructure, they must first have an understanding of the Active Directory design elements and, equally important, an understanding of the business for which the Active Directory infrastructure is being designed. The process that occurs in developing an Active Directory infrastructure involves an analysis of the business's current administrative model, goals it wants to achieve, as well as any future plans. With proper business analysis, an Active Directory infrastructure can meet the needs of the business's current administrative model while easily allowing for future growth and expansion.

Active Directory is implemented as a service that allows network administrators to centrally organize and manage objects such as users, computers, printers, applications, and profiles. This means that locating and managing network resources is now much simpler. Objects that are stored in Active Directory are then accessible to users throughout an organization. Users do not need to know the physical location of the objects because they are logically grouped into a central location. The specific structure of Active Directory can be customized to meet the needs of almost all business environments.

This chapter will briefly discuss each of the design elements within the Active Directory infrastructure. A more detailed description of each design element will be covered in later chapters. The examples provided throughout the chapter will be based on a fictitious corporation named XYZ. XYZ is the main division within the company, with a second division being recently established—called ABC. The two divisions each have their own Internet presence and wish to remain somewhat independent of one another. The headquarters for XYZ is located in Paris, and the headquarters for ABC is located in New York. There are also several branch offices in various locations.

Major Design Elements of Active Directory

The structure of Active Directory is hierarchical. It consists of five main design elements:

➤ Forests

➤ Trees

➤ Domains

➤ Organizational Units

➤ Sites

It is important to have a thorough understanding of these elements to effectively design an Active Directory structure. When you're planning an Active Directory structure, it is also important to analyze the organization's current administrative needs—both its current administrative structure and plans for future changes—in order for each design element to be properly implemented.

Forests

The first design element that will be discussed is the *forest*. A forest is the boundary of the scope of an Active Directory implementation. In its simplest form, a forest is a single domain. Forests can contain multiple domains, and each new domain created with its own unique namespace establishes a new tree within the forest (trees will be discussed later in the chapter). Take a look at the structure of the XYZ Corporation in Figure 2.1.

The first domain created in the forest is **xyz.corp**. The Paris domain and NY domain are created within this tree and share a portion of their namespace with

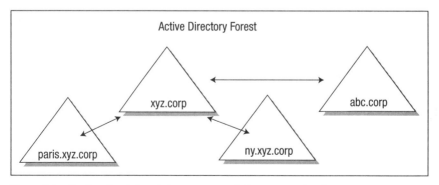

Figure 2.1   The forest root domain is **xyz.corp**, and **abc.corp** requires its own namespace. Together, the two namespaces form an Active Directory forest.

xyz.corp. For administrative purposes, the ABC domain requires a separate namespace and is established as a new tree within the same forest.

The first domain created within the forest is the *forest root*. This domain cannot be renamed or deleted. For this reason, it is important to plan which domain will become the forest root domain for an organization. Careful planning during this phase can help avoid the possibility of having to completely reorganize the Active Directory structure in the future. Once the forest root domain has been configured, new domains can be added to this tree or they can be established as new trees within the forest.

When you're designing the forest structure, remember that simpler is usually better. With Active Directory, it is possible to create multiple forests, but a single-forest environment is much easier to administer and maintain. It is also easier on users because they do not need to know where resources are located within the Active Directory forest. In some cases, however, it may be necessary for organizations to create more than one forest in order to meet their administrative needs.

Domains within a single forest share some common information:

➤ Schema

➤ Configuration container

➤ Enterprise admin

➤ Schema admins

Having common information among domains within a single-forest environment is easier to administer. Conversely, this can also be the reason why an organization would opt to create a multiforest structure. The next two sections should clarify this statement.

Schema

The schema maintains a list of all objects that can be stored within Active Directory as well as the attributes associated with each object. The schema is made up of two main components:

➤ The class-schema object

➤ The attribute-schema object

An example of a class-schema object within an Active Directory would be the Users class. An attribute associated with this class may be the user's first name. Each attribute, such as the user's first name, will have an attribute-schema object associated with it that defines items such as the syntax of the attribute. For the most part, the default schema should meet the needs of an organization, but components can also be added or modified within the schema if needed. For example, an organization may require that employee IDs be a required field for all users. In a case such as this, the schema can be modified to include this attribute.

When planning a forest structure, the design team will have to consider the schema policy. If the default schema policy does not meet the needs of the entire organization, it may be necessary to create multiple forests. For example, if two organizations work together but require different schema policies for their domains, it will be necessary to create a multiple-forest hierarchy.

Note: You can modify the schema within the Microsoft Management Console using the Schema snap-in. In order to modify the schema for a forest, you must be a member of the Schema Admins group.

Configuration Container

A forest also contains a single configuration container that is copied to all domain controllers within the forest. This container stores configuration information about the entire forest, such as which subnets have been combined into sites and the site links connecting them. This information can be used for tasks such as replication. The configuration container can be examined when determining links between sites and the best route for replication if multiple links exist. Having a forest-wide configuration container means that configuration information does not need to be created for each domain. This makes the administration of multiple domains much easier.

Global Catalog Server

All domains within a forest also share a single Global Catalog Server. The Global Catalog Server stores certain attributes pertaining to each object within the forest. This is beneficial for clients, because they do not need to go searching for objects in different domains. Think of a Global Catalog Server in terms of the Yellow Pages, which stores certain attributes for businesses in a city. You use the Yellow Pages when you want to quickly determine the location of a business or find its phone number. When searching for objects within the forest, you can query the Global Catalog Server to determine their location instead of having to perform an extensive search. This is a welcome change from Windows NT 4.0, where users who wanted to locate an object within the network would have to do a search of the entire domain and any trusted domains.

Default attributes are automatically included within the Global Catalog. Organizations have the option of adding attributes and customizing the information stored in the Global Catalog Server to meet their needs. If the XYZ Corporation requires that the employee ID attribute be added to the information stored in the Global Catalog Server, an administrator would simply have to use the Active Directory Schema snap-in (see Figure 2.2).

Figure 2.2 To add an attribute to be replicated to the Global Catalog Server, use the Active Directory Schema snap-in in the MMC. For any additional attributes you want to have stored in the Global Catalog, select the Replicate This Attribute To The Global Catalog checkbox.

A Global Catalog server is not needed in a single-domain environment. If a forest contains more than one domain, a Global Catalog server is required for successful network logon. Therefore, it is essential that one be placed at every site.

By default, the first domain controller within the forest is designated as the Global Catalog Server. An organization can thereafter designate its domain controller of choice as the Global Catalog Server. For a Windows 2000 network running in native mode, a Global Catalog Server is required for the logon process. Therefore, it may be necessary to designate a domain controller in each site as a Global Catalog Server so that users do not have to log on via a wide area network (WAN) link. The XYZ Corporation may find it necessary to designate another server as a Global Catalog Server within its New York site if its current Global Catalog is in Paris. Designating another server as a Global Catalog Server can be done through Active Directory Sites and Services, under the administration tools (see Figure 2.3).

Trusts

Windows 2000 has also made the process of providing access to resources across multiple domains much simpler. In previous versions of NT, in order for users in one domain to access resources in another domain, at least a one-way trust had to be manually set up between the two domains. Assuming the domain controllers

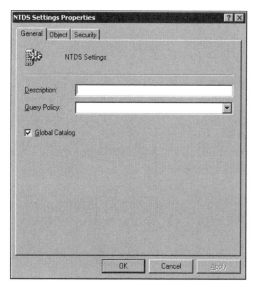

Figure 2.3 Accessing the NTDS Settings property box through Active Directory Sites and Services allows an organization to delegate another domain controller as a Global Catalog Server.

in Figure 2.1 are running NT 4.0, if users in the Paris domain needed access to resources in the NY domain, the administrators would have to manually set up a one-way trust where NY would trust Paris. With Active Directory, two-way, transitive Kerberos trusts are automatically established between all domains in the same forest. For example, if the Paris and NY domains are in the same forest, complete trusts would automatically be established between them, which would give users in each domain access to others' resources. This eliminates the need for trusts to be manually created between domains. It is important to keep in mind that in a multiforest environment, in order for users in one forest to access resources in another, an explicit trust must first be established.

Note: In an organization that has a combination of Windows 2000 and Windows NT 4.0 domains, trusts can still be established, but they must be set up manually.

 Two-way transitive trusts are new to Windows 2000. They are created automatically between parent and child domains, and between root domains within a forest. Old-style, one-way trusts can still be manually created between domains in different forests, as well as between Windows NT and Windows 2000 domains. These one-way trusts are identical to NT trusts, and are not transitive.

Now let's take a look at how domains are organized within an Active Directory forest.

Trees

Within a forest, any domains that share a contiguous namespace form a *tree*. Once a tree has been established within a forest, any new domains added to an existing tree will inherit a portion of its namespace from its parent domain.

In the example shown in Figure 2.4, the Paris domain is added to an existing tree within the forest and inherits a portion of its namespace from its parent domain—in this case, **xyz.corp**. Any new domains added to the forest that require a unique namespace can be established as new trees. A tree structure similar to the one shown in Figure 2.4 may be appropriate for organizations that have more than one registered DNS domain name and wish to maintain each of them. If the organization itself consists of multiple divisions with distinct and separate roles that require their own unique namespaces, it may be appropriate to create a new tree in the forest for each division.

Note: To create a new domain with its own unique namespace, choose to create a new tree within an existing forest during the installation of Active Directory.

With NT 4.0, each time a new domain is added, an administrator must manually configure a trust along with any other domains that it needs to share resources with. If the environment consists of multiple domains configured in a multiple-master domain model, the administrators would have to establish several trusts. The trusts that are set up by the administrator are also not transitive, meaning that if A trusts B and B trusts C, A and C do not trust each other.

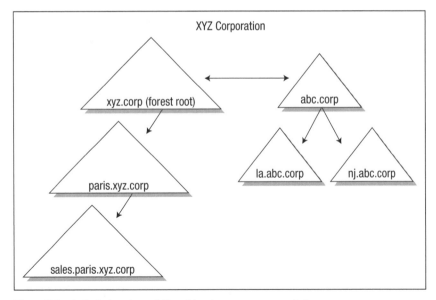

Figure 2.4 A single forest consisting of two trees: **xyz.corp** and **abc.corp**.

Conversely, in Active Directory, two-way transitive trusts are immediately set up between the new domain and its parent domain without the intervention of an administrator. This means that if A trusts B and B trusts C, then A and C also trust each other. When a new tree is created, two-way transitive trusts are also established between the new tree and any other trees within the forest. Trusts within Active Directory will be covered in greater detail later in this chapter.

Domains

The main components of the Active Directory hierarchy are domains and Organizational Units. The *domain* is the main object within Active Directory. *Organizational Units* are created within the domain to organize objects based on the organization's administrative model.

Domains determine both the security and administrative boundaries within the Active Directory hierarchy. Think of a domain as a container, and all the objects within the container share the same administration, replication process, and security requirements. In most cases, the same security requirements can be applied to an entire business. If a business requires separate security policies to meet its administrative structure, it may be necessary to create more than one domain. Objects would then inherit the security policy from the domain in which they are located.

A new feature in Windows 2000 and Active Directory is the multiple-master replication model. Within a domain, all domain controllers are considered to be equal, meaning they all contain a working copy of the directory. In previous versions of NT, there was only one working copy of the directory database for the domain that was stored on the primary domain controller (PDC). The backup domain controllers (BDCs) only maintained copies, which they received from the PDC. If a PDC was taken offline, it was necessary to promote a BDC to take its place so that a working copy of the directory database was available. Within Active Directory, each domain controller can receive changes to the directory and then replicate the changes to other domain controllers in the domain.

Active Directory can also contain domains within domains, known as a *parent-child relationship*. An example of this type of relationship is shown in Figure 2.5 below. Using this relationship, an organization can create a central root domain for administrative purposes and allow the different departments or geographical locations to remain as their own domains by making them child domains to the root. An analysis of the organization's administrative needs will need to be done to determine whether child domains will be necessary.

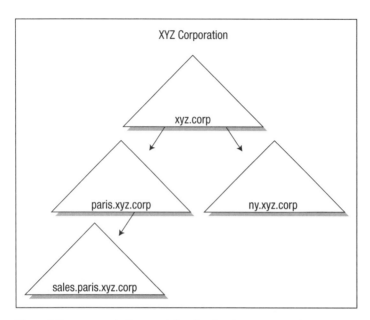

Figure 2.5 **xyz.corp** is the parent domain of **paris.xyz.corp** and **ny.xyz.corp**. **paris.xyz.corp** is also the parent domain of **sales.paris.xyz.corp**.

Organizational Units

Another design element within Active Directory is the Organizational Unit. *Organizational Units* are container objects used to organize objects within a domain. They are not based on the physical structure of the network. When you're planning Organizational Units within Active Directory, it is important to base them on the business's current administrative model. For example, a business may decide to create an Organizational Unit for each department (Accounting, Human Resources, and so on) to establish the hierarchy. Further Organizational Units could then be created to organize the objects in each department.

Note: Creating an Organizational Unit within another Organizational Unit is known as nesting.

For example, within the **ny.xyz.corp** domain, the administrators may decide to create Organizational Units for each department. If the domain consists of three separate departments, three Organizational Units could be created (see Figure 2.6).

By creating these Organizational Units, administrators can delegate control of the objects to other users in the organization. This way, domain administrators do not need to remain responsible for every administrative aspect pertaining to their organization. For example, within the structure shown in Figure 2.6, an Organizational Unit could be created within each department for network printers, and

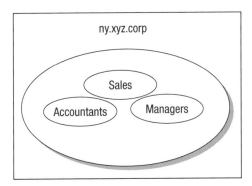

Figure 2.6   The **ny.xyz.corp** domain has created Organizational Units based on departments.

delegation of control over this Organizational Unit can be assigned to another individual or group of individuals.

All domains within a forest maintain their own hierarchy of Organizational Units. This allows administrators in different domains to establish a hierarchy that best meets their needs. Likewise, if all domains within a forest require the same hierarchy of Organizational Units, they can be modeled on one another. For example, if a central IT team manages the entire XYZ Corporation, this team can develop a structure of Organizational Units within Active Directory that can then be implemented by each domain in the forest.

Not only can Organizational Units be created to assign a user or group control over the objects contained within them, but they can also be used to group objects that require a similar Group Policy (for an in-depth discussion of Group Policies, refer to Chapter 6). By applying a Group Policy to an Organizational Unit, an administrator can limit the abilities or restrict the environment of the objects contained within it. A group of users that require a similar desktop environment can be grouped into an Organizational Unit, and the Group Policy can then be applied to that specific container.

Sites

The last major design elements within the Active Directory structure are sites. A *site* is basically a group of IP subnets that are connected by high-speed, reliable links with a lot of available bandwidth. Sites are created within the Active Directory infrastructure to optimize replication between domain controllers. A site topology is designed around the physical location of IP subnets within a domain and the type of link connecting them. As with the other design elements previously discussed, a careful analysis of the physical structure will have to be done to determine the number of sites needed.

When planning for sites, the first thing you'll need to determine is where the domain controllers are going to be located. Clients are usually going to prefer a quick response time, so in most situations, at least one domain controller will be placed in each of the sites (there may be instances when it is determined that a site does not require a domain controller, such as if a site has a very small number of users). Once the domain controllers have been placed, a careful examination of the type of links connecting them and how much network use each one will experience needs to be done. Once connectivity and available bandwidth has been assessed, you can then determine where site links will be established.

If the **ny.xyz.corp** domain shown in Figure 2.7 consists of five IP subnets, the design team would have to look at the speed of the connection between them and the current amount of network traffic. Through analysis, it is determined that IP subnets 1 and 3 are connected by a fast, reliable link and are associated with one site—site A. Replication between these subnets does not need to be controlled. The connection between them has sufficient bandwidth to support replication traffic as well as any other network traffic. The remaining three subnets within the NY domain have been grouped to form another site (site B), because the physical connection between these three is also high speed and reliable, capable of supporting a large amount of traffic. Replication within each site (intrasite) will occur within five minutes of a change.

If there are subnets within a domain that are linked via a connection that cannot support a lot of replication traffic because it is an unreliable, slow link or already heavily used, multiple sites can be created. During the analysis, it is determined

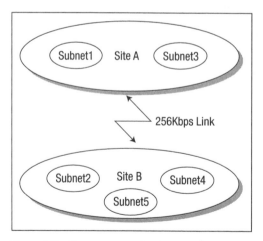

Figure 2.7   The **ny.xyz.corp** has been segmented into two separate sites to optimize replication. Through an analysis, it is determined that the 256Kbps connection will not be able to support the regular traffic generated by replication.

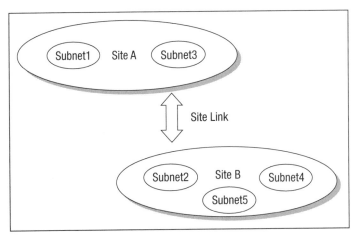

Figure 2.8 The 256Kbps connection will not be able to support the regular replication traffic. Two separate sites with a site link connecting them are created so that replication across the connection can be controlled.

that the connection between site A and site B cannot support regular traffic generated through replication because it is already heavily used (see Figure 2.8).

By creating two separate sites, administrators can then create a site link between them, connecting the two sites. The site link allows replication between subnets to be controlled. The site link can be assigned a cost and a schedule, limiting when replication occurs and which site link is used if multiple site links exist. By specifying a polling interval, you can also control how often a domain controller will check for updates. Once a site link is established, any information sent across the link will be compressed.

Note: Compression of data across a site link does not actually occur until the amount of traffic is greater than 50K.

The site links that are created are transitive as well. Therefore, if a link is created between sites A and B and also between sites B and C, it is assumed that the domain controllers in sites A and C can communicate.

DNS and DNS Namespace Planning

Windows 2000 has adopted the DNS naming convention for naming objects within Active Directory. Each DNS name within the DNS databases is derived from a root name, forming a hierarchical structure. A host's DNS name identifies its position within the hierarchy. This is the same naming structure that has now been implemented within Active Directory. The naming scheme is simple and logical for administrative purposes but also descriptive of the object's location within the hierarchy. The domains within an Active Directory structure are identified by the name they have been assigned, and their domain names identify their positions within the Active Directory hierarchy. When you're choosing a DNS name for an organization, it is once again important to assess its structure and future plans.

Note: If you establish the forest root domain and then determine that it requires a new domain name, Active Directory will need to be reinstalled and a new forest created. Avoid this by carefully choosing an appropriate forest root name.

The DNS naming standards are now applicable to the objects stored within Active Directory to ensure that all names remain unique. By implementing this type of naming scheme, the names that users use on their intranet are also compatible and ready for use on the Internet. Users no longer need to remember two different names—their logon name and their email name. For example, with Active Directory, a user can log on to the network with a name such as JohnD@xyz.corp and can also use the same name as his email address.

The naming scheme implemented by Active Directory also adheres to the same naming requirements as DNS names so that all names within a hierarchy remain unique. When assigning DNS names, keep the following points in mind:

➤ A child domain can only have one parent domain. Looking at the example from the XYZ Corporation, **xyz.corp** is the parent domain of **paris.xyz.corp**. The Paris domain can only have one parent; it cannot be the child of both XYZ and ABC.

➤ If two children share the same parent domain, they must each be assigned unique names. Referring back to Figure 2.5, LA and NJ are both child domains of **abc.corp**. To ensure uniqueness throughout the hierarchy, LA and NJ have to be assigned unique domain names.

Contiguous and Disjoint Namespaces

Within the Active Directory structure, there are basically two types of namespaces:

➤ Contiguous namespace

➤ Disjoint namespace

A *contiguous namespace* is one in which a child object has inherited a portion of its namespace from its parent object. Looking again at the namespace within the XYZ Corporation, **xyz.corp** and **paris.xyz.corp** form a domain tree, which is an example of a contiguous namespace. The Paris domain has inherited a portion of its namespace from the XYZ domain.

A *disjoint namespace* is one in which a child domain has a namespace that is independent from the parent root domain. Within the XYZ Corporation, **abc.corp** is an example of a disjoint namespace because its namespace is independent from the forest root domain, **xyz.corp**.

Here's an easy way to differentiate between the two types of namespaces within a forest: A contiguous namespace forms a tree structure, whereas a disjoint namespace establishes a new tree within the forest.

Practice Questions

Case Study: Paxil Pharmaceuticals

Paxil Pharmaceuticals, based in Princeton, NJ, has business locations in the United States, Canada, and Europe. The majority of its 50,000 employees work in the U.S. offices, with 5000 employees in Europe and 2000 in Canada.

Paxill recently acquired Ritter Health Products, a U.S.-based firm with 10,000 employees. The merger has not gone especially smoothly, both from a management and an IT perspective.

LAN/Network Environment

Paxil's environment consists mainly of Windows NT 4.0 Server and Workstation. Very few computers run any version of Windows 9x, and these are primarily laptops.

Ritter is primarily UNIX-based, with Windows 98 found in the administrative offices and a sizeable population of Macintosh computers.

Both companies are very well networked within locations.

Proposed LAN/Network Environment

The merged companies will migrate to Windows 2000 as quickly as possible. The Paxil Active Directory design was already complete, and deployments were under way when the Ritter acquisition was announced.

The decision to move to Windows 2000 has met with some resistance at Ritter, and certain UNIX-based applications will continue to run on the UNIX hardware after the migration is complete.

WAN Environment

Both Paxil and Ritter have excellent WAN links in North America. Full 1.5Mbps T-1 circuits connect the eight Paxil and three Ritter locations. Temporarily, a 128Kbps VPN circuit is used to connect Paxil and Ritter headquarters locations.

In Europe, Paxil offices use 256Kbps connections. Paxil's European headquarters in London is connected to the Princeton headquarters with a 64Kbps line. This connection is typically saturated during overlapping business hours.

Proposed WAN Environment

No changes are planned at this time. Eventually, the Paxil and Ritter headquarters offices will be linked by T-1, and the Europe circuit will be upgraded, but no timetable has been set yet.

Directory Design Commentary

CEO: We need to "digest" the Ritter acquisition before we make any major changes to our computer systems. We will go ahead with the migration to Windows 2000 and include Ritter, but the applications will stay the same for the foreseeable future.

Director, IT: The Ritter merger was the last thing we needed. We had our Active Directory plans all set, and had migrated two datacenters and four of our locations to Windows 2000. We will have to include them in our plans now, but we need to keep them somewhat separate for resource management.

VP, Sales: We need to be sure to work as a team with Ritter. Its sales force needs access to Paxil data, and vice-versa, if we are to take advantage of our two companies' strengths.

Internet Strategy

Both Paxil and Ritter have a wide range of Internet initiatives. With registered domain names of **paxilpharm.com** and **ritterhealth.com**, respectively, both companies have extensive Web and FTP sites, as well as employee email. Both have developed extranets for use by medical professionals.

No changes are planned, and both companies will retain their domain names.

Question 1

What is the first domain created in an organization's Active Directory called?

- ○ a. The root domain
- ○ b. The forest
- ○ c. The forest root
- ○ d. The schema

The correct answer is c. Answer a is incorrect because although the forest root is also a root domain, the forest root domain has special importance in Active Directory, which other root domains will not have. Answer b is incorrect even though the creation of the forest root occurs at the same time as the creation of the forest. The schema is the logical definition of Active Directory. Therefore, answer d is incorrect also.

Question 2

> Can both the Paxil and Ritter domains share the same forest?
>
> ○ a. No, there can only be one domain in a forest.
>
> ○ b. Yes, there can be more than one domain name in a forest.
>
> ○ c. No, only one root domain is permitted in an Active Directory forest.

The correct answer is b. Active Directory permits more than one root domain in a forest. Answer a is incorrect because there is no limit to the number of domains in a forest. Answer c is incorrect because it is possible to have more than one domain in a forest, creating a disjoint namespace.

Question 3

> Paxil's Active Directory design has a root domain of **paxilpharm.com**, with child domains of **na.paxilpharm.com** and **eur.paxilpharm.com**. By default, can users in **na.paxilpharm.com** access resources in **eur.paxilpharm.com**?
>
> ○ a. No. A cross-link trust must be created between na.paxilpharm.com and eur.paxilpharm.com.
>
> ○ b. No. Trusts in Active Directory are not transitive.
>
> ○ c. Yes. Two-way Kerberos trusts are automatically created between parent and child domains as well as between root domains in a forest.
>
> ○ d. Yes. Trusts are created automatically between every domain in a forest.

The correct answer is c. Two-way transitive Kerberos trusts are created automatically whenever a new domain is added to a forest. The trust goes from child domain to parent domain or between root domains in a disjoint namespace. Although you can create a cross-link trust between two domains to speed Kerberos validation, answer a is incorrect because this trust is not necessary. Answer b is incorrect because the default trusts established between domains are indeed transitive. Finally, answer d is incorrect because trusts are not created between every domain but rather from parent to child and between root domains in the forest.

Question 4

During the migration to Windows 2000 at Paxil, users in a Windows 2000 domain need access to file and print resources in an NT 4.0 domain. What kind of trust can be created to allow access to the NT 4.0 domain?

- O a. No trust relationships can exist between Windows 2000 and Windows NT 4.0 domains.
- O b. A two-way transitive Kerberos trust can be created.
- O c. A two-way nontransitive Kerberos trust can be created.
- O d. A one-way nontransitive NTLM trust can be created.

The correct answer is d. "Old-style" NTLM trusts can be established between Windows 2000 domains and Windows NT domains. These trusts are nontransitive. If a two-way trust is required, two one-way trusts can be set up, just as was done under NT. Therefore, answer a is incorrect. Answers b and c are also incorrect because Windows NT does not support Kerberos authentication or trust relationships.

Question 5

Management at the Paxil headquarters office in Princeton would like to be able to view basic employee information contained in Active Directory for the entire corporation. However, it is concerned that doing this will create an inordinate amount of WAN traffic whenever the query is performed, which is definitely not desirable given the slow and congested link to Europe. How can Paxil management view the employee information without placing a burden on the WAN?

- O a. Place a Global Catalog Server in the Sydney office.
- O b. Locate a domain controller for the Asia and Europe domains in the Sydney office.
- O c. Create an LDAP script to extract information from the Europe domain and use LDIF to import it into the root domain.
- O d. There is no way to query basic employee information in all domains without crossing the WAN.

The correct answer is a. The Global Catalog contains a subset of all attributes for all objects in all domains in an Active Directory forest. By placing a Global Catalog Server in the Princeton office, management can obtain reports on all basic employee information by searching the Global Catalog. Answer b is technically correct, but it is not as good as answer a because extra replication traffic would be generated and custom queries would still have to be written. Answer c is incorrect because this solution would create duplicate user accounts in the forest. Answer d is also incorrect. Although Global Catalog replication traffic will cross the WAN, causing some overhead, the employee information queries will not.

Question 6

Because of political issues regarding the Paxil/Ritter merger, management is considering leaving the companies in separate forests for the next 12 months but would like to be able to merge the two organizations' Global Catalogs. Can this be accomplished, and how?

O a. No. It is not possible to merge Global Catalog contents of two separate forests.

O b. Yes. Create a Kerberos trust between the forest root domains of the two forests, and the Global Catalogs will automatically update each other.

O c. Yes. Run an LDAP script to extract the contents of each Global Catalog and use LDIF to import the other forest's data.

O d. Yes. In the Active Directory Domains and Trusts MMC snap-in, select domain controllers from both forests and create a Global Catalog replication path.

The correct answer is a. The Global Catalog is forest-wide in scope and is read-only, so no updates can be performed. It may be possible to write ADSI or LDAP scripts to query both Global Catalogs, but there is no way to automatically merge them. Aside from this, answer b is incorrect because you can only create a one-way, nontransitive NTLM trust between domains in different forests. Answer c will not work because the Global Catalog is only updated through replication between domain controllers. Answer d is incorrect as well because there is no such feature in Active Directory using any snap-in.

Question 7

To support a Human Resources application being installed at Ritter, three attributes of the User object class must be added to the Global Catalog. Who can perform this operation?

O a. A member of the Domain Admins global group in the domain where the application is installed.

O b. A member of the Enterprise Admins global group.

O c. A member of the Schema Admins global group.

O d. Attributes cannot be added to the Global Catalog without permission from Microsoft.

The correct answer is c. Only members of the Schema Admins group can modify the schema. The Active Directory Schema MMC snap-in is used to mark an attribute as one that should be replicated to the Global Catalog. Answer a is incorrect on two counts—schema modifications affect the entire forest, not a single domain, and domain admins do not have the rights to modify the schema. Answer c is incorrect also, although the initial Administrator account created in the forest root domain is a member of both the Enterprise Admins and Schema Admins groups. Finally, answer d is incorrect because the Active Directory design allows an organization complete flexibility in modifying the schema.

Note that this update to the Schema will affect not only the Ritter domain, but all of the Paxil domains as well.

Question 8

The Active Directory design team is discussing the types of servers that will be needed in various locations across the merged companies. Below is a list of sites, and a list of servers. Place the appropriate server type under the name of the site where it should be placed. You may use a server type in more than one location.

Locations:

Paxil—Berlin office

Ritter—Dallas headquarters

Paxil—Princeton headquarters

Server types:

DNS server

Global Catalog server

Domain Controller

Schema Operations Master

The correct answer is:

Paxil—Berlin office

DNS server

Global Catalog server

Domain Controller

Ritter—Dallas headquarters

> DNS server

> Global Catalog server

> Domain Controller

Paxil—Princeton headquarters

> DNS server

> Global Catalog server

> Domain Controller

> Schema Operations Master

Note that each site should have at least one Domain Controller, Global Catalog server, and DNS server, but only the site where the forest root domain is located will have a Schema Operations Master.

Question 9

The Active Directory design team at Paxil wants to manage replication traffic for the Ritter locations. Using the following list, arrange the steps necessary to create an effective replication topology across the Ritter WAN links.

Tasks:

Specify a replication schedule for each site link

Define subnets in Active Directory for all Ritter locations

Create site links as necessary

Create sites

Assign subnets to sites

The correct answer is:

> Define subnets in Active Directory for all Ritter locations

> Create sites

> Assign subnets to sites

> Create site links as necessary

> Specify a replication schedule for each site link

Question 10

Paxil's European headquarters is connected to the Princeton office by a 64Kbps circuit. During the hours of 7 AM until 2 PM, this link is at almost full capacity. To prevent replication from occurring during these hours, a replication schedule should be set for each site.

○ a. True

○ b. False

Answer b is correct. Replication schedules are set for site links, not sites. Replication frequency (every 15 minutes, every hour) is set at the site level, but not the schedule.

Need to Know More?

 Microsoft Corporation. *Windows 2000 Active Directory Services.* Microsoft Press, Redmond, Washington, 2000. ISBN 0-7356-0999-3.

 The *Microsoft Windows 2000 Server Resource Kit* contains in-depth information about the design elements within Active Directory.

 Try searching the TechNet CD or use Microsoft's online version at **www.microsoft.com** and search for keywords such as "tree," "forest," and "Organizational Unit."

Gathering Information and Analyzing Requirements

Terms you'll need to understand:

✓ Scope

✓ Centralized organizational model

✓ Decentralized organizational model

✓ Bandwidth

✓ LAN/WAN connectivity

Techniques you'll need to master:

✓ Determining the organizational model

✓ Centralized

✓ Decentralized

✓ Determining the organizational structure

✓ Geographical

✓ Divisional

✓ Functional

✓ Determining LAN/WAN connectivity

✓ Assessing the available bandwidth

✓ Determining a business's performance requirements

✓ Assessing the impact of Active Directory

This chapter is broken up into three main sections, each of them equally important. These sections are "Gathering and Analyzing Business Requirements," "Gathering and Analyzing Technical Requirements," and "Assessing the Impact of Active Directory." As you work through this chapter, don't forget to keep in mind the terms you'll need to understand and the techniques you'll need to master, as shown on the chapter's title page.

Throughout this chapter some reference will be given to a fictitious business called XYZ Corporation. The XYZ Corporation is comprised of two main departments: training and external IT. XYZ Corporation has several locations throughout the world and has established several partnerships with other organizations worldwide. **xyz.corp** is in the process of designing an Active Directory infrastructure.

Gathering and Analyzing Business Requirements

The first step in implementing an Active Directory infrastructure for an organization is to analyze its administrative structure, needs, and goals. This is one of the most important steps because the information gathered from the analysis will influence the design of the Active Directory structure. An effective business analysis will offer a clear understanding of the business and allow for the creation of an Active Directory structure that will meet the needs of everyone in the organization. The information gathered about the business should be reflected in the design plans.

The following sections cover what you'll need to do to complete this analysis. These tasks include determining scope, assessing organizational models, assessing business processes, identifying business priorities, and determining client computing requirements.

Determining Scope

During this phase of designing an Active Directory infrastructure, the design team will need to determine the scale of the rollout. Determining the areas within the organization that are to be included in the plan will help you design an Active Directory structure that meets the requirements and needs of the business. The following are a few general questions that should assist you in determining the scope of the business's plan:

➤ Is the Active Directory structure to include the entire organization or just certain areas?

➤ Does the organization foresee any growth within the next five years and, if so, should this information be included in the plan?

➤ Does the organization have any clients or partners that should be included in the Active Directory design plan?

Using the example of the XYZ Corporation, you could use the following questions to determine the scale of the Windows 2000 rollout:

➤ Is the rollout going to include the entire XYZ Corporation or will it just include specific departments?

➤ Does the XYZ Corporation foresee any growth within the next five years?

➤ Does the scope include the partners and clients that the XYZ Corporation has established?

Assessing Organizational Models

When performing the assessment of a business, it is imperative that you determine the organizational model (also referred to as the *administrative model*) that is being used.

There are basically three different types of models that can be implemented: the centralized organizational model, the decentralized organizational model, and the centralized-decentralized organizational model.

Centralized Organizational Model

In a centralized model there is usually an upper management group responsible for most of the decision-making within the business, as illustrated in Figure 3.1. Administration is very much centralized; one group is responsible for making decisions and implementing them at all levels throughout the business.

Decentralized Organizational Model

Within an organization that implements a decentralized organizational model, each business unit or department would be responsible for its own administration (localized administration). This type of model would work well for an

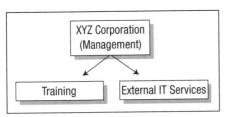

Figure 3.1   The XYZ Corporation may choose to implement a centralized organizational model. Central management within the XYZ Corporation would hold all decision-making authority for the training division and the external IT division.

organization comprised of several businesses. Each business unit would be able to make its own decisions based on its own needs, without affecting the other business units.

If the XYZ Corporation chose to implement a decentralized model, the diagram shown in Figure 3.1 would be slightly different. As shown in Figure 3.2, there would be no centralized management and both divisions within the organization would be able to make decisions based on their own needs.

Centralized-Decentralized Organizational Model

The third model is actually a combination of the first two. A business that implements this model usually recognizes a need for some form of centralized management, but certain administrative tasks have been delegated to different groups to maintain a level of localized administration. In a model such as this, there may be a centralized IT team that is responsible for overall network development while certain tasks, such as creating user accounts, may be delegated to the IT teams within each business unit. Using the XYZ Corporation as an example, this type of model is shown in Figure 3.3.

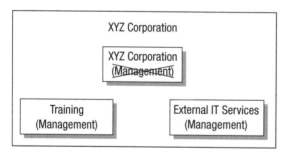

Figure 3.2   If the XYZ Corporation implemented a decentralized organizational model, there would be no central management group. Each division—training and external IT—would be responsible for its own administration. Administration within the organization becomes localized.

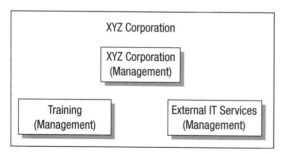

Figure 3.3   If the XYZ Corporation implemented a centralized-decentralized organizational model, there would be a central management group but each division would still be given administrative authority over certain tasks.

Note: The type of organizational model that a business implements should be reflected in the Active Directory design.

Once you've determined the organizational model that is being implemented within the business, you can then determine how the business is actually structured. Under the central management group, how is the business structured? Assessing the organizational structure will be important in determining how administration is actually distributed throughout the business. There are basically three organizational structures that can be implemented:

➤ *Geographical*—Is the structure of the business based on the locations of its offices?

➤ *Functional*—Is the structure based on the different job functions (that is, purchasing, accounting, and manufacturing) found within the business?

➤ *Divisional*—Has the business implemented an organizational structure based on the different divisions within itself? For example, the XYZ Corporation is comprised of two separate divisions (training and external IT consulting) and may choose to structure itself around them.

Taking the time to assess the organizational model and organizational structure of the business will help allow for the creation of an Active Directory structure that will fit in with the current design. The organizational model and organizational structure that a business has implemented should be reflected in the Active Directory structure that will eventually be implemented. The information gathered will have an impact on how the different design elements (forests, trees, domains, and Organizational Units) are implemented.

Assessing Business Processes

It is important to assess the current business processes within an organization because they will have an impact on the design of the Active Directory structure. Examining this aspect of a business will allow the design team to see how Windows 2000 will fit with these processes and even make them more efficient.

Even the smallest changes can have an immense impact on an organization; therefore, it is important to prepare and plan for any changes. If the rollout of Windows 2000 is going to affect any of the business's current practices, be sure to document these changes and make the appropriate people fully aware of them.

For example, it is common practice for the XYZ Corporation to move users from one division to the other, and this causes an increase in replication traffic to occur. The design team will have to consider this business practice when creating sites within the Active Directory structure so that replication traffic within the XYZ Corporation can be optimized.

Identifying Business Priorities

Identifying the priorities that a business has will assist the design team in creating an Active Directory structure that will meet the business's needs and expectations. The technology features that will be implemented within Active Directory will be based on the priorities that the business has expressed. Assess what the business has laid out for itself in terms of short-term and long-term goals and what the business hopes to achieve. Then it can be determined how Windows 2000 is going to help the business meet its goals.

For example, one of the priorities of the XYZ Corporation may be to allow the divisions within the organization to maintain control over their own users and network resources. Knowing that this is a priority for the XYZ Corporation, the design team would create an Active Directory structure that would allow the corporation to maintain this localized administration.

Determining Client Computing Requirements

The Active Directory structure that is designed must not only meet the needs of administration but also the needs of the users within the organization. Therefore, it will also be necessary to do an assessment of the client computing requirements. Assess the following information when determining the computing needs of the clients within an organization:

➤ What type of configuration do the clients' computers require?

➤ Do clients require a preconfigured desktop?

➤ What tasks do the clients perform and what do they need in order to perform them?

➤ What are the computer requirements for client workstations if an upgrade is needed? Keep in mind the minimum requirements for Windows 2000 Professional (these are the requirements to run the OS). If the clients will be running any applications, the minimum will not be sufficient.

➤ What applications do the clients need access to?

➤ What network resources do users need access to and where are they located?

➤ What types of security do they require?

Gathering and Analyzing Technical Requirements

When you're gathering and analyzing information about a business, it is important to not only consider the business requirements but also the technical, security, and performance requirements as well. These three requirements are going to have a major impact on the design of the Active Directory structure and must be carefully considered.

These factors will be covered in the next three sections: "Determining the Technical Environment," "Assessing Security Requirements," and "Determining Performance Requirements." Keep in mind that these topics are equally important as the previous ones discussed and are crucial in designing an effective Active Directory structure.

Determining the Technical Environment

To get a good overall picture of the technical environment within an organization, it is important that you look at the following aspects:

➤ LAN/WAN connectivity

➤ Available bandwidth

➤ Server and workstation distribution

LAN/WAN Connectivity

Begin the assessment of LAN/WAN connectivity by determining the topology of the network. Document the network topology and the size of the network. Once the layout of the network has been established, you can assess the connectivity within the business structure. Documenting the connectivity within a business will assist you in designing an Active Directory structure that complements the physical layout. Not doing a thorough assessment of the connectivity between and within the different locations can result in such things as regular replication occurring over a slow network connection.

The easiest thing to do to get an overall picture of the network structure is to draw a diagram representing the physical structure of the network. An example of this type of diagram is shown in Figure 3.4 (this will help give you an overall picture of the physical layout). Once you've documented the physical layout, you can then determine the type and speed of connections within the different locations as well as the speed of the links between them.

Determining the appropriate speed of the links within an organization will depend on the amount of network traffic that is generated. Further analysis as to the amount of network traffic generated throughout the business will need to be done to determine whether or not a connection will be sufficient.

Note: Completing these assessments will help the design team determine the best replication routes within the business and the optimum location for its servers.

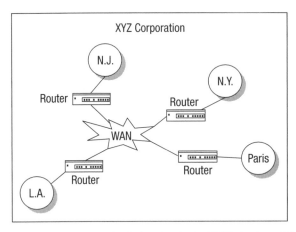

Figure 3.4   An example of what the physical WAN structure of the XYZ Corporation might look like. The design team may choose to document the physical structure in a similar way to get a better overall idea of the structure. In your diagram, be sure to also include the LAN structure.

Available Bandwidth

Assessing the amount of bandwidth available is necessary in determining the location of Active Directory sites. A connection between two locations may be high-speed and reliable but if it is already heavily used, it may not have enough bandwidth available to support regular replication. This information may lead the design team to create sites on either side of the connection. Only a thorough analysis of the network traffic generated within an organization will give you a good picture of the available bandwidth. Using a network analyzer such as Network Monitor will help you determine the amount of traffic currently being generated.

 The physical LAN and WAN infrastructure will influence not only site design but also domain design and server placement within a domain.

Figure 3.5 shows the speed of the WAN connections between the different locations within the XYZ Corporation (when doing an actual assessment of connectivity, be sure to include LAN connectivity as well as WAN). Creating a diagram similar to this one will help the design team establish an overall picture of the links available. Once the type of connectivity has been established, the next step will be to determine how much bandwidth is available over each link.

When determining the amount of traffic that is generated on the network and the available bandwidth, consider some of the following traffic-generating events and how often they occur:

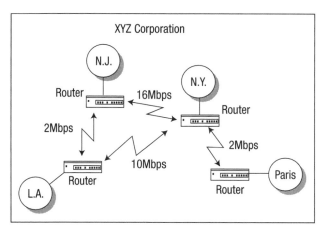

Figure 3.5 This figure shows the design team the exact speed of the connections between the different locations. You would then have to assess the usage of each link to determine whether it will be capable of handling traffic generated by Active Directory replication.

➤ How often are users required to change their passwords?

➤ How many users log on to the network?

➤ When do the bulk of the logons occur?

➤ How many DNS queries are performed throughout the day?

Server and Workstation Distribution

The design team will be responsible for assessing how the servers and workstations are currently distributed throughout the organization. Once the physical setup of the network has been documented, the design team will need to determine how many workstations are in each location, the number of servers within the business, and their current placement as well. The design of Active Directory sites will be dependent on the number of workstations in each location. The decision as to where domain controllers should be placed will be partially dependent on the number of workstations in the different business locations.

For example, the design team working for the XYZ Corporation may determine during its assessment that one of the locations has a very small number of workstations. Information such as this will help the design team in later determining whether a domain controller should be placed in this location.

Note: It may be beneficial to add this information into your diagram of the physical network so you can get an overall picture of how the servers and workstations are distributed throughout the network.

Assessing Security Requirements

The security requirements of a business will have a major impact on the design of the Active Directory structure. The security plan that is developed by the design team should be based on the security requirements of the business. Security has become a hot issue when designing a network infrastructure. As the need for enterprise networks increases and the need to distribute internal data among employees becomes more important, businesses are implementing strict security policies to secure their network resources. When assessing the security requirements that a business has, you'll need to consider user security needs and local (geographical) security requirements.

User Security Needs

Most businesses implement some form of security for their users to protect network resources and to reduce the total cost of ownership (TCO). The security requirements that a business implements for its users, such as data encryption for mobile users, application restrictions, and account restrictions, need to be considered when designing the Active Directory structure.

For example, the XYZ Corporation may require some of the following security requirements for its users:

➤ Preconfigured desktop for all users

➤ Limited capability for users to modify the configurations assigned to them

➤ Secure logon

➤ Application restrictions

➤ Sensitive data available to select groups

➤ Encrypted data for mobile users

The design team needs to be aware of these security needs so the Active Directory structure can support them.

Local (Geographical) Security Requirements

Not only will the security of the users need to be assessed, but consideration will also need to be given to the security needs of the different locations. There are often instances where one location within an organization has very different security needs than another location. If this is the case, the design of the Active Directory infrastructure will need to reflect this.

For example, the XYZ Corporation has several locations throughout the world. After completing an assessment of the local security needs, it may be determined that the offices in L.A. and the offices in Paris have different security requirements.

L.A.	Paris
High Desktop Security	Minimal Desktop Security
Startup and Shutdown Scripts	Data encryption
Application Restrictions	Smart Card Logon
Strict Account Policies	

Figure 3.6   A list of some of the different security requirements that two of the locations within the XYZ Corporation may have.

Figure 3.6 shows a few of the security requirements for each of the geographical locations.

The design of the Active Directory infrastructure for the XYZ Corporation will need to reflect individual security needs that the locations within the business have. In order to meet the different security needs of Paris and L.A., the design team may decide to create separate domains for each location. This would allow each of them to implement its own security. The point is that a company's security requirements will have a major impact on the creation of forests, trees, domains, and Organizational Units. Therefore, it's an aspect that deserves attention.

 In particular, a critical aspect of domain design is understanding all of the security requirements of an organization. Almost all security policy decisions are made at the domain level, so if a part of an organization requires specialized security, this need may force the creation of an additional domain.

Determining Performance Requirements

The performance requirements define the business and employee expectations for their network. The information gathered during this assessment will assist you in creating a design that will meet the expectations that have been expressed. Your goal should be to understand the performance requirements that a business has and ensure that they are incorporated into the Active Directory design plans. Assess the performance requirements of both those in management positions as well as the end users.

One of the expectations that the XYZ Corporation has expressed is that it does not want the WAN link between Paris and N.Y. (refer to Figure 3.5) to become saturated with replication traffic. Being aware of this performance expectation, the design team could create two separate Active Directory sites between the two locations. This would allow the XYZ Corporation to schedule when replication traffic can occur over the WAN connection.

Assessing the Impact of Active Directory

One of the things that need to be considered during the design phase is the impact that Active Directory is going to have on different areas of the business. Your goal should be to make the entire process go as smoothly as possible for everyone involved. Focus on the areas discussed in the following sections ("Existing Systems and Applications," "Technical Support Requirements," and "Scheduled and Planned Upgrades and Rollouts") when determining the impact the upgrade will have on the business.

Existing Systems and Applications

It is important to gather and document information pertaining to the current systems in use. Information about the existing systems and how they will integrate with Active Directory needs to be included in the initial design plans. Use the following questions as a guide when documenting this information:

➤ Do the current systems meet the hardware requirements?

➤ Is the hardware currently used supported by Windows 2000?

➤ What operating systems are currently in use? What service packs have been applied?

➤ How will these operating systems integrate with Active Directory?

➤ Will any operating systems need to be upgraded to another version (NT 4.0) before installing Windows 2000?

➤ Does the business have any DNS servers configured and how will they interoperate within Active Directory?

Not only do the systems have to be assessed but attention also needs to be given to the applications that the business is running on them. What applications does the business currently use? What applications do the business and its employees require to perform their job tasks? Once it has been determined which applications are required, be sure to test them to see how they will integrate within Active Directory.

Note: This may seem like an unimportant step in the design of Active Directory, but it will be a lot easier for you and the organization if it is known beforehand that some systems or applications need to be upgraded.

Technical Support Requirements

The rollout of Windows 2000 is bound to have an impact on the technical support within an organization. The current technical support requirements will need to be assessed to determine how they will be affected. If a business currently relies on internal staff for technical support, what impact will Active Directory have on this? The skill set of the current technical support staff will need to be assessed and a training plan put into place. The IT staff will require highly specialized training on the Active Directory features and functions that are being implemented. Nothing could be worse than to implement a rollout of Windows 2000 only to discover afterwards that the IT staff is unable to provide the technical support necessary to maintain the new structure.

When designing the training plan, consider including end users as well as the IT staff. Providing end users with some basic training on the Active Directory infrastructure being implemented may help to reduce the technical support requirements as the upgrades and rollouts occur.

If a business currently outsources all or some of the technical support requirements to external companies, the impact that the rollout will have on these arrangements will need to be considered. Once the business begins to migrate to Windows 2000, consider whether the company currently responsible for the business's technical support will still be able to meet its needs. If not, this job will need to be managed by a company that is fluent in the Active Directory technologies.

One of the jobs of the design team is to ensure that the upgrades and rollouts go as smoothly as possible for everyone.

Scheduled and Planned Upgrades and Rollouts

Scheduling and planning when the upgrades and rollouts are going to occur will make the transition process less chaotic for the business and its employees. One of the most important things you should do is try to schedule the upgrades and rollout to occur during the business's off-hours. Implementing the changes during peak hours is sure to have an impact on the employees.

Proper communication during this phase is crucial and will help reduce confusion within the business. If you can establish a good line of communication early on, the upgrade and rollout should be less of a disruption for employees. Consider the following points:

➤ Explain to employees how the upgrade process will impact on their jobs, essentially making them easier.

➤ Inform the employees about the deployment process, keeping in mind that some may need more detailed information than others.

➤ Determine how you are going to keep the employees within the business informed of the deployment status.

The more informed you keep the employees about the deployment process, the less of an impact the process will have and the smoother the transition will go.

Chapter Summary

In order to effectively design an Active Directory infrastructure, consider the issues and questions presented in Table 3.1.

Table 3.1 Business Issues and Questions to Address.	
Business Issue	**Question(s)**
Scope	What areas within the business will be included in design plans?
Organizational model	What is the organizational model—centralized, decentralized, or centralized-decentralized?
Business Processes	What are the current processes (practices)? How will they be affected?
Priorities	What has the business laid out for itself in terms of short- and long-term goals?
Client computing requirements	What do clients require to perform their day-to-day tasks?
LAN/WAN Connectivity	What types of connections exist between the different locations?
Available bandwidth	How much bandwidth is available over each connection?
Server and workstation distribution	How are the servers and workstations currently distributed throughout the network?
User security needs	What type of security is currently in place for users in the organization?
Local security needs	What are the security needs of the different locations within the organization?
Performance requirements	What kind of expectations does the business and its employees have in regards to network performance?
Existing systems and applications	How will the systems and applications in use be affected by the rollout? Will any systems need to be upgraded? Are there any unsupported applications that need to be tested?

(continued)

Table 3.1	Business Issues and Questions to Address *(continued)*.
Business Issue	**Question(s)**
Technical support requirements	What are the current technical support requirements for the business and how will they be impacted by the upgrade?
Upgrades and rollouts	When should the upgrades and rollouts be performed? How will employees be kept up-to-date on the progress of the upgrades and rollout?

Practice Questions

Case Study: Melody Music

Melody Music is a musical instrument manufacturer with locations in North America, Asia, and Europe. It consists of three divisions: guitars, electronics, and percussion, and these divisions are spread across the three continents.

LAN/Network

Melody Music has a Windows NT 4.0 server infrastructure, with a single accounts domain and resource domains for each continent's operations. Client computers are predominantly Windows 98, with some NT 4.0 Workstation at the headquarters office in Los Angeles.

10 Mbps twisted-pair Ethernet is used at all Melody Music locations.

Proposed LAN/Network

Melody Music has decided to implement Windows 2000 and Active Directory in all locations, including the joint venture factory in Germany. It has registered the DNS domain name **melodymusic.com,** which it intends to use for internal as well as external naming.

WAN Connectivity

The company has four facilities in North America, connected by full T-1 links. The two European plants are connected to each other with a 256Kbps circuit, and the two Asian facilities are linked with a 256Kbps Virtual Private Network (VPN). All these links are relatively underutilized.

The headquarters office in Los Angeles is connected to both the European and Asian locations via a 64Kbps link. This circuit is very heavily used, especially during Los Angeles business hours.

Proposed WAN Connectivity

No changes are proposed at this time, although management has recognized that the 64Kbps circuit between Europe, North America, and Asia will need to be upgraded eventually.

Directory Design Commentary

CIO: Each of the divisions outside of North America enjoys a fairly autonomous existence, with little intervention from the home office. IT, however, is currently centralized in Los Angeles. Melody Music plans to grant the local network administrators much greater authority in the future, however.

CEO: Melody Music has entered into a joint venture with Klavier, AG, a German manufacturer of pianos. The joint venture makes pianos for sale under the MK Pianos brand. MK Pianos is located in a former Klavier factory, and employees are paid by Melody Music. Melody Music management needs full access to MK Pianos' information.

Internet

Melody Music currently has no Internet presence.

Future Internet

Melody Music has registered the melodymusic.com domain name, will set up email servers, and will develop a Web site.

Question 1

What should the name of the forest root domain be?

○ a. ad.melodymusic.com

○ b. klavier.de

○ c. melodymusic.com

○ d. www.melodymusic.com

The correct answer is c. Melody Music intends to use the melodymusic.com domain name for internal as well as external namespaces. Because of this requirement, answer a is not correct—it places the Active Directory domain below the root. Answer b is incorrect because it is the name of another company and is not at all appropriate as the forest root. Answer d is the DNS name of the Melody Music Web site, so that is incorrect as well.

Question 2

Melody Music management decides to create an Internet presence for the joint venture company, MK Pianos, and registers the DNS domain name of mkpianos.com. How should the Active Directory design be modified for this new domain?

○ a. Create a child domain of melodymusic.com called mkpianos.melodymusic.com

○ b. Create a child domain of melodymusic.com called melodymusic.mkpianos.com

○ c. Create a new domain tree with a root domain of mkpianos.com

○ d. Create a new forest with a root domain of mkpianos.com

The correct answer is c. Because mkpianos.com is a different DNS namespace from Melody Music, it is best to create a new domain tree rather than use the approach suggested by answer a. Answer b is incorrect because the child and parent domain names are reversed. Because Melody Music management requires full access to MK Pianos data, including Active Directory contents, answer d is also incorrect.

Question 3

How many child domains should be created off the forest root domain?

○ a. None

○ b. One—mkpianos.com

○ c. Three—one for each continent

○ d. Three—one for each division

The correct answer is c. Because each of the continents is relatively autonomous, and there are definite WAN considerations, this solution is better than answer d. Answer a is incorrect because of the same WAN speed and capacity restrictions. Finally, answer b is incorrect because mkpianos.com is a different namespace from melodymusic.com.

Question 4

In which domain will the Enterprise Admins and Schema Admins groups be created?

○ a. melodymusic.com

○ b. mkpianos.com

○ c. na.melodymusic.com

○ d. root.melodymusic.com

The correct answer is a. The root domain of the forest should be melodymusic.com, and the forest root is the only domain to have the Enterprise Admins and Schema Admins groups. Answer b is incorrect because although mkpianos.com may be a root domain, it is not the forest root. The same is true for answers c and d, which are also incorrect. na.melodymusic.com is a child domain, not the forest root.

Question 5

> What kind of trust relationship exists automatically between melodymusic.com and mkpianos.com?
>
> ○ a. None
>
> ○ b. Two-way transitive Kerberos trust
>
> ○ c. One-way nontransitive NTLM trust
>
> ○ d. Cross-link trust

The correct answer is b. A two-way Kerberos trust is automatically created between root domains of a disjoint namespace in the same forest, which means that answer a must be incorrect. No one-way trusts are automatically created in Windows 2000, so answer c is incorrect. Answer d is also incorrect because cross-link trusts are manually created between domains that do not have a direct trust relationship between them. Cross-link trusts speed Kerberos credential validation by shortening the validation path through the forest.

Question 6

> Melody Music has decided that a small administrative group on each continent should have control over all Active Directory resources. Control will be assigned on a divisional basis. Based on this plan, arrange the entities below in order, from the domain through lowest-level Organizational Unit.
>
>   Plant location
>
> Computers
>
>   Functional department
>
> Division
>
>   Continent

The correct answer is:

Continent

Division

Plant location

Functional department

Computers

Note that Continent is a domain, and all other entities are Organizational Units.

Question 7

As part of the migration planning process, the Melody Music Active Directory design team has listed a number of issues, both business and technical. Place the issues in list two under the appropriate issue type in list one. You may use the same issue more than once.

Type of issue:

Business

Technical

Active Directory Design Issues:

Organizational model

Client computing requirements to run a specialized application

WAN available bandwidth between North America and Asia

Special security requirements in Asia

Scope of Active Directory

Timing of upgrades and rollouts

The correct answer is:

Business:

Organizational model

Special security requirements in Asia

Scope of Active Directory

Timing of upgrades and rollouts

Technical:

Client computing requirements to run a specialized application

WAN available bandwidth between North America and Asia

Special security requirements in Asia

Timing of upgrades and rollouts

There is overlap on these lists, because many issues require both a business and a technical approach.

Question 8

Melody Music management is considering changes in how the company is run that will result in more centralized control. However, a consultant has told Melody Music management that it may need to completely redo the Active Directory design because permissions from Organizational Units in top-level domains are not inherited by like-named OUs in lower-level domains. Is the consultant correct in her statement?

○ a. Yes

○ b. No

The correct answer is a. The consultant is right. Permissions do not flow across domain boundaries, regardless of what the Organizational Units are named.

Question 9

A new office is opened in Sydney, Australia, and the IT director wants to know whether a new domain should be created for the Australian continent. Business plans call for an expansion of operations to include 2000 employees at three locations within two years. What factors should the IT director consider in making her decision? [Check all correct answers]

❑ a. Security requirements specific to Australia

❑ b. Number of employees

❑ c. Local administration of resources

❑ d. The size of Active Directory

❑ e. Replication traffic and wide area link availability

The correct answers are a and e. Security policies are set at the domain level, so if there are requirements specific to the Australian operation, a separate domain should be considered. Also, if wide area links are slow, congested, or unreliable, a new domain will allow use of the SMTP protocol for Active Directory replication over the slow link.

Answers b and d are not correct. The tested limits of Active Directory are over 50 million objects, so it is not necessary to create additional domains to handle 2000 additional employees.

Finally, answer c is not correct because administration can be delegated at the Organizational Unit level, thus eliminating the need to create a domain to achieve administrative granularity.

Question 10

Klavier AG launches a successful hostile takeover of Melody Music soon after Melody's successful implementation of Windows 2000. Because it has not yet begun its own Windows 2000 implementation, Klavier management decides to simply rename the melodymusic.com domain to klavier.de. Will this approach work?

○ a. Yes

○ b. No

The correct answer is b. It is not possible to rename domains at this point, and the forest root domain, which in this case is melodymusic.com, may never be renamed.

Need to Know More?

 Minasi, Mark. *Windows 2000 Resource Kit*. Sybex, 2000. ISBN 0782126146. This in an advanced book that provides you with in-depth information pertaining to all aspects of Windows 2000 Server, including Active Directory.

 The *Microsoft Windows 2000 Server Resource Kit*, Microsoft Press, 2000, ISBN: 1572318058, contains in-depth information about planning an Active Directory structure.

 Try searching the TechNet CD or use Microsoft's online version at **www.microsoft.com**. Search for keywords pertaining to Active Directory.

Designing a DNS Implementation Strategy

Terms you'll need to understand:

✓ BIND (Berkeley Internet Name Daemon)
✓ Delegated domain
✓ Domain
✓ Dynamic update
✓ Incremental zone transfer
✓ Internal and external names
✓ Root domain name
✓ SRV record
✓ Standard primary DNS server
✓ Standard secondary DNS server
✓ Zone
✓ Zone transfer

Techniques you'll need to master:

✓ Understanding DNS names and hierarchies
✓ Installing and configuring DNS servers
✓ Delegating zones to multiple DNS servers
✓ Configuring different external (public) and internal (AD) DNS namespaces
✓ Understanding interoperability issues with Microsoft and non-Microsoft DNS servers

Microsoft Windows 2000 and Active Directory depend heavily upon a well-designed and reliable Domain Name System (DNS) infrastructure. In this chapter, you will learn how to design an effective DNS strategy for an organization, and how DNS servers provide essential services for Windows 2000 and Active Directory. You will learn different techniques for integrating Microsoft's DNS into an existing non-Microsoft DNS infrastructure, and how to identify potential interoperability issues. In addition, naming strategies will be covered here, as they relate to an overall Active Directory naming strategy.

Overview of DNS and Windows 2000

One of the major changes to Windows 2000 is its reliance on DNS as a locator service—not just for the traditional servers and hosts but also for operating system services such as Kerberos and LDAP, the Lightweight Directory Access Protocol. Under Windows NT, NetBIOS name services were used instead. A NetBIOS name was a 16-character string, in which the first 15 characters identified the computer and the 16th character contained a hexadecimal value identifying specific services. A Microsoft networking host computer would register itself with one or more NetBIOS service records, using the 16th character of the NetBIOS name to identify the services available on that particular machine. But reliance on NetBIOS has been one of the major criticisms of Windows NT over the years, and Microsoft has moved to reduce the need for NetBIOS in Windows 2000. As a result, Windows 2000 and Active Directory depend upon a reliable DNS infrastructure for proper operation.

Although NetBIOS naming is retained in Windows 2000 for backward compatibility with older Microsoft operating systems such as NT and Windows 98, DNS has become the primary name-resolution mechanism. Domains and computers are given DNS names, with NetBIOS names derived from their DNS counterparts. Where previously computer or domain names could be almost anything as long as all names were unique, Windows 2000 forces a more standardized naming approach. Names must conform to DNS standards, as spelled out in RFCs 1034, 1035, and 1123, especially in organizations where Microsoft and non-Microsoft DNS servers will coexist. Naming standards will be explored later in this chapter.

Microsoft first included an "official" DNS server component with the release of NT 4. The Windows 2000 DNS implementation is a far more ambitious product. With an eye towards supporting the needs of Active Directory and an enterprise-wide deployment of Windows 2000 servers and workstations, Microsoft has added a slew of features to its new DNS, including the following:

➤ *SRV record support*—SRV (Service Locator) records are used to locate services running under Windows 2000. The concept is similar to the having services register NetBIOS names with a special 16th character under prior Microsoft networking products.

➤ *Dynamic update*—Dynamic update allows host computers to automatically update DNS. Optionally, these updates can be secured, thus preventing unauthorized modifications to DNS.

➤ *Incremental zone transfers*—Incremental transfers reduce the amount of data moved over the network during a zone transfer between the primary and a secondary DNS server. Instead of having a scheduled transfer of an entire zone file, which is initiated by the secondary, with incremental transfer, only new and updated records are sent down to the secondary server. Also, the transfer occurs when updates are made, and the primary DNS server notifies the secondary.

➤ *Active Directory integration*—Probably the most controversial feature of Windows 2000 DNS is AD integration. Converting a zone to Active Directory integration means that updates can occur at any AD-integrated DNS server, not just a primary server. Also, zone transfers follow the AD replication topology rather than a separate DNS topology.

Only one of these technologies is required by Windows 2000, namely SRV record support. The SRV records replace the NetBIOS service registration records found in Windows NT, and they provide some additional functionality as well. Windows 2000 hosts will use "site" SRV records to locate nearby servers and resources, thus minimizing wide area network traffic.

Although not mandatory, dynamic update capability is very strongly recommended on primary DNS servers. When a Windows 2000 Server is being promoted to domain controller (DC), it registers a large number of SRV records during the process. These records must be manually entered into DNS if dynamic update capabilities are not available on the primary DNS server. Delegation of the Active Directory zones to Windows 2000 DNS servers may provide a workaround in this case, however.

Finally, it is not even necessary to use Windows 2000 DNS. It is possible to use BIND (Berkeley Internet Name Daemon), the most prevalent Unix-based DNS service. There are many different versions of BIND, and these will be discussed.

As is the case with much of Active Directory design, a successful implementation will start with an analysis of the business requirements of an organization. Let's look into some of the business needs that will influence the DNS and AD designs.

Identifying Business Needs

An Active Directory design will always begin by defining scope, as discussed in Chapter 3. How much of an organization will be included in the proposed Active Directory? Will all branches, regions, subsidiaries, joint ventures, and the like, be included in a single enterprise directory or will the organization be split somehow? How much merger, acquisition, and divestiture activity is in progress or forecast for the future?

Does the organization have an Internet presence? If so, how many different names are used? If the company has several names on the Internet, will business continue in this manner or will the number of names be reduced or expanded?

Finally, is there a need to separate the internal Active Directory domains from the external Internet presence? In many cases, security considerations may require a different internal name from the external Internet name recognized by the public.

Evaluation of the answers to these questions will help you develop a sound naming strategy. This naming strategy must then be translated into an approach for implementing a new DNS infrastructure, enhancing existing DNS services, or interoperating with non-Microsoft DNS servers.

Throughout this chapter, we'll use the XYZ Corporation example presented in earlier chapters. XYZ consists of two divisions: the eponymous XYZ division and a recently opened division called ABC. The two divisions each have their own Internet presence and wish to remain somewhat independent of one another. The headquarters for XYZ is located in Paris, and the headquarters for ABC is located in New York City. XYZ also has several branch offices in various locations.

BIND DNS servers are located in Paris and New York. The Paris DNS server runs BIND 4.9.7, whereas New York runs 8.2.2. A branch office in Chicago hosts a third DNS server on a Windows NT 4.0 member server with Service Pack 4 installed.

DNS and Active Directory

Unlike Windows NT, with Windows 2000, a domain name is a DNS domain name. There are several basic guidelines for developing a naming scheme for new Windows 2000 implementations.

Domain Names

Domain names should follow RFC standards. Although Microsoft Windows 2000 DNS will permit relaxed RFC compliance for names, and even allow Unicode names to be registered, it is a good idea to follow RFCs 1034, 1035, and 1123 when naming domains and computers (see the "Need to Know More" section at the end of this chapter). This is an especially important rule to follow when interoperability with non-Microsoft DNS is of prime concern. If, however, only Microsoft Windows 2000 DNS servers will be used, you may relax the naming restrictions. Name checking can be relaxed using the DNS MMC snap-in, selecting the Server Properties page, and clicking the Advanced tab, as shown in Figure 4.1.

Registered Domain Names

Companies wishing to conduct business on the Internet must obtain a registered domain name. Getting a registered name means that two companies cannot have or own the same name.

It is possible to install Active Directory using a nonregistered name, but this is a very unwise idea. First, it will be impossible to set up email or Web servers with Internet access without a registered name. Even if an organization has no plans in the near future to connect to the Internet (hard to believe!), it will be impossible to connect at a later date if some other company has registered the name in the meantime. Name registration is extremely inexpensive and should be a required step for any new Active Directory installation.

The other problem with a nonregistered name is that it is possible for a merger to occur where both companies have selected the same nonregistered domain name.

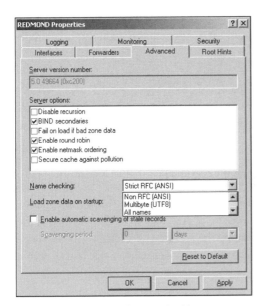

Figure 4.1   Relaxing DNS name checking.

Although the probability of such a merger occurring may be statistically small, Murphy's Law suggests that the likelihood is far, far greater.

It is critical to register the Active Directory root domain name. The root domain (the first domain created in Active Directory) is also the forest root, and it is impossible to rename this domain. Should business needs change and the root domain name prove to be unusable, it may be necessary to uninstall Active Directory and reinstall from scratch. Clearly this is not a desirable option.

Differences between DNS and Active Directory Domain Names

Depending on the business requirements of an organization, the externally recognized DNS domain name and the Active Directory domain name may be different. In some cases, the Active Directory domain name may just be a subdomain of the DNS name. For example, if the external DNS name is **xyz.corp**, the Active Directory root domain may be **ad.xyz.corp**.

A second option is a completely different domain name. Using the preceding example, the Active Directory root may be named **xyz.local**. In this case, configuration of Proxy Server and email may prove challenging.

These options are discussed in greater detail in the following paragraphs.

Regardless of the DNS design approach used, the following "best practices" should be employed when creating DNS host and domain names for use with Windows 2000:

➤ Use RFC-compliant DNS names, especially when working in a heterogeneous DNS environment.

➤ Register the root domain (forest root) name before creating the first Windows 2000 domain controller.

➤ Register any other domain roots before creating the first domain controller for that domain tree.

DNS Infrastructure Design

A successful DNS infrastructure design must meet both business and technical requirements. The business needs must be addressed first so that existing applications and systems are not impacted by the addition of Windows 2000, Active Directory, and a new DNS. Technical requirements include availability, reliability, security, and scalability.

Integrating Windows 2000 DNS with BIND

BIND (Berkeley Internet Name Daemon) is the most prevalent Unix-based DNS service. Many organizations, even those with predominantly Windows-based hosts, have implemented BIND for external and internal name resolution. Because DNS is a critical service, many IT departments are reluctant to modify an existing, functional implementation of DNS to support Windows 2000 and Active Directory.

Fortunately, it is possible for Windows 2000 DNS to interoperate with BIND. Different solutions will be required based on the installed version of BIND because the later versions include features not found in earlier BIND implementations.

As mentioned earlier, Windows 2000 processes use service locator records (SRV records) in DNS to find a nearby domain controller that is hosting a desired service. A Windows 2000 Professional client computer may be running an application wanting to access the Global Catalog, for example. SRV record support is mandatory for any DNS server accessed by Windows 2000 domain controllers. BIND version 4.9.7 and above supports SRV records.

Although not mandatory, it is strongly suggested that any DNS used for Windows 2000 domain controllers also support dynamic update. Dynamic update allows a host computer to register its own DNS records. You'll find dynamic update extremely useful when adding a new domain controller because a large number of SRV records must be registered. The exact number depends on the number of services to be hosted on that server. The records are written to the %systemroot%\system32\config\netlogon.dns file when the new domain controller's dcpromo process completes successfully. To avoid the need for tedious and error-prone manual update, it is best to use a DNS server that permits dynamic update. BIND version 8.2.2 is the first reliable version of BIND to perform dynamic updates successfully.

Note: You may find references to BIND 8.2.1 in older documentation. BIND 8.2.1, however, crashes when updated by a Windows 2000 computer and is therefore not very well suited to a Windows 2000 implementation.

A sample netlogon.dns file follows:

```
xyz.corp. 600 IN A 10.10.1.1
_ldap._tcp.xyz.corp. 600 IN SRV 0 100 389 redmond.xyz.corp.
_ldap._tcp.pdc._msdcs.xyz.corp. 600 IN SRV 0 100 389
redmond.xyz.corp.
_ldap._tcp.gc._msdcs.xyz.corp. 600 IN SRV 0 100 3268
redmond.xyz.corp.
_ldap._tcp.558f59cf-0aad-4841-9d85-
9dcb91989ee2.domains._msdcs.xyz.corp. 600
```

```
 IN SRV 0 100 389 redmond.xyz.corp.
gc._msdcs.xyz.corp. 600 IN A 10.10.1.1
8bbc38db-c18e-48bb-a7a3-e3154617862d._msdcs.xyz.corp. 600 IN CNAME
  redmond.xyz.corp.
_kerberos._tcp.dc._msdcs.xyz.corp. 600 IN SRV 0 100 88
redmond.xyz.corp.
_ldap._tcp.dc._msdcs.xyz.corp. 600 IN SRV 0 100 389
redmond.xyz.corp.
_kerberos._tcp.xyz.corp. 600 IN SRV 0 100 88 redmond.xyz.corp.
_gc._tcp.xyz.corp. 600 IN SRV 0 100 3268 redmond.xyz.corp.
_kerberos._udp.xyz.corp. 600 IN SRV 0 100 88 redmond.xyz.corp.
_kpasswd._tcp.xyz.corp. 600 IN SRV 0 100 464 redmond.xyz.corp.
_kpasswd._udp.xyz.corp. 600 IN SRV 0 100 464 redmond.xyz.corp.
_ldap._tcp.Default-First-Site._sites.xyz.corp. 600 IN SRV
  0 100 389 redmond.xyz.corp.
_ldap._tcp.Default-First-Site._sites.gc._msdcs.xyz.corp. 600 IN
SRV
  0 100 3268 redmond.xyz.corp.
_kerberos._tcp.Default-First-Site._sites.dc._msdcs.xyz.corp. 600
IN SRV
  0 100 88 redmond.xyz.corp.
_ldap._tcp.Default-First-Site._sites.dc._msdcs.xyz.corp. 600 IN
SRV
  0 100 389 redmond.xyz.corp.
_kerberos._tcp.Default-First-Site._sites.xyz.corp. 600 IN SRV
  0 100 88 redmond.xyz.corp.
_gc._tcp.Default-First-Site._sites.xyz.corp. 600 IN SRV
  0 100 3268 redmond.xyz.corp.
```

The following subsections look at some common options based on the version of BIND in use.

BIND Version Prior to 4.9.7

BIND implementations using versions prior to 4.9.7 support neither SRV service locator records nor dynamic update. These servers cannot be used alone to support Active Directory but may be used in conjunction with later BIND servers or Microsoft Windows 2000 DNS servers to provide the necessary functionality.

Two basic options exist. First, the four Active Directory zones can be delegated to DNS servers with SRV record support. The delegated servers can be running BIND 4.9.7 or higher, or Windows NT 4.0 DNS (with Service Pack 4) or higher.

Second, a separate Active Directory subdomain can be created, again on a BIND or Microsoft DNS server that supports at least SRV records and preferably dynamic update.

These options are discussed in a following section, "DNS Naming Strategies."

BIND Versions 4.9.7 through 8.2.1

These versions of BIND allow for SRV records but either do not support dynamic update at all or do not perform it reliably for Microsoft hosts. The options described previously for earlier versions of BIND apply here as well. A third option is to perform manual updates of the DNS server using the contents of the netlogon.dns file created during the dcpromo operation. Note that updates must also be done whenever a new site or Global Catalog Server is added.

BIND 8.2.2 or Higher

These versions of BIND permit SRV records and also can be reliably updated by Microsoft Windows 2000 hosts. It is not necessary to run Windows 2000 DNS if the existing DNS infrastructure consists of BIND 8.2.2 or higher.

Other DNS Servers

Microsoft Windows NT 4.0 DNS will support SRV records if Service Pack 4 has been applied. NT 4 DNS will not perform dynamic updates, so the Active Directory SRV records must be manually updated every time a domain controller, Global Catalog Server, or site is added or deleted.

 Windows 2000 domain controllers must use a DNS server with SRV record support. Dynamic update is strongly recommended, because changes in the domain controllers or Active Directory may require updates to SRV record information. Note that only a standard primary DNS server needs to support dynamic update. Secondary DNS servers pull updates from the primary server and therefore do not need dynamic update capability.

Ensuring Availability

Because DNS is so critical to the proper operation of Windows 2000 and Active Directory, the DNS design must be fault tolerant. You can take several approaches to ensure that a DNS server is always accessible, regardless of failures in hardware, software, or LAN/WAN connections.

Use One DNS Server Per Site

The first rule of thumb is to place at least one DNS server in each site. Sites are areas of good network connectivity, and a multisite environment typically has wide area links connecting the sites. WAN links are usually more prone to failure than LAN connections, so it stands to reason that a DNS server per site will provide a good measure of fault tolerance.

Delegate Subdomains Off the Root

A traditional DNS implementation consists of one primary DNS server, which receives periodic updates, and one or more secondary DNS servers, which obtain read-only copies of the zone file from the primary.

Note: DNS primary and secondary servers operate in a manner similar to primary and backup domain controllers under Windows NT 4.0. Updates can only be made at the primary DNS server, and secondary DNS servers periodically pull an updated copy from the primary.

The biggest problem with the traditional approach is that, if the primary DNS server is down, no updates can take place. In a nondynamic environment, this does not present a major issue because updates are manually entered. It matters little if a host record update, for example, occurs now or in one hour. However, if DNS is being updated dynamically, server availability becomes much more important. If client computers are configured to update DNS, either by themselves or through DHCP, server availability is critical.

One solution is to delegate all subdomains off the root domain. For example, assume that the XYZ Corporation has subdomains for Europe, Asia, and North America. The European and Asian subdomains should be delegated to servers located in those geographic areas. Delegation will improve reliability and performance because DNS updates will not need to cross wide area networks. In addition, to further minimize WAN traffic, the DNS server that is the primary server for a given subdomain, such as **eur.xyz.corp**, should be the secondary server for all the other domains and subdomains in the enterprise. Configuring multiple DNS servers as secondaries also provides a level of fault tolerance. Therefore, the DNS server in Europe would contain not only the zone file for Europe but also would be secondary for all other zones. In addition to being primary for Europe, this DNS server would also have a read-only (secondary) copy of the Asian, North American, and root zones.

Use Active Directory-Integrated Zones

Active Directory-integrated zones are exclusive to Windows 2000 DNS. A new zone may be created as "Active Directory integrated" or may be changed from a standard zone at any time. Simply right-click the zone file name in the DNS MMC snap-in, select Properties, and click the Change button on the General tab of the Properties page, as shown in Figure 4.2.

Active Directory-integrated zones can have several advantages over the standard zone types. The most significant of these is that AD-integrated zones are multimaster. If there are two domain controllers at a site and both are DNS servers with Active Directory-integrated zones, updates can occur at either server.

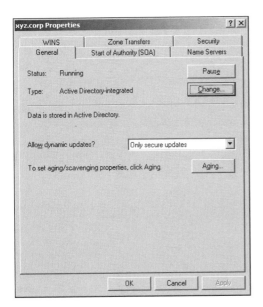

Figure 4.2   Active Directory-integrated zones.

Fault tolerance is greatly enhanced, and updates are far more likely to remain local rather than cross slower and possibly more congested WAN links.

Because the zone information is stored in Active Directory, replication now follows the same path as regular Active Directory replication. Traditional DNS requires a separate replication topology, which can complicate zone transfer troubleshooting.

An additional benefit of Active Directory integration is the ability to secure the dynamic update process. When the Only Secure Updates option is selected, as shown previously in Figure 4.3, updates to DNS are signed and encrypted. Encryption prevents unauthorized persons from "sniffing" or monitoring the network to pick up information about servers and workstations by examining DNS traffic. Packet signatures validate that the DNS update request was sent by the proper entity, thus curtailing name theft.

Traditional zone transfers, either incremental or full, are sent in clear text so that someone monitoring the network has a complete picture of all servers and workstations registered with DNS. Note that it is possible to use IPSec to secure transmissions between standard DNS servers. IPSec can be configured to sign, encrypt, or both sign and encrypt all IP traffic between specified computers. Because IPSec security is applied low in the IP stack, it is not necessary for applications to be aware of the existence of IPSec. This means, however, that IPSec must be configured separately from DNS, so the security features are not available automatically.

In a mixed DNS environment, non-Microsoft secondary DNS servers can still receive updates from an Active Directory-integrated DNS server because a BIND-style zone file is still maintained.

DNS Naming Strategies

You have four basic design options when planning a DNS domain name strategy. In all cases, however, the most important consideration is that the root domain for any Active Directory domain tree must be registered with a naming authority. Otherwise, you'll run the risk of conflicts when connecting your organization to the Internet.

The options are:

➤ Use the same DNS domain name for the internal network as the external network.

➤ Use existing DNS servers and delegate Active Directory subdomains to new Microsoft DNS servers.

➤ Create a subdomain of the external Internet domain for use internally.

➤ Create a private internal network name that's different from the external name.

Each option has its pros and cons, which will be discussed in the following subsections.

Use the Same DNS Domain Name Internally as Externally

Using this option, there is no difference between the internal and the external DNS names. The network is effectively split at the firewall, with external resources resolved by one or more external DNS servers and internal resources resolved by the internal servers. Any external resources, such as Web, mail, and FTP servers, must have host records added manually to the internal DNS. Likewise, any internal resources that can be accessed from the Internet, such as Virtual Private Network (VPN) servers, must be defined in the external as well as the internal DNS servers.

This approach is simple and effective, but care must be taken if the external DNS servers are capable of dynamic update. For security reasons, it is not a good idea to publish the SRV records from the internal hosts to the external DNS, so it is imperative that dynamic update be turned off outside the firewall. Although it may be common sense to ensure that Internet visitors can neither view the internal network nor update DNS, it is very easy to accidentally turn on dynamic update capabilities.

Use Existing DNS Servers and Delegate Active Directory Zones

A company with an older DNS infrastructure, and no need or desire to upgrade, will give this option serious consideration. The four Active Directory subdomains, _msdcs, _sites, _tcp, and _udp, are delegated to either Windows 2000 DNS servers or any other DNS that supports SRV records and, ideally, dynamic update. Delegation means that responsibility for maintaining the subdomain is transferred to another DNS server or set of servers. In this case, when a domain controller attempts to dynamically update the locator SRV records, it is initially directed to one of the default non-Microsoft DNS servers, which in turn passes the request on to the delegated server. Even if the primary DNS servers do not support either SRV records or dynamic updates, as long as the delegated servers do, the updates will occur correctly and Active Directory will function properly.

As with the one domain name solution mentioned previously, this approach is simple and also maintains a single domain. Figure 4.3 shows the Active Directory subdomains that should be delegated when using this approach.

Create a Subdomain of the External Internet Domain for Use Internally

When you're integrating Windows 2000 in an environment where an existing DNS infrastructure already exists to support non-Windows hosts (and changes should be minimal, if any), it is often best to create a special subdomain for

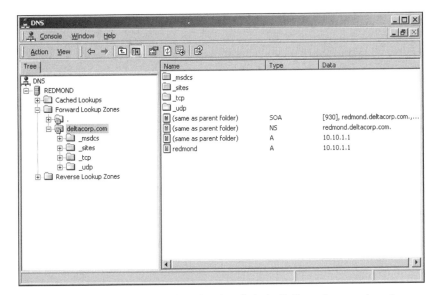

Figure 4.3   Active Directory-related subdomains all start with the underscore character.

Windows 2000 hosts. This subdomain will permit Windows 2000 servers and workstations to be managed separately from other non-Windows computers. It will also clearly differentiate between the internal Windows 2000 network and the external network. The internal network will be easily recognized, as it will be a subdomain off the registered first-level domain name.

If the XYZ Corporation were to use this approach, the current namespace, used both for external (Internet) and internal name resolution, would remain unchanged. A new Windows 2000 subdomain would be created called **ad.xyz.corp** or something similar. Windows 2000 DNS servers would handle Microsoft client name resolution only. Resolution requests for the **xyz.corp** domain, as well as any external resources, would be forwarded to the existing DNS servers. In all likelihood, the **ad** subdomain would not be delegated from the **xyz.corp** root for security reasons.

Create an Internal Network Name that's Different from the External One

By creating a completely different internal DNS namespace, public and private resources are clearly distinguished from one another. This approach is somewhat more complicated than the preceding three, because two independent domain names must be registered. There could be some confusion among system users, who might not understand why their logon IDs, which map to the internal network, are different from the external "public" corporate DNS namespace. Email addresses may also be different from Windows 2000 logon IDs, depending on where the corporate email servers are located.

DNS server configuration will be simpler, however. There is no need to delegate or forward requests to other servers because each domain has a distinct namespace. Also, unlike single-domain solutions, there is no need to create duplicate host records for shared resources inside and outside the firewall.

Common Goals of DNS Namespace Design Options

Ultimately, the goals of DNS namespace planning are simple:

➤ Accommodate the existing DNS infrastructure as required by the organization.

➤ Ensure that internal client computers can resolve names both inside and outside the firewall.

➤ Ensure that external client computers can resolve names as permitted outside and possibly inside the firewall.

➤ Simplify user access to resources and minimize end-user training expense.

DNS Integration Options

If a DNS infrastructure already exists and is running reliably, many organizations will be reluctant to replace their DNS servers to support Windows 2000. Fortunately, Windows 2000 and existing non-Microsoft DNS can coexist peacefully and efficiently. In fact, many Windows 2000 implementation plans recognize the existence of and the need to interoperate with BIND and other Unix-based DNS installations. Depending on the Active Directory design, the current DNS infrastructure may require but a few minor changes, such as adding delegated zones or just a few host records.

Four basic options are available to integrate Windows 2000 into an existing DNS infrastructure. These options are:

➤ Use BIND version 8.2.2 or higher.

➤ Segregate DNS implementations at the firewall.

➤ Create a separate Active Directory DNS domain for Windows 2000.

➤ Delegate only Active Directory zones to Windows 2000 DNS servers.

Let's explore these options in detail, starting with the simplest.

Use BIND Version 8.2.2 or Higher

The Berkeley Internet Name Daemon (BIND) is the most popular DNS server implementation. The current version of BIND supports both SRV records and dynamic update. BIND version 8.2.2 or higher will support all Windows 2000 requirements. Note that although version 8.2.1 supports dynamic update, it will fail whenever a Windows 2000 host attempts an update, making it rather unsuitable for Windows 2000 deployments. Earlier versions of BIND do support SRV records, but not dynamic updates, making this an undesirable option.

Using this option, hosts are configured as usual. The Windows 2000 DHCP server can be configured to dynamically register non-Windows 2000 clients, or not to register them, as desired. A Windows 2000 server, when being promoted to domain controller, simply registers its set of SRV records, which are then used by hosts to locate Windows 2000 services.

Segregate DNS Implementations at the Firewall

The most critical DNS server at any organization is its authoritative DNS server—the server used to resolve IP addresses for external hosts. By dividing DNS responsibilities "at the firewall," the existing DNS environment used to resolve external requests is left untouched, and the requirements of Windows 2000 are met internally by Windows 2000 DNS.

The Windows 2000 DNS servers should be configured to forward requests they cannot resolve locally to the external DNS server, and host records defined on the external servers must be manually added to the internal DNS.

For security, the firewall configuration should only allow DNS traffic between internal and external DNS servers, because external hosts should not be allowed to query the internal Windows 2000 DNS information, and internal requests for Internet name resolution will be forwarded by the internal DNS to the external DNS for resolution.

Create a Separate Active Directory DNS Domain for Windows 2000

If a separate "child" domain is created for an organization's Windows 2000 implementation, the net result is similar to the prior scenario. However, this approach is more appropriate in environments where there is a substantial number of non-Microsoft hosts, and the existing DNS is used to support internal as well as external name resolution.

The Active Directory domain can be defined in the main corporate DNS and delegated, allowing access to Windows 2000 servers from any host in the organization.

Delegate only Active Directory Zones to Windows 2000 DNS Servers

The final option is appropriate when client computers will not dynamically update DNS, but servers will. In this case, the existing DNS can be configured to delegate the four Active Directory service locator zones only. These four zones are:

➤ _msdcs

➤ _sites

➤ _tcp

➤ _udp

Only domain controller-generated SRV records are added to these zones, which can be delegated to one or more Windows 2000 DNS servers. Note, however, that domain controllers will not be able to dynamically add their own host or reverse-lookup records, unless the standard primary DNS server supports dynamic updates. As a result, if the primary DNS is not capable of dynamic update, the "A" and "PTR" records for new domain controllers should be added before the dcpromo operation is run. This will ensure that the new DC has the proper host entries on the primary DNS servers, and only the delegated servers will need to be updated.

Deciding on a DNS Integration Strategy

Clearly, there are several options for maintaining an existing DNS infrastructure when deploying Windows 2000. There is no "right" answer, just a lot of decisions and trade-offs to make.

If an organization is using BIND 8.2.2 or higher, the choice is fairly simple—just keep what is working today. However, if an earlier version of BIND is deployed and supports the needs of the organization, most DNS administrators would be reluctant to replace something that works, even if it is just a newer version of the same product.

Segregation of DNS architectures "at the firewall" may be a viable solution. There are some configuration challenges in organizations that use a proxy server to manage access to the Web and other Internet resources, but these are not insurmountable.

Creating an Active Directory "child" domain and delegating the zone to Windows 2000 DNS is also a workable option. However, starting the DNS root in Active Directory at a lower level can raise Active Directory design issues; this approach should be understood by both the DNS administrators and the Active Directory design team before it is selected.

Finally, delegation of only the Active Directory locator zones is a slightly more complex solution, but it avoids the need to create a lower-level Active Directory domain root. The biggest challenge is to ensure that host and PTR records are manually entered on the corporate DNS whenever new domain controllers are added. These records should be added well before starting the dcpromo process to create the domain controller.

Whichever approach is chosen, it should be clearly understood that a migration to Microsoft Windows 2000 will not require the replacement of an existing DNS infrastructure, and the integration of Microsoft and non-Microsoft DNS servers is simple and straightforward.

Practice Questions

Case Study: Acme Bowling Ball Corporation

The Acme Bowling Ball Corporation is a multinational corporation with offices in sixteen different cities on three continents—North America, Europe, and Asia. Acme's headquarters is in New York City, and the centralized IT department is located there; it supports the 10,000 Acme employees worldwide. Acme recently acquired Able Wax, a small manufacturer of bowling alley wax in Chicago.

Acme is also partnered in a joint venture with two other companies: a major financial services firm and a construction company. This joint venture is called MMW Holdings. The 900 employees in this joint venture are located in Acme facilities in North America, but are paid as employees of MMW Holdings.

LAN/Network Structure

Acme Bowling Ball Corporation has a mixed environment consisting of UNIX servers, Windows NT 4.0 servers, and Windows NT 4.0 workstations. Acme's NT domain structure consists of three master account domains, one for each continent, and sixteen resource domains, one at each corporate location. While Acme has a DNS infrastructure, it is not used internally. Instead, WINS is used for NetBIOS name resolution.

An additional master accounts domain was created last year to support the MMW Holdings employees.

Able Wax runs Windows NT 4.0 servers with predominantly Windows 95 workstations. Able uses a single domain for its employees, and runs NT 4.0 DNS for name resolution.

Acme's LAN uses twisted-pair Ethernet, with a 100Mbps backbone and 10Mbps out to the desktop. Able Wax's network is entirely 10Mbps twisted-pair Ethernet.

Proposed LAN/Network Structure

Acme is migrating to Windows 2000 at all North American locations. Desktop deployments of Professional have already begun, and the server migration project will begin soon. The European and Asian locations will not migrate for at least one year.

The Able Wax migration will start when Acme completes the upgrade in its North American facilities. Able will need to replace most of the existing servers and workstations to support Windows 2000.

No physical network changes are planned at this time.

WAN Connectivity

Acme locations throughout North America are connected via full 1.5Mbps T-1 circuits. Most of these circuits are underutilized today. The New York office has an additional T-1 connection to the Internet for the corporate Web site and e-mail. 256Kbps leased lines link the three European facilities, and these connections are rarely saturated. Acme's four Asian offices are connected by 64Kbps links, which are very heavily utilized during normal business hours.

The New York headquarters office is connected to London and Singapore by 64Kbps leased lines. While the circuits are seldom saturated, the New York—Singapore line has been unreliable lately.

Able Wax is not currently connected to either Acme or the Internet.

Proposed WAN Connectivity

Asian locations will be upgraded to full T-1 circuits by the end of the year. These shared voice/data links will have 512Kbps dedicated to data transmission. At the same time, the New York/Singapore link will be moved to a new carrier, in hopes of improving reliability.

A T-1 circuit will be installed at Able Wax, linking it to the Internet. A Virtual Private Network (VPN) link will connect Able to Acme through the Internet.

No other changes will be made in North America or Europe.

Directory Design Commentary

Chief Technology Officer: Our DNS infrastructure may not support our Windows 2000 deployment without some major upgrades. The business requirements that must be supported with the new DNS design include:

➤ Maintenance of existing BIND DNS servers at Acme

➤ An upgrade, if necessary, of Able Wax's Windows NT 4.0 DNS server

➤ Maintenance of existing Web presence for Acme and MMW Holdings

➤ Support for email and a Web presence for Able Wax with an ablewax.com domain name

➤ Reliable access to DNS from remote locations

Director, Human Resources: We need to be able to consolidate information from Acme, our new Able Wax subsidiary, and the MMW joint venture. We currently have to put in a lot of manual effort to compile employee lists, organization charts, and the like.

President, Able Wax: We need to get our products out on the Internet. We were a small company, and are very much behind the times. Still, we want to be sure to maintain the Able Wax brand name.

Internet Positioning

Acme has had an Internet presence for many years and maintains a registered domain name of **acme.com**. Primary and secondary DNS servers running BIND version 4.8.3 handle external (Internet) name resolution.

Able Wax does not have an Internet presence, nor has it registered a domain name yet, but is using Microsoft Windows NT 4.0 DNS internally.

MMW Holdings has a Web site with a registered domain name of **mmwholdings. com**. Currently, the MMW Web site is being hosted by Acme, and that is expected to remain the case for the foreseeable future. Employees in this joint venture are located in Acme facilities but have mmwholdings.com email addresses. The organization's domain model is shown graphically in Figure 4.4, below.

Future Internet Positioning

There are plans to create a new Able Wax Web site and to give employees **ablewax.com** email addresses.

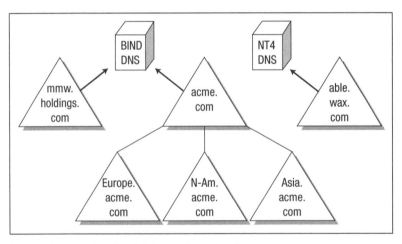

Figure 4.4 Acme Bowling Ball Corporation—domains.

Question 1

Should the Able Wax domain be made a subdomain of the Acme parent company domain?

- ○ a. Yes
- ○ b. No

The correct answer is b. The business requirements call for an **ablewax.com** domain, and making Able Wax a subdomain of Acme would create an **ablewax.acme.com** domain name.

Question 2

If no additional DNS servers are deployed, can the current DNS servers at Acme and Able Wax be used to support Windows 2000 and Active Directory without upgrades? [Check all correct answers]

- ❑ a. Yes, the current DNS servers will work with Windows 2000 and Active Directory.
- ❑ b. No, the BIND server will not support SRV records.
- ❑ c. No, the Windows NT 4.0 Server will not support dynamic update.
- ❑ d. No, the Windows NT 4.0 Server will not support SRV records.
- ❑ e. No, BIND servers cannot be used in the same enterprise as Windows NT 4.0 DNS.

The correct answers are b and d. BIND version 4.9.7 is required for SRV record support, and Acme is currently running version 4.8.3. Microsoft Windows NT 4.0 DNS will support SRV records if Service Pack 4 or higher has been applied. Because Able Wax is at Service Pack 3, its DNS server will not work.

Although it is true that Windows NT 4.0 DNS servers do not support dynamic update, dynamic update is not a requirement for Windows 2000.

Finally, answer e is incorrect, because BIND and Windows NT 4.0 DNS are compatible.

Question 3

> Because the availability of DNS is so crucial to the operation of Windows 2000, Acme's IT director has asked the Network Services manager to devise a plan for ensuring DNS availability at all locations. Which of the following options would be appropriate for the manager to consider when creating her DNS infrastructure design? [Check all correct answers]
>
> ❏ a. Use Active Directory integrated zones for all DNS servers.
>
> ❏ b. Place one forwarding-only DNS server in Europe and one in Asia.
>
> ❏ c. Delegate the Europe and Asia subdomains to DNS servers located in those two regions.
>
> ❏ d. Place at least two DNS servers in each region (continent).
>
> ❏ e. Ensure that all Windows 2000 DNS servers are manually updated with host records for the Acme corporate Web site and email server.

The correct answers are a and d. Using Active Directory-integrated zones will allow dynamic hostname registration to occur even if one DNS server is unavailable. If there are at least two servers per region, a WAN link failure will not affect DNS operation, even if one server is down as well.

Answer b is incorrect because forwarding-only DNS servers are used for performance, not fault tolerance. Delegation of Europe and Asia subdomains is a step in the right direction, but other domains, such as North America and the root, would need to be replicated to these servers as well for a true fault-tolerant solution. Therefore, answer c is incorrect. Finally, although answer e is certainly something that needs to be done, it has no bearing on fault tolerance.

Question 4

> You are ready to create the first domain controller in the **acme.com** domain. Arrange the DNS-related tasks from the following list in the proper order. You may not need to use all of the tasks.
>
> Manually copy SRV records from the netlogon.dns file to the root zone of the primary DNS server.
>
> Install at least one Windows 2000 DNS server.
>
> Run the "dcpromo" utility to create a Windows 2000 domain controller.
>
> Enable dynamic update on the Windows 2000 DNS server.
>
> Verify that the Windows 2000 server to be promoted is pointed to a Windows 2000 DNS server.
>
> Use the domain name of **acme.com** when creating the Active Directory domain.

The correct answer is:

Install at least one Windows 2000 DNS server.

Enable dynamic update on the Windows 2000 DNS server.

Verify that the Windows 2000 server to be promoted is pointed to a Windows 2000 DNS server.

Run the "dcpromo" utility to create a Windows 2000 domain controller.

Use the domain name of **acme.com** when creating the Active Directory domain.

Note that it will not be necessary to copy SRV records from the netlogon.dns file as long as the DNS server supports dynamic update.

Question 5

> The IT director wants to know some of the advantages of Active Directory-integrated zones. Which of the following are real advantages of Active Directory integration? [Check all correct answers]
>
> ❑ a. Compression of zone transfer traffic reduces network load.
>
> ❑ b. Single-replication topology shared with AD replication simplifies troubleshooting.
>
> ❑ c. Secure dynamic updates prevent name theft and "sniffing" of DNS network traffic.
>
> ❑ d. Any DNS server can receive updates, thus improving fault tolerance.
>
> ❑ e. Active Directory integration is required for proper Windows 2000 operation.

The correct answers are a, b, c, and d. Since only updated records are transferred, network load is reduced compared with standard full zone transfers. Active Directory integration of DNS means greater fault tolerance because all servers act as "primary" and can receive updates, which results in a more secure dynamic update environment and a shared replication topology with regular Active Directory updates. Answer e is incorrect because any DNS with SRV record support will work with Windows 2000.

Question 6

A consultant has told the network manager at Able Wax that his Windows NT 4 DNS server cannot be used with Windows 2000, even if updated with the latest service pack. The reason he gives is that Active Directory-integrated DNS servers cannot perform standard zone transfers with down-level secondary DNS servers. Is this reason true or false?

○ a. True

○ b. False

The correct answer is b. Any Windows 2000 DNS server can supply a standard secondary DNS server with a valid zone file transfer, even one that's Active Directory-integrated.

Question 7

In reviewing the Active Directory design documentation for Acme, an auditing firm has questioned the use of the same DNS name inside and outside the firewall. It has recommended using different names for the private and public networks. What are some of the advantages of using different DNS names for the internal and external network? [Check two answers]

❏ a. The internal (private) naming hierarchy is not exposed to the Internet.

❏ b. Only one DNS domain name needs to be registered.

❏ c. It is easier to manage resources because there is no confusion as to which resources are available to the Internet and which are internally accessible only.

❏ d. Users may be confused by the different domain names used for internal and external resources.

The correct answers are a and c. By using a different DNS namespace, internal DNS information is not available to users on the Internet. It is easy for the network management staff to distinguish between servers and other resources located internally versus external to the firewall because of the different DNS hostnames. Answer b is incorrect because both the private and the public DNS names should be registered. Answer d is incorrect because this is a *disadvantage* of having separate internal and external namespaces.

Question 8

If Acme decides to use a delegated subdomain name (such as **ad.acme.com**) for the internal network, what will need to be done with the existing BIND 4.8.3 DNS servers?

○ a. The servers will have to be upgraded to BIND 4.9.7.

○ b. The servers will have to be replaced by Windows 2000 DNS servers.

○ c. The servers will have to be upgraded to BIND 8.2.2.

○ d. No changes will be needed to the existing BIND servers.

The correct answer is d. No changes are necessary to the existing DNS infrastructure. Delegating the **ad.acme.com** subdomain means that the current servers will not handle name registration or resolution for the Windows 2000 network. Therefore, answers a and c are incorrect; since SRV record support is not needed, the older BIND servers can be retained. Answer b is incorrect for much the same reason, and also would go counter to the business requirement of keeping the existing BIND servers.

Question 9

Acme has decided to use standard primary and secondary DNS servers. However, the network services manager is concerned about excessive zone transfer traffic when the secondary servers pull updates from the primary. How can the impact of zone transfer traffic be reduced on the Acme network? [Check all correct answers]

❑ a. Configure the DNS servers for incremental zone transfer.

❑ b. Create two forwarding-only DNS servers on the network.

❑ c. Schedule zone transfers for off-peak hours only.

❑ d. Configure the DNS servers to use UTF-8 character encoding.

The correct answers are a and c. Incremental zone transfers copy only new or updated DNS records from the primary to the secondary servers. For large zones, where most records do not change, this can result in a significant reduction in network traffic. If the DNS servers do not support incremental zone transfers, the transfers can be scheduled for times when the network is not busy. Answer b is incorrect because forwarding-only name servers do not have any impact on zone transfer traffic. Answer d is incorrect because UTF-8 encoding allows for non-RFC-compliant DNS hostnames and also does not affect zone transfers.

Question 10

> Match the DNS servers in the first list with the features in the second list. You may use a feature more than once.
>
> DNS Servers
>
> > BIND 4.9.7
> >
> > BIND 8.2.2
> >
> > Windows NT 4.0—SP 2
> >
> > Windows NT 4.0—SP 3 or higher
> >
> > Windows 2000
>
> Features
>
> > Secure dynamic update
> >
> > Incremental zone transfer
> >
> > SRV (Service Locator) record support
> >
> > Dynamic update
> >
> > Active Directory integration
> >
> > WINS integration

The correct answer is

BIND 4.9.7

> SRV record support

BIND 8.2.2

> Incremental zone transfer
>
> SRV record support
>
> Dynamic update

Windows NT 4.0 – SP 2

> WINS integration

Windows NT 4.0 – SP 3 or higher

> SRV record support
>
> WINS integration

Windows 2000

Secure dynamic update

Incremental zone transfer

SRV (Service Locator) record support

Dynamic update

Active Directory integration

WINS integration

Need to Know More?

 Liu, Cricket, and Paul Albitz. *DNS and BIND, 3rd Edition*, O'Reilly & Associates. Sebastopol, CA, 1998. ISBN 1565925122. This is *the* definitive book on DNS. If you don't have a copy yet, go out and get one. Then read it from cover to cover—twice.

 The *Microsoft Windows 2000 Server Resource Kit* contains lots of information about Active Directory.

 Try searching the TechNet CD or use Microsoft's online version at **www.microsoft.com**. Search for keywords pertaining to DNS and Active Directory.

 To read the RFC's mentioned in this chapter (and all of the rest), go to Internet Engineering Task Force (IETF) web site: **www.ietf.org/ rfc.html**, or **www.ietf.org/rfc/rfcNNNN.html**, where NNNN is the number of the RFC.

Designing Active Directory for Delegation

. . . .

Terms you'll need to understand:

✓ Administrative model

✓ Delegation

✓ Delegation of Control Wizard

✓ Inheritance

✓ Inheritance modification

Techniques you'll need to master:

✓ Identifying the administrative needs within an organization and determining the impact this will have on Active Directory

✓ Developing an administrative model based on the needs of the IT organization

✓ Designing a strategy for delegation

✓ Assigning authority using the Delegation of Control Wizard

✓ Using inheritance and inheritance modification to determine the scope of administration

✓ Designing an Organizational Unit (OU) hierarchy for delegation of authority

One of the most important new features of Windows 2000 is *delegation*, which allows an administrator of an organization to grant administrative rights to other individuals or groups. This eliminates the problem of having one person or group being entirely responsible for all the administrative tasks. By grouping objects into containers within Active Directory, delegation of control over the objects can be assigned to specific individuals or groups.

During this phase of designing an Active Directory infrastructure, a delegation plan will be implemented. A thorough assessment of different aspects of the business will need to be performed to determine which administrative model to implement as well as which individuals and groups will be assigned delegation of control over which administrative tasks.

This chapter is broken down into four major topics: identifying business needs, determining the type of IT organization, developing a model for administration, and developing strategies for delegation. Also keep in mind the terms and techniques that you'll need to become familiar with listed at the beginning of this chapter.

Identifying Business Needs

In today's world of enterprise networks, delegation of the administrative tasks becomes very important. The purpose of delegation is to distribute administrative tasks among users and groups. Before this can be done, a thorough understanding of the business's structure and needs is necessary. In order to effectively design delegation within Active Directory that will meet these needs, it is important to first perform a thorough assessment of the current IT structure. During this assessment you'll want to determine the administrative model and identify who is responsible for administering resources.

Determining the Administrative Model

Determining the administrative model that a business has implemented is crucial in designing a delegation plan. The administrative model basically determines who holds the decision-making authority within a business and who is responsible for implementing these decisions throughout all levels. As was discussed in Chapter 3, there are basically three administrative models that can be implemented: centralized, decentralized, and centralized-decentralized. Table 5.1 summarizes these three administrative models.

Table 5.1 The three administrative models.	
Model	**Description**
Centralized	A central group holds all decision-making authority within an organization (centralized administration).
Decentralized	Different units within a business are responsible for their own administration (localized administration).
Centralized-decentralized	A central group maintains some level of decision-making authority while certain administrative tasks are assigned to each business unit.

Identifying Responsibilities for Administering Resources

Once the administrative model within the organization has been identified, the next step is to identify who is currently responsible for administering network resources. When determining administrative responsibilities, consider the following questions:

➤ Who is responsible for what?

Determine which individuals or groups within the business have administrative privileges and what exactly their responsibilities are. For example, there may be a group of individuals who have been given the responsibility of administering user accounts, whereas another group may have administrative privileges over network printers.

➤ Where do these privileges apply?

Do the permissions apply throughout the organization or only to certain areas? For example, in an enterprise network, if a user has been given administrative authority over user accounts, should this privilege apply to all domains and OUs or just specific ones? Is he or she responsible for all user accounts or just certain ones? In other words, what is the scope of the administrative privilege?

➤ What type of privilege is assigned?

Does the individual or group have full administrative privileges or only control over certain aspects? For example, what level of control does the individual or group have over user accounts? Does the individual or group have full control or only control over certain aspects of user accounts?

Determining the answers to these questions will help in developing a delegation plan that can easily integrate into the business's current administrative model and its current way of distributing administrative tasks among its employees.

Determining the Type of IT Organization

In order to effectively delegate authority within Active Directory, the current structure of the IT organization within the business needs to be assessed. Once the current structure is documented, the design team can work with the business to determine if there are any areas that need improvement or areas that can be restructured for easier administration. This information will assist in creating a delegation plan that meets the requirements of the business.

Centralized Vs. Decentralized Management

When assessing how the IT organization within a business is structured, determine the model that is currently in place. Is the network administration centralized or does the business allow for distributed administration (decentralized)? Determining this will ensure that the needs of the IT organization are identified and reflected in the administrative model that is developed.

 An organization can also have decentralized management, but a centralized IT function, or vice-versa. Do not assume that decentralized management means decentralized IT.

Centralized Management

This type of model is hierarchical in structure. It is characterized by one individual overseeing all network development and administration to whom the IT organization would report. Some of the day-to-day administrative tasks may be assigned to select individuals or groups outside the IT organization, but most network administration remains centralized. The IT organization would maintain decision-making authority as well as the responsibility of ensuring that all decisions are implemented throughout all levels within the business.

Figure 5.1 shows the hierarchical structure of this model. If the XYZ Corporation implemented this type of model, decision-making authority and most network administrative authority would be maintained in the upper level of the hierarchy.

There is also a slight variation to this model where the IT organization is still centralized but day-to-day management is decentralized. The central IT organization would be responsible for overseeing network development, and the IT groups within the different business units would be responsible for the day-to-day administrative tasks.

For example, the XYZ Corporation may maintain a centralized IT organization that is responsible for overseeing network development and implementing standards throughout the business while decentralizing the day-to-day administrative tasks by assigning them to the IT groups within each unit (see Figure 5.2).

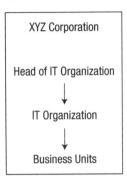

Figure 5.1   The structure of a centralized IT management model is hierarchical. The IT organization reports to the individual at the top of the hierarchy. Network administration is very much centralized and is the responsibility of the central IT organization.

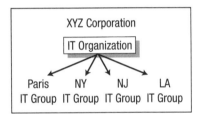

Figure 5.2   The central IT group would maintain some form of centralized authority over all the business units but the day-to-day tasks would be assigned to each of the IT groups within the different units.

Decentralized Management

With decentralized management, there is no longer one person or group holding all the decision-making and network administrative authority; in other words, there is no hierarchy or central IT organization overseeing all network development. Each business unit would maintain its own IT organization and implement its own IT model based on its needs. When it comes to technical issues affecting the entire organization, the different IT groups from each of the business units would have to work together. For example, if a business were planning a rollout of Windows 2000, each of the IT groups from the different business units would need to be involved.

The type of IT organization that a business implements will not have a direct impact on the Active Directory structure. It is still crucial to characterize the current IT organization that a business has implemented because this will help the design team determine the type of administrative model to use. The administrative model will, however, directly impact the organization of the different elements within the Active Directory structure.

Table 5.2	Contrasts the centralized and decentralized management models.	
Model	**Advantages**	**Disadvantages**
Centralized	Ability to maintain central decision-making authority	Business units have little say over decisions affecting entire organization
	One group responsible for ensuring decisions implemented throughout business	One individual or group holds all decision-making authority within the organization
Decentralized	Each business unit can maintain decision making authority over its own department or location	No central hierarchy makes it difficult to ensure that organization-wide decisions are implemented at all levels
	Allows business units to make decisions based on their own needs	Different groups must work together for decisions affecting the entire organization

Table 5.2 summarizes some of the advantages and disadvantages of each model.

Developing a Model for Administration

Once you've characterized the type of IT organization a business has in place, the next step is to develop a model for administration. The model for administration that is chosen will determine the organization of the Active Directory structure. The type of model that is developed should be based on the structure of the IT organization (centralized versus decentralized). There are basically four models for administration:

➤ Geographical (location)

➤ Organizational (business unit or department)

➤ Functional (role)

➤ Hybrids (combinations of the preceding types)

 The administrational model chosen will directly affect the Active Directory design, specifically the top-level domains or organizational units.

Geographical (Location)

If you choose to implement a model for administration that is based on geographic location, the Active Directory structure will be organized around the different locations within the business. This type of model would be well suited for a business that maintains a central IT organization while decentralizing management by assigning the responsibility of performing day-to-day administrative tasks to the different IT groups within the business units (see Figure 5.3).

For example, the XYZ Corporation maintains offices in Europe and the U.S. The design team may decide to create two domains—one for each country—and then create OUs within each domain for the specific offices.

 Before implementing this type of model, make sure there is an individual or group of individuals at the different locations capable of performing these day-to-day tasks.

One of the positive features of an administrative model based on location is that it is fairly immune to reorganization and expansion. Usually when a company changes its structure, it will reorganize departments but not the geographical locations of the business. Accommodating expansion can be as simple as having to create a new domain or OU for the new location.

Organizational (Business Unit or Department)

If a business has implemented a decentralized IT organizational model and allowed the different departments to implement their own IT models, a model for administration that is organizational may be best. The organization of the Active Directory structure would be based on the different business units or departments within the company.

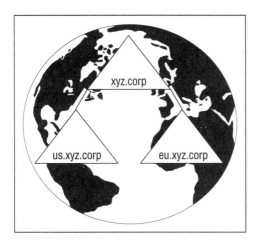

Figure 5.3   The model for administration is based on the different geographical locations within the business. Two domains are created—one for Europe and one for the U.S. Organizational Units within each domain can be created for the specific offices.

Using the XYZ Corporation as an example, let's take a look at the structure of this model (see Figure 5.4). The XYZ Corporation has two distinct divisions: training and external IT consulting services. If the design team opted to use a model based on organization, two separate domains could be created, one for each of the business units within the company.

One of the nice features of this model is that it allows a business to maintain its departmental divisions. Each business unit is still able to maintain control over itself. However, in a model based on departments, if the departments are reorganized, it could mean a reorganization of the Active Directory structure.

Functional (Role)

This type of model is based on the different job roles within a business, without considering the different geographical locations and departments. For some businesses that implement a decentralized IT organization and have job roles that span multiple divisions, a functional model may be more suited to their administrative needs than an organizational model. The model based on organization may not work for the XYZ Corporation because it may have job roles (such as marketing) that span both of the divisions. In this case, it may be more appropriate to implement a model based on function (see Figure 5.5).

This model is more manageable within a smaller business because users are more easily grouped into general functions. The larger the business, the more variance in job roles, and the harder it is to group users. However, large organizations with many mobile users might find this model very attractive

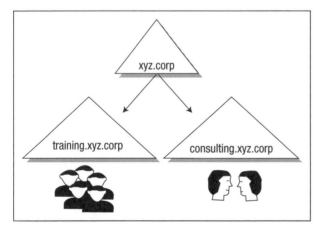

Figure 5.4 With this type of model, the Active Directory structure is organized around the different departments or business units. The XYZ Corporation consists of two divisions—training and external consulting—so two domains are created based on these divisions.

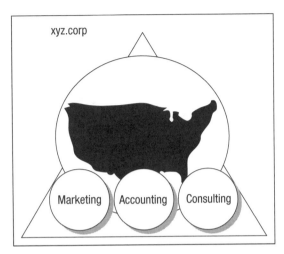

Figure 5.5 A model for administration based on function would create domains or OUs based on the different roles in the business.

Because this model is based on the different roles within the business, it is basically immune to reorganization. Reorganizations within a business most often affect departments, whereas job roles are not usually impacted.

So far we've covered three different models for administration that a business could implement. The fourth model is basically a combination of the three models just discussed.

Hybrids

Sometimes, in order to design an Active Directory structure that will meet the administrative needs of the IT organization, it may be necessary to combine several models. These new types of models are known as *hybrids*. Two of the common hybrid designs are "geographical, then organizational" and "organizational, then geographical."

Geographical, then Organizational

With this type of model, the upper layers within the Active Directory structure are organized by location, whereas the lower layers are organized by business unit. This type of model is well suited for a business spanning geographical locations. Because the lower levels of the structure are based on business units, it also allows a business to maintain departmental independence. If the XYZ Corporation were to implement this type of model, the upper layers of the Active Directory structure would be based on the different geographical locations within the business. Two domains could be created—one for the U.S. and one for Europe (refer to Figure 5.3). The lower layers would be organized around the departments within the corporation. Within the locations, Organizational Units could be created for the two departments—training and external IT consulting services (see Figure 5.6).

The geographical organization of the upper layers of the Active Directory structure makes it immune to company reorganizations. However, a reorganization of the company may result in some restructuring of the lower layers because they are based on departments.

Organizational, then Geographical

The second type of hybrid model is the opposite of the one just discussed. The upper levels of the hierarchy are based on the different business units or departments within the company, whereas the lower levels are based on the geographical locations. This model is ideal for those businesses that need to maintain independence between the different departments for security purposes. Basing the lower levels on the physical structure (geography) also allows the business to distribute administration among the IT groups in the different locations.

Figure 5.7 shows the structure of this model as it may apply to the XYZ Corporation. The upper layers in the Active Directory structure would be based on the different departments—in this case training and external IT consulting services. The lower layers would be based on the geographical locations within the corporation.

You may recall the discussion on models for administration based on departments and how they are affected by reorganization. This model will be affected by any reorganization that occurs within the business and may result in an entire restructuring of the Active Directory.

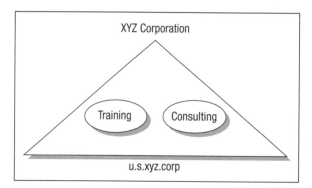

Figure 5.6   This hierarchy is based on location, then organization. The upper layers of the Active Directory structure are organized by geographical location (**us.xyz.corp**) and the lower levels are organized by department (training and consulting).

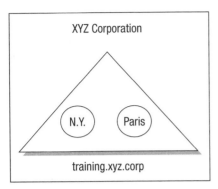

Figure 5.7 The upper layer within the Active Directory structure will be based on department (training). The Organizational Units within the training domain will be based on the different geographical locations within the business.

 Designing the Active Directory structure around the different locations instead of the departments will make good use of the physical connections between the locations. Using the model shown in Figure 5.7 will result in the possibility of domains spanning large geographical locations.

Once the model for administration has been designed, the next step will be to develop a strategy for delegation.

Developing a Strategy for Delegation

Delegation is the process of decentralizing network administration by assigning some of the administrative duties to other individuals or groups within the business. Individuals or groups can be assigned specific administrative privileges to certain objects within the Active Directory structure without having control over all objects. For example, an administrator from one location can be given control over objects within that location and that location only. This is a welcome change from NT 4.0, where a user who is given privileges to administer user accounts can administer all user accounts within the domain.

Creating a strategy for delegation will determine at what level in the Active Directory structure administrative permissions should be assigned: site, domain, or Organizational Unit. The level at which the permissions are applied will be determined by the scope of the administrative duties. Keep in mind that it is most common to delegate authority at the Organizational Unit level because it is much easier to manage. If you start delegating authority on specific objects and object attributes, you'll soon find it difficult to track the permissions that have been assigned (remember, your goal is to make administration easier, not more complex).

Before you begin developing a strategy for delegation, make sure you've determined the answers to the following questions:

➤ Who will be assigned administrative privileges?

➤ What will they be administering?

➤ What is the scope of their administrative duties?

This section of the chapter will cover the Delegation of Control Wizard, inheritance and inheritance modifications, designing an Organizational Unit hierarchy for delegation, and design guidelines.

The Delegation of Control Wizard

Anyone who has worked with Windows should be familiar with wizards and what they are used for. Wizards walk you through the process of completing a task such as adding a printer or creating a user account. The Delegation of Control Wizard serves the same purpose. This wizard walks you through the process of assigning administrative control over an Organizational Unit or container. Within the wizard you'll assign the user or group permissions over an Organizational Unit or container.

Use the following steps to delegate control using the Delegation of Control Wizard:

1. Open the Active Directory Users and Computers MMC snap-in.

2. Select the Organizational Unit or container that you wish to delegate control over.

3. From the Action menu, choose Delegate Control.

4. The Delegation of Control Wizard appears, as shown in Figure 5.8.

5. Once you click Next, the dialog box that appears will allow you to select additional users or groups for delegation. The list is always empty when you first start the wizard (see Figure 5.9).

6. Once you click Next, the dialog box that appears will allow you to select the users or groups that will be administering the Organizational Unit or container (see Figure 5.10).

7. Once you've selected the users or groups, you can then select the tasks to delegate. You have two options. The first option is to select the common tasks from the list presented in Figure 5.11. For example, if a user needs administrative control over passwords, the user could be assigned the Reset

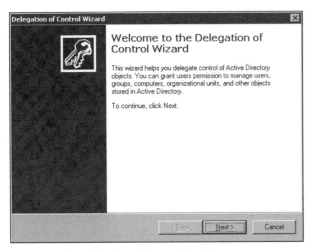

Figure 5.8 The Delegation of Control Wizard's welcome screen.

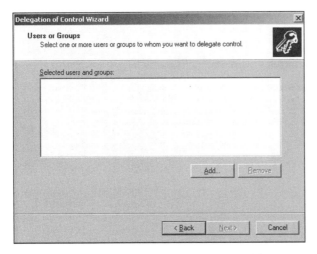

Figure 5.9 From this dialog box, you can begin to add the users or groups to whom you want to assign administrative permissions.

Passwords on User Accounts Permission option. If the common tasks do not meet your requirements, the second option is to create a custom task to delegate (see Figure 5.12).

8. If you choose to use the common tasks, select from the list the tasks for which the users or groups will be responsible. The next dialog box to appear will allow you to summarize who has been given control and the type of permissions they have been assigned. From this box you can select Finish (see Step 11). It may be a good idea to pay attention to the summary just to make sure no errors have been made.

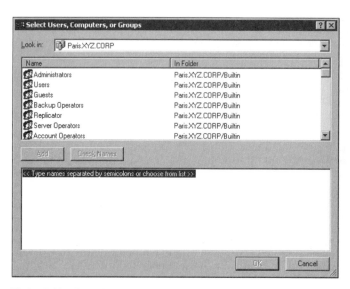

Figure 5.10 From this dialog box you can select the users or groups from the list of domain accounts.

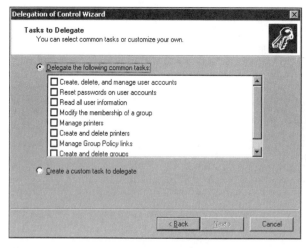

Figure 5.11 Choose the tasks you wish to delegate. You can choose from the list of common tasks or choose the second option and create a custom task to delegate.

9. If you choose Create A Custom Task To Delegate, you're not finished yet; there are a few more steps to complete. The dialog box shown in Figure 5.12 will appear; it's where you can specify the scope of the control. Will it apply to all objects within the container and any new objects created? Or is control limited to only specific objects within the container?

10. Once the scope of control has been configured, you'll then be prompted to select the permissions you want to assign to the users or groups (see Figure 5.13).

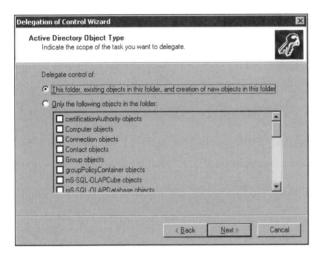

Figure 5.12   From this dialog box you can specify the scope of a user's or group's control.

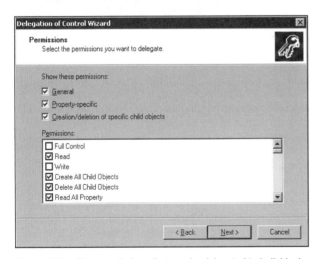

Figure 5.13   The permissions that can be delegated to individual users or groups.

11. Once you've selected the types of permissions you want to assign, the last dialog box will show you a summary of who has been assigned what permissions (see Figure 5.14).

Table 5.3 summarizes the three options presented in the permissions window (shown in Figure 5.13).

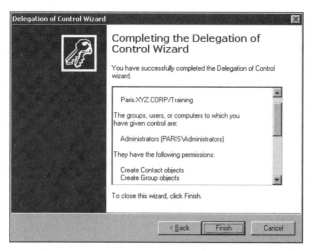

Figure 5.14   The last dialog box in the Delegation of Control Wizard will show you a summary of who has been assigned what permissions over the container object.

Table 5.3	The three options available when assigning access rights to users and groups.
Options	**Description**
General	The general permissions are common permissions that can be assigned to the container object.
Property-specific	This option will allow you to specify the permissions on the attributes associated with the object. For example, one of the attributes associated with an object may be an administrative description. You can assign a user or group permission to Read adminDescription. If the user or group needs to be able to change the administrative description, you can assign Write adminDescription.
Creation/Deletion of Specific child objects	Select this option if you want to assign the individual or group the permission to create or delete child objects. Once you select this option you'll have to specify the types of objects that can be created or deleted. For example, if a user needs to be able to create printer objects within the container, he or she can be assigned permission to only create this type of object.

Inheritance and Inheritance Modification

Objects in Active Directory typically inherit permissions from the parent object. This behavior is appropriate in most circumstances. However, the occasion may arise where a child object must be managed independently of the parent. In such a case, use inheritance modification to override the default inheritance rules.

Inheritance

Inheritance in Active Directory allows you to apply permissions that have been set on a parent object to the child objects within. It is the same idea as folder and file permissions. When you set permissions on a folder, you have the option of specifying whether those permissions should apply to the subfolder and files within. The permissions may only have to be set once, thus simplifying the process.

With inheritance, a user or group can be assigned permission to a container and all the objects it contains. Permissions can be set once on a container, as opposed to having to set the permissions on each individual object, and can save administrators a lot of time and effort.

For example, within the **paris.xyz.corp** domain shown in Figure 5.15, there is an OU created for the training department (parent object). Child objects have been created within the Training OU for administrative purposes. If a group of users within the Paris domain need administrative privileges over the Training OU and all its child objects, permissions only need to be set once by using inheritance.

 To take advantage of inheritance, make sure the Allow Inheritable Permissions from Parent to Propagate to This Object option is selected (this is selected by default).

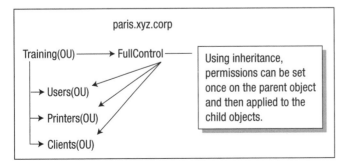

Figure 5.15　Using inheritance, permissions can be set once on the parent object and applied to the child objects.

Inheritance Modification

Conversely, if you do not want permissions to apply to all the child objects within a parent object, you can modify inheritance. You can use inheritance modification to specify which child objects should inherit permissions and which ones should not.

Using the example in Figure 5.15, if it is determined that the Full Control permission set on the Training OU should not apply to the Clients OU, inheritance modification could be used to block it. Blocking inheritance is as simple as clearing the Allow Inheritable Permissions from Parent to Propagate to This Object checkbox.

Use the following steps to block inheritance on a child object.

1. Open the Active Directory Users and Computers MMC snap-in.

2. Select the object you want to block inheritance on and from the Action menu choose Properties.

3. Select the Security tab from the object's Property dialog box.

4. To block inheritance, clear the Allow Inheritable Permissions from Parent to Propagate to This Object checkbox.

Once you've cleared this checkbox, you'll be prompted to choose whether you want to copy previously inherited permissions to this object or remove inherited permissions and only keep those permissions that have been explicitly set on the object.

Designing an Organizational Unit Hierarchy for Delegation

Organizational Units are created within a domain to logically group objects for administrative purposes. Once OUs are created, a user or group can be assigned the task of administrating the objects contained within. Creating OUs allows you to limit the scope of administrators' control and, as a result, any administrative errors they make will only affect the areas they have control over.

The OU structure that's designed should be relative to the way that administration is currently dispersed throughout the business and will be dependent on how the administrative tasks are delegated. Here are some questions to keep in mind:

➤ Is the delegation of administration based on location? Are there individuals in each geographical location responsible for administration?

➤ Have the administrative tasks been divided into different roles such as user account administration and printer administration?

➤ Is the delegation of administrative tasks based on department? Are there individuals or groups within each department responsible for administration?

The OU structure that's designed should be based on the current delegation of tasks. For example, if the XYZ Corporation has divided the administrative tasks into different job roles, this should be reflected in the OU structure that's implemented (see Figure 5.16). This will allow the corporation to continue with its current strategy of distributing administrative authority.

Because the XYZ Corporation divides the administrative tasks into separate roles, OUs can be created for each of the roles. The individual or group responsible for a role will be assigned delegation of control over the appropriate OU. When you're designing the OU hierarchy, keep in mind that the structure should allow the business to continue to use the same strategy of assigning administrative control that it's currently using.

One of the important features of using OUs is that they can be nested within one another, and this becomes a benefit when delegating control. Objects within one OU can be subdivided in child OUs. Referring back to the Paris domain in Figure 5.15, a hierarchy of OUs is created by nesting the OUs within one another. You may be asking yourself why you would want to do this, but it makes perfect sense for delegating authority. If an OU is created to hold all user accounts, you may not want to assign one user or group control over all of them. In this case, you can divide the user accounts into child OUs (Clients and Employees), which

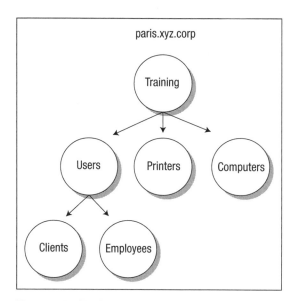

Figure 5.16   The OU hierarchy should represent the current strategy for assigning administrative authority.

would be contained in the parent OU (Users). This way, a user or group can be assigned administrative permissions over certain user accounts without having control over all of them.

Nesting is a very powerful feature in Windows 2000, but keep in mind that creating an OU hierarchy that is very deep can soon become difficult to keep track of and manage.

Design Guidelines

When designing Active Directory for delegation, keep the following guidelines in mind:

➤ Perform a thorough assessment of the business and its internal IT organization so their needs are identified.

➤ Make sure the model you create allows for flexibility and growth within the business. Growth or reorganization within a business should not have a major impact on the Active Directory structure.

➤ The OU hierarchy should reflect the structure of the organization.

➤ When at all possible, delegate authority at the OU level and use inheritance. This will make the tracking of permissions much simpler.

➤ If an individual needs authority over an OU, assign the appropriate administrative permissions. Avoid putting the individual into the Domain Admins group, because this will give him or her privileges throughout the domain. Assign the most restrictive permission that will allow the user (or group) to perform the required tasks.

Practice Questions

Case Study: Smith and Deutsch Candy

Smith and Deutsch is a candy manufacturer based in Sydney, Australia, with offices throughout the world. Currently, Smith and Deutsch maintains regional headquarters in the following locations:

➤ Australia (Sydney)

➤ Asia (Hong Kong)

➤ Europe (Berlin, Germany)

➤ North America (Los Angeles)

➤ South America (Bogota, Columbia)

The Sydney, Australia regional headquarters also serves as the company's home office.

LAN and Network Structure

The regions run a mixture of Windows 95, 98, and NT 4.0 client computers on mostly twisted-pair Ethernet. Servers are predominantly NT 4.0, but some regions, most notably South America, still run some NT 3.51 servers.

Proposed LAN and Network Structure

All companies are scheduled to be upgraded to Windows 2000 within 12 months. The LAN infrastructure is basically sound, and only a few smaller offices in Asia and South America will require upgrades.

WAN Connectivity

The regional offices are linked to headquarters using fractional T-1 data circuits. Each region has at least a 512Kbps data connection, with generally less than 50 percent utilization.

Within the regions, data connections range from fractional T-1s to 19.2Kbps circuits in some of the more remote offices.

Proposed WAN Connectivity

Several remote offices will upgrade to VPN connections with bandwidth of at least 128Kbps.

Directory Design Commentary

Vice President, South America region: Several of our offices are in remote areas. These offices typically have very poor data connections to our central office in Bogota. Some of these offices are large, so we need to upgrade our network soon.

CIO: As part of our Windows 2000 migration strategy, we plan to use the delegation of administration features of Active Directory extensively. In particular, we are looking to delegate most simple user management tasks to individual departments. However, management at headquarters is also interested in maintaining oversight of each of the regions.

Executive Vice President: Decision-making at Smith and Deutsch is handled primarily at the regional offices. Only major corporate policy directions come from the home office. The IT function is managed in a similar manner. Although certain high-level decisions are made at the home office, most day-to-day management is performed regionally. Some of the regions have distinct security policies as a result of management decisions or local regulations.

Internet Positioning

Smith and Deutsch has an Internet presence, with a registered domain name of **sdcandy.com**. The company's Web servers are located in the Los Angeles office.

Question 1

Based on the scenario, how should domains be structured at Smith and Deutsch?

○ a. Single domain called **sdcandy.com**

○ b. Three domains, **sdcandy.com**, **regions.sdcandy.com**, and **www.sdcandy.com**, all in a single forest

○ c. Six domains, with a root domain of **sdcandy.com** and five regional child domains, all in a single forest

○ d. Five forests, one for each region

The correct answer is c. Because individual regions may require discrete security policies, it is necessary to create individual regional domains. Although this requirement could also be met with answer d, creating multiple forests will make the enterprise very difficult to manage. Answer a is also incorrect, because it will be impossible to maintain separate security policies. Answer b is incorrect for the same reason, because a single region's child domain does not provide the ability to independently set security policy.

Question 2

The administrative model for Smith and Deutsch appears to be which of the following? [Check two answers]

❏ a. Centralized management

❏ b. Centralized IT

❏ c. Decentralized management

❏ d. Decentralized IT

The correct answers are c and d. Both management and IT are decentralized, with strong local decision-making and control of IT resources.

Question 3

Using the following list of Active Directory objects and the list of object names appropriate for Smith and Deutsch, place the object names under the appropriate Active Directory objects. An object name may be used more than once or even not at all.

Active Directory objects:

Root domain

Domain

Organizational Unit

Object names:

namerica.sdcandy.com

Finance

finance.sdcandy.com

Manufacturing

Human Resources

sdcandy.com

australia.sdcandy.com

Computers

Color Printers

The correct answer is:

Root domain:

> **sdcandy.com**

Domain:

> **sdcandy.com**
>
> **australia.sdcandy.com**
>
> **namerica.sdcandy.com**

Organizational Unit:

> Finance
>
> Manufacturing
>
> Human Resources
>
> Color Printers

Note that Computers is *not* a valid Organizational Unit because it is one of two default objects of the type Container created in Active Directory.

Question 4

Smith and Deutsch has created an Organizational Unit called "Information Technology" in each of the six domains in the forest. A manager has been given administrative privileges for the Information Technology OU in the root domain. Will this give him administrative privileges to the other Information Technology OUs in all the child domains?

○ a. Yes

○ b. No

The correct answer is b. Administrative privileges cannot be inherited across domains. Domains are security boundaries. The administrator could be made a member of a universal group, and that universal group could be given administrative privileges to each Information Technology OU in each domain of the Smith and Deutsch forest.

Question 5

In planning for delegation of administration, the Active Directory design team has interviewed the director of Human Resources. She gave them the following statement:

"Managers in the HR department should be responsible for creating new user accounts, managing computers, and managing printers in the department. In addition, supervisors in HR should also be able to manage their own user accounts and manage all printers in the department. HR clerks should not be allowed to manage anything."

Using the diagram in Figure 5.17, drag the appropriate OU name to the Organizational Unit in order to create the delegation structure described by the director of Human Resources.

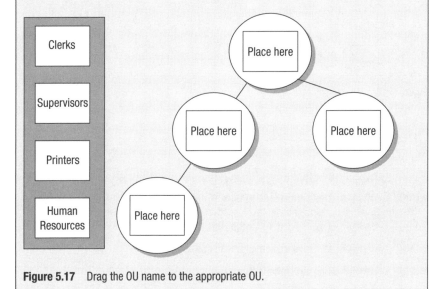

Figure 5.17   Drag the OU name to the appropriate OU.

The Human Resources OU is the top-level Organizational Unit defined for the hierarchy, and managers' user accounts will be placed in this OU. Supervisors and Clerks are second-level OUs, because managers must have administrative privileges to manage these accounts. Printers are placed in the third-level OU so that both managers and supervisors have delegated administrative rights. Figure 5.18 shows the correct answer.

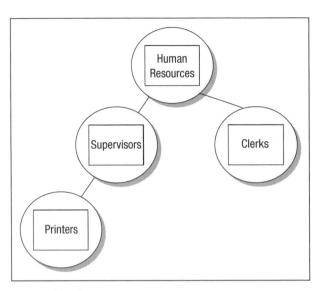

Figure 5.18 The correct answer.

Question 6

Normally, permissions "flow," or are inherited from, the top-level Organizational Units to OUs below. However, in designing the OU hierarchy for the manufacturing department, it has been determined that inheritance should be blocked from a low-level OU. When blocking inheritance, what two options are available for the administrator? [Check two answers]

❏ a. Copy previously inherited permissions to this object.

❏ b. Delete all existing permissions for this object.

❏ c. Only keep permissions that have been explicitly set on this object.

❏ d. Allow full control to all attributes for this object.

The correct answers are a and c. When blocking inheritance, either all previously inherited permissions can be copied to the object, or only the explicit settings are retained. The option you choose will depend on what you are trying to do with the object after blocking the permission. Answer b is incorrect because explicitly set permissions are always retained. Answer d is incorrect because, when blocking inheritance, there is no option for allowing full access to the object.

Question 7

> A consultant has suggested that Smith and Deutsch should use the single-domain model. His rationale is that because administrative permissions cannot cross domain boundaries, the home office IT staff will lose control of the regional domains. Is the consultant's rationale correct?
>
> ○ a. Yes
>
> ○ b. No

The correct answer is b. The root domain contains the Enterprise Admins group, which has administrative rights to the entire forest.

Question 8

> In the sales department, three administrative assistants will be responsible for resetting passwords for the sales staff. Do the administrative assistants have to be in the same OU as the salespeople?
>
> ○ a. Yes
>
> ○ b. No

The correct answer is b. Permissions can be delegated to user accounts or, better yet, group accounts defined in any Organizational Unit or container object within the domain.

Question 9

> The CIO has questioned a portion of the Smith and Deutsch Active Directory design document. Specifically, she is concerned about the safeguards preventing a user from obtaining administrative capabilities without authorization. Which of the following points can you make to reassure the CIO that delegation of administration is safe? [Check all correct answers]
>
> ❑ a. Delegation is more controlled than creating additional administrators, as was necessary with Windows NT 4.0.
>
> ❑ b. Users who have been granted permission to perform administrative tasks are not necessarily able to delegate those tasks to others.
>
> ❑ c. Active Directory does not allow standard users to delegate administrative tasks—you must be an administrator to delegate.
>
> ❑ d. Users who have been delegated permissions to administrative tasks are placed automatically in a DelegatedUser built-in security group.

Answers a and b are correct. Delegation of control is much safer than simply adding more users to the Domain Admins security group. Delegation is very granular, so it is possible to allow a user to perform a task without allowing the user to delegate that task to others. Answer c is incorrect because users can be given the right to delegate administration. Answer e is incorrect because there is no DelegatedUser built-in group.

Question 10

The South American region of Smith and Deutsch is sold to a Swiss chocolate firm. What changes will need to be made to the delegation settings for the other four regional domains as well as the home office?

○ a. None. Domains are security boundaries, and administrative tasks cannot be delegated to users from other domains.

○ b. The one-way trusts between **samerica.sdcandy.com** and the five other domains must be broken.

○ c. Any security accounts from the **samerica.sdcandy.com** domain should be removed from security groups in the other regional domains as well as the root domain.

○ d. All user accounts from the **samerica.sdcandy.com** domain must be deleted from the **sdcandy.com** root domain.

The correct answer is c. Any references to security principals from the **samerica.sdcandy.com** domain should be removed from group accounts in the other domains. In this way, administrative privileges, which may have been assigned to groups, will no longer be assigned to members of the samerica domain. Answer a is incorrect because global and universal groups can contain members from other domains and can be directly or indirectly allowed administrative privileges. Answer b is incorrect because one-way trusts must be manually created in Windows 2000 and have no bearing on standard security. Answer d is incorrect because users should not be defined in more than one domain in a forest.

Need to Know More?

 Microsoft Press. *Windows 2000 Active Directory Services.* Microsoft Corporation. Redmond, WA, 2000. ISBN 0735609993. Sections of this book provide some general information on how to assign delegation of authority to individuals and groups.

 Minasi, Mark. *Windows 2000 Resource Kit.* Sybex. San Francisco, CA, 2000. ISBN 0782126146.

 The *Microsoft Windows 2000 Server Resource Kit* contains in-depth information about designing Active Directory for delegation.

 Try searching the TechNet CD or use Microsoft's online version at **www.microsoft.com**. Search for keywords such as *delegation, delegation of control,* and *inheritance.*

Designing Active Directory for Group Policy

Terms you'll need to understand:

✓ Blocking

✓ Filtering

✓ Group Policy Object (GPO)

✓ Inheritance modification

✓ Local Group Policy Object

✓ Override

✓ Security groups

Techniques you'll need to master:

✓ Understanding the purpose of Group Policies

✓ Defining General Policy settings that can be configured through Group Policy

✓ Determining how Group Policy is processed

✓ Filtering GPOs using security groups

✓ Modifying inheritance using blocking and override options

✓ Understanding techniques to optimize Group Policy

✓ Delegating authority over GPOs

✓ Implementing design and testing guidelines for GPOs

Within a networking environment, administrators need some way of employing standards for clients' computers and supervising their computing environments. *Group Policy* is an administrative tool that can be used to administer different aspects of the client computing environment, from installing software to applying a standardized desktop.

If you recall from Windows NT 4.0, the tool used to administer the client computing environment was Policy Editor. Group Policy in Windows 2000 serves the same purpose, only it is much more powerful and flexible. It is designed to function within the hierarchy of Active Directory. Group Policies can be created for users and computers and is linked to the different levels (site, domain, and Organizational Unit) within the hierarchy, depending on to whom or to what the policy needs to apply. Group Policy can be inherited within the hierarchy or filtered using security groups. Before creating and linking Group Policies, you'll need to assess the business's needs to determine the level of management it requires. This is an important step because it will have an impact on the creation of lower-level OUs within the hierarchy.

This chapter is broken down into five main topics: business needs for Group Policy, applying Group Policy, Group Policy planning issues, designing Group Policy, and testing Group Policy. Also, keep in mind the previously listed terms and techniques while working through the chapter.

Business Needs for Group Policy

Before implementing a Group Policy, you'll need to perform an assessment of the business's needs to determine where in the business management is required and the level of management that needs to be implemented. Use the following questions as a guideline when assessing the needs of the business:

➤ What areas of the client's computing environment need to be controlled?

➤ What areas within the business require administration?

➤ Do all areas within the business require the same level of management? Are there some areas that require a high level of management and other areas that require minimal management?

Determining the different levels of management required throughout the business is important because they will have an impact on the creation of lower-level OUs in the Active Directory hierarchy. Because Group Policies can be likened to the different levels within the Active Directory hierarchy, using the preceding questions as a guide will also help the design team determine where in the hierarchy the policies should be linked to best serve the needs of the IT organization.

In order to determine this, you must first understand what Group Policy can actually do.

What Does Group Policy Do?

Group Policy is a tool that allows for centralized administration. It can be used to configure and set standards for the computing environment (both client and computer) within a business. Group Policies are linked to containers within the Active Directory hierarchy. All objects within the container are affected by the policy settings. This is unlike policies in Windows NT 4.0, which are specifically applied to groups, users, and computers. Figure 6.1 shows the general settings that can be configured for both users and computers.

The Microsoft Management Console (MMC) snap-in is used to manage Group Policy settings. The snap-in is available automatically when using the Active Directory Users and Computers, or the Active Directory Sites and Services snap-in. You may also create a custom MMC console to use exclusively for modifying Group Policy. Use the following steps to open the Group Policy snap-in:

1. Launch the Microsoft Management Console by clicking Run from the Start menu and typing in MMC.

2. From the Console menu, choose Add/Remove Snap-In.

3. Select Add from the dialog box that appears.

4. Choose the Group Policy snap-in and click Add.

5. Click Finish and then Close to make the Group Policy snap-in available.

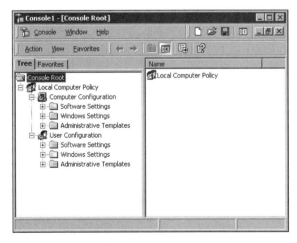

Figure 6.1   The general settings that can be applied to users and computers. Each setting has specific options that can be configured.

6. You may wish to save this console. Select the Console menu, and select Save As, then specify the name and location of the MMC configuration (.msc) file that stores the console settings, and can be used subsequently to launch the MMC with the configured snap-ins.

Software Settings

Using Group Policy, administrators can manage the distribution and installation of software from a central location. Software can be installed, removed, updated, repaired, assigned, and published from a central location. This makes the administration and distribution of software much simpler, especially in an enterprise environment.

One of the strongest features of Group Policy is that it gives administrators the ability to assign or publish applications to users in a selected Group Policy Object (GPO). A Group Policy Object contains the policy settings that are applied to users and computers. Assigning an application makes that application mandatory, and it cannot be uninstalled by the user. If you have a group of users who require an application to perform their job, you may choose to assign it to them. Publishing an application makes it available to the users, and they have the choice of whether to install it.

Note: Applications can be assigned to both users and computers. Applications can only be published to users, not to computers.

Windows Settings

Group Policy can also be used to apply security settings throughout the Active Directory hierarchy. Windows settings allow you to configure script settings and security settings for both users and computers. The security settings that can be configured define the security configuration for the user or computer. Figure 6.2 shows the Windows settings that can be applied.

The security settings that can be applied to a computer include password policies, account lockout policies, and audit policies. Security policies for computers are most commonly applied to (and should be applied to) domain controllers and other servers within the network. For example, a security policy can be applied to domain controllers that governs who is able to log on to them locally.

 One of the nice features of Group Policy in Active Directory is that different account policies can be created for different areas within a domain. If you recall from Windows NT 4.0, only one account policy could be created per domain, and it affected all users. Now separate policies can be created, allowing for better administrative control.

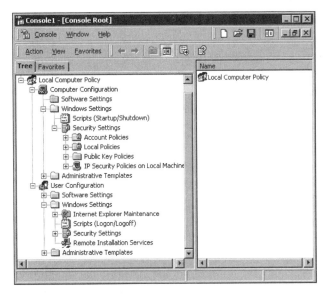

Figure 6.2   The software and Windows settings that can be applied to users and computers through Group Policy.

Through the Windows settings in the Group Policy snap-in, logon/logoff and startup/shutdown scripts can be configured. The logon/logoff scripts are applied to users regardless of which computer they log on from. The startup/shutdown scripts are applied to the computers regardless of which user logs on.

Administrative Templates

By using the administrative templates, Registry settings for users and computers can be configured. Through the administrative templates, the user interface can be preconfigured and enforced. For example, by using the options available under Administrative Templates, a standard configuration can be applied to groups of users and computers. If both users and computers within a specific department require a common desktop configuration, a Group Policy can be applied to enforce the necessary configuration.

Over 400 options can be configured, including the user's Start menu, Taskbar, desktop, and network connections. Figure 6.3 shows the general settings under the administrative templates, each of which have several configurable options.

A number of options can be configured through Group Policy for users and computers. Which options are used and where in the hierarchy the GPO is linked is dependent on the administrative model and the level of management required.

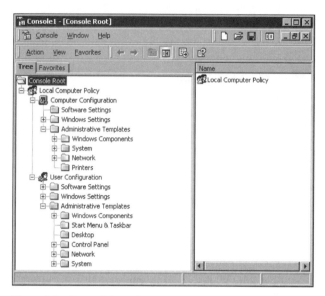

Figure 6.3   Some of the options that can be configured through the administrative templates.

Applying Group Policy

Group Policy Objects can be linked to any of the three levels within the Active Directory hierarchy. The level at which the GPO is linked will determine its scope. In other words, where in the hierarchy the GPO is linked will determine the number of users and computers that are affected. For example, applying a GPO to a domain will affect more users and computers than if it were applied to an OU within the domain. This section looks at the effect a GPO will have when linked to the three different levels in the Active Directory hierarchy. A thorough understanding of this is crucial in determining where to link GPOs.

Where Can Group Policies Be Applied?

To effectively apply Group Policies, it is important to understand the effect a GPO will have when it is applied at a certain level in the Active Directory hierarchy. Linking a Group Policy at the site level will have a different effect from a Group Policy that is applied at the OU level. The needs of the business will determine where in the hierarchy Group Policies should be linked. As already mentioned, there are three levels at which GPOs can be linked: site level, domain level, and OU level (SDOU).

Site Level

The first level at which a GPO can be linked is the site level. If you recall from Chapter 2, a *site* is basically a collection of IP subnets. This means that one GPO can be applied to a group of subnets.

A GPO linked at the site level will affect all users and computers within those particular IP subnets. You may be asking yourself why you would ever want to link a GPO at this level instead of applying it at the domain or OU level. Linking a GPO at this level allows a business to take advantage of the physical connections (remember the reason why these subnets are grouped into a site; refer to Chapter 2 for a review).

In order to take advantage of the high-speed connections within a site, administrators may choose to create a GPO for publishing applications and apply it at this level. A GPO can be applied to Site A so that users do not have to install applications over a relatively slow WAN link and the high-speed connections within the site can be utilized (see Figure 6.4).

 Remember that in order to link a GPO to a site, you must be a member of the Enterprise Admin group.

Domain Level

The next level in the Active Directory hierarchy to which a GPO can be linked is the domain level. When a GPO is applied at this level, it affects all the users and computers belonging to that particular domain. If an organization requires all computers within a domain to have the same account policy or lockout policy, a GPO could be linked to the domain level. Therefore, if the XYZ Corporation applies a GPO to the Training.xyz.corp domain, all users and computers belonging to this domain would be affected (see Figure 6.5). Users and computers in the Consulting domain would not be affected by the policy.

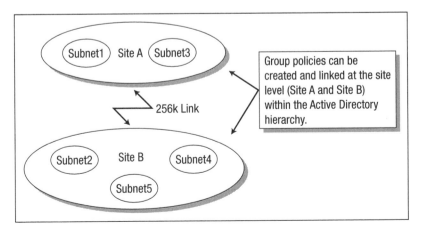

Figure 6.4   A GPO can be linked to the site level to take advantage of the physical links connecting subnets within a site.

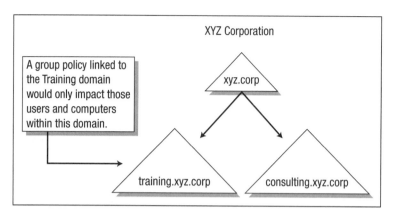

Figure 6.5 Group Policies can be linked at the domain level. A policy can be linked to the Training domain that would not impact any other domains in the organization.

When applying a GPO at this level in the Active Directory hierarchy, you need to be aware of a couple of issues. If you recall from the previous chapter, one of the reasons why OUs are created is to delegate control over their contents to another user or group. When a GPO is applied at the domain level, all the OUs within the domain inherit the policy settings. The policy has to be administered at the domain level, and authority over the policy cannot be delegated to administrators responsible for administering the OUs. In other words, in order to delegate authority, it has to be done at the domain level. The administrators for the different OUs will have no administrative control over the policy.

Also keep in mind that when a policy is linked to a domain that is a parent domain, the child domains are not affected by the policy. The policy is not passed down from parent domain to child domain. If the Training domain is the parent domain to NY and Paris, any policy linked to the Training domain will not affect the users and computers in the two child domains (see Figure 6.6).

 Domains are security boundaries, so no Group Policy settings are inherited by child domains. This means if you want to create Group Policy at the domain level, you must link a GPO to each domain in a forest. Likewise, settings from a Group Policy Object linked to an Organizational Unit in a parent domain are not inherited by OUs in a child domain.

If the child domains require the same Group Policy settings, there are two options. The first is to link the GPO to the child domains. The only problem with linking GPOs across domain boundaries is that it increases traffic, because the policy has to be retrieved from another domain. This becomes a major concern if the link between the domains is slow. The preferred method would be to create another GPO with the same settings and apply it to the child domain.

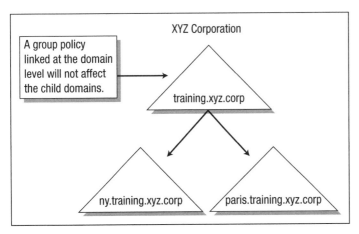

Figure 6.6   Policies applied to a parent domain are not applied to child domains.

OU Level

The third level at which a GPO can be linked within the Active Directory structure is the OU level. Applying GPOs at this level provides administrators with the most control. Users and computers can be grouped into an OU, and a GPO can be created and applied to that container.

For example, within the **training.xyz.corp** domain, mobile computers may require a different security policy than all other computers within the domain. To support this, two separate OUs could be created within the domain and a Group Policy with the required security settings applied to each one.

One advantage of linking a GPO at this level is that delegation of authority over the GPO is still possible without giving the user or group privileges throughout the domain. In other words, a user or group can be given the responsibility of administering the Group Policy at the OU level (unlike applying a GPO at the domain level). This allows an organization to maintain its decentralized administrative model.

If you recall from the previous chapter, OUs can be nested; therefore, when you're linking a GPO at the OU level, careful planning is required. At this level, GPOs are inherited from parent to child (unlike GPOs applied at the domain level). Within the Training domain, the Clients and Employees OUs will also inherit a GPO that is applied to the Users OU (see Figure 6.7).

Keep in mind that GPOs do not have to be applied at a single level only. They can be applied at all three levels within the Active Directory hierarchy. It is important to understand how GPOs are processed when there are multiple policies applied throughout the hierarchy. The GPO that is processed last will overwrite settings applied by the other GPOs. Here are some key points to keep in mind:

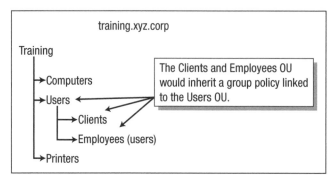

Figure 6.7 Policies applied at the OU level are passed down from parent (Users) to child (Clients and Employees).

➤ Each computer running Windows 2000 has a Group Policy Object that is stored on the local computer (Local Group Policy Object). This is the policy that is processed first.

➤ Any policies that have been linked to the site level are processed after the local policy.

➤ GPOs linked to the domain level are processed next.

➤ The last GPOs to be processed are those linked to the OU level.

Note: If there are multiple policies linked at each level, the administrator will specify the order in which they should be processed.

Now that we've covered the different levels at which Group Policies can be applied, let's take a look at some of the issues that need to be considered when planning for Group Policies.

Group Policy Planning Issues

When designing Active Directory for Group Policy, you need to consider several issues. The planning issues that require consideration are filtering using security, inheritance modification, and optimizing Group Policy performance. For example, the user or group who is responsible for the administration of a domain or OU may need to remain exempt from a GPO. When you filter a GPO, you are exempting a group from those settings.

Filtering Using Security

By default, all objects within a container are affected by a Group Policy that has been applied. However, there may be instances where not all objects should be affected by the Group Policy. In such cases, filtering can be used. *Filtering* is a feature that allows an administrator to exclude certain groups from being affected by a Group Policy (by limiting the scope of the policy). When you filter a GPO, you exempt a group from the settings within the policy.

Note: GPOs are applied to containers within Active Directory. Filters, on the other hand, are applied to groups.

The Group Policies that are applied to a container will affect all users who have Read permission for the GPO. This is the default permission given to all users for a GPO. This means that all users within a container will, by default, be affected by the policy. To change the scope of the GPO and exclude certain users from being affected, simply create a security group containing the users who need to be excluded and deny the group access to the GPO.

Note: Security groups in Windows 2000 are used to assign a group of users permissions to resources on the network.

If a Group Policy is applied to the Users OU (as shown previously in Figure 6.7), it may be necessary to limit its scope so that it does not affect the users or the group responsible for administration.

If the policy applies restrictions to the users' computing environment, some of the restrictions might not be required for administrative purposes. In this case, a filter can be applied to exempt those users responsible for administration of the OU from the policy.

Inheritance Modification

In some instances, a GPO applied to a parent container should not be applied to its child containers (remember, a GPO applied at the OU level is passed down from parent container to child container). Referring back to Figure 6.7, a GPO applied to the Users OU will be inherited by the Clients and Employees containers. In such a case, blocking inheritance can prevent the GPO settings applied to a parent OU from being applied to a child OU.

Blocking

Using a feature called *blocking*, the inheritance of a GPO can be modified so that it is not passed on from parent container to child container. Any policy applied at the site, domain, or OU level can be blocked. If the Group Policy applied to the Users container should not apply to the Clients container (as shown previously in Figure 6.7), then inheritance of the GPO can be blocked. The Employees container will still be affected, but not the Clients container.

The block is not applied to the GPO itself but rather to the site, domain, or OU that should be exempt from the policy. All policy settings are blocked, not just those from a single GPO.

Use the following steps to block the inheritance of a GPO:

1. Open the Active Directory Users and Computers MMC snap-in.

2. Right-click the site, domain, or OU that should be exempt from the policy and choose Properties.

3. Select the Group Policy tab and select the Block Policy Inheritance checkbox, as shown in Figure 6.8.

By selecting this checkbox, the Clients container would no longer be affected by the Group Policy linked to the Users container.

Note: There is no way to block only certain settings within a GPO from applying. If you require some of the settings from a GPO to apply, but not all, you will have to create another Group Policy.

The only time that the Block Policy Inheritance option will be ignored and the policy still applied is if the No Override option is set.

No Override

The No Override option means exactly that. If this option is set, any Group Policies linked to a parent container will be applied to the child containers, regardless of whether the Block Policy Inheritance option is set. This option will prevent any other GPO from overwriting the settings contained within it. Any GPO that has the No Override option set will not be overwritten by another policy.

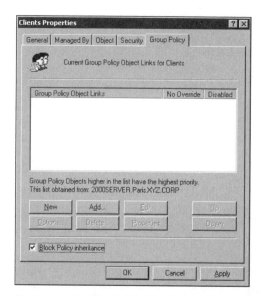

Figure 6.8 Checking the Block Policy Inheritance option causes this container to be exempt from any policy applied to the parent container.

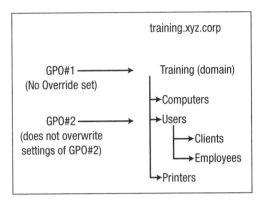

Figure 6.9   Setting the No Override option on the GPO link at the domain level will prevent any other GPOs from overwriting its policy settings.

Using the XYZ Corporation to see how this option can affect inheritance, refer to Figure 6.9. Suppose a GPO has been linked to the Training domain and another GPO has been linked to the Users OU. Without any inheritance modification, the GPO at the domain level would be processed first, and the GPO at the OU level would be processed second, overwriting previous settings (remember local policies would be applied before any others). If the No Override option is set on the first GPO link at the domain level, its settings will not be overwritten when the second GPO is applied.

Use the following steps to specify the No Override option:

1. Open the Active Directory Users and Computers or the Active Directory Sites and Services MMC snap-in. If you are setting the No Override option at the Site level, use the Sites and Services snap-in. Use the Users and Computers snap-in to set No Override at the domain and OU levels.

2. Right-click the site, domain, or OU that the GPO is linked to and choose Properties.

3. Choose the Group Policy tab, select the GPO you want to set the No Override option to apply to, and choose Options.

4. From the dialog box that appears, check the No Override checkbox (see Figure 6.10).

Optimizing Group Policy Performance

One of the overall goals when designing any network infrastructure is to optimize the performance of the network. There are some issues to keep in mind and some settings that can be configured to optimize the performance of Group Policies. When designing Active Directory for Group Policy, keep the following points in mind to ensure performance is optimized:

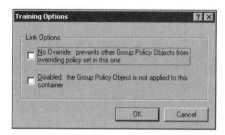

Figure 6.10 By checking the No Override option, you can prevent other Group Policies from overriding the policy applied at this level.

➤ Some settings, but not all, within Group Policy can be configured to process if only there is sufficient bandwidth. For example, if applications are being published through a Group Policy, consider configuring this option to only be processed when there is sufficient bandwidth.

➤ If you recall from Windows NT 4.0, when a change is made to a system policy, the user must log off and then log on again for the new settings to be applied. Group Policies in Windows 2000 refresh themselves by default every 90 minutes (this means the user does not need to log off for new settings to apply). Consider increasing the refresh interval to increase performance.

➤ All GPOs within the Active Directory hierarchy are processed from the site level down to the OU level. To increase performance, try to limit the number of policies that are used—the more policies you have, the busier the network will be. Also, each time a user logs on, the policies will have to be processed. Therefore, the more there are, the longer it will take for the users to log on. Remember that *less* is usually best.

➤ The more GPOs that users are affected by, the longer it will take to process them, and in turn the longer it will take for users to log on. Consider using security groups to exempt users from policies that are not applicable to them. This way, there are fewer GPOs to process.

➤ If you are linking GPOs between sites and domains, consider the impact that this will have on performance. Remember, linking GPOs between sites and domains will increase traffic, because the GPO has to be retrieved. If the physical links between them are already slow, performance will only decrease. Consider creating separate GPOs with the same settings and linking them to each site or domain so that the GPO doesn't have to be retrieved.

➤ Whenever possible, limit the use of inheritance blocking and overriding. Overuse of these two options will make it difficult to track and troubleshoot GPO processing.

Designing Group Policy

When designing Group Policy, the design team will need to determine the best way to implement it for management purposes. It will be important to design the GPOs in such a way that allows for the current IT organization to easily manage them. There should be some sort of standard set in place so that the creation and organization of GPOs can remain consistent throughout the network. In designing Group Policy, you'll once again need to consider how administration is distributed throughout the network (centralized versus decentralized). The design team will also need to determine who will be responsible for administering the GPO and the level of administration he or she will be assigned.

When organizing GPOs, you have basically three options: single policy, multiple policy, and a dedicated policy. Keep in mind that the implementation that you choose will affect a number of things, including the maintainability of the GPO, logon times as Group Policy is processed, and the ability to delegate GPO maintenance tasks.

➤ In a single-policy implementation, a separate policy is created for each of the different policy options. Separate Group Policies could be created for application settings, security settings, and desktop settings. With this type of implementation, different users or groups can be given authority over different areas of Group Policy. If this type of option is implemented within the XYZ Corporation, there could be several GPOs applied to the Users container, each with different settings. This implementation would best meet the needs of a business that distributes the administrative tasks among different users or groups (decentralized).

➤ The second option is to implement a multiple policy. With this type of implementation, one GPO contains all the settings that need to be applied to a container. One GPO would contain all the application, security, Windows, and administrative settings. This option would be best suited to a business that implements a centralized administrative model.

➤ A dedicated policy contains settings that are divided into two general categories. One GPO would be created to hold the computer settings, and another GPO would contain the user settings.

When designing Group Policy, also take into consideration which users or groups will be assigned delegation of control over the GPOs and the type of permissions they will require. Will the user or group be given the right to create new GPOs, modify existing policies, link policies between sites and domains, or will they be given full control? The type of permissions assigned to users will again be determined by how the business currently distributes administrative tasks.

The previous chapter discussed delegation of authority for distributing administrative duties among users and groups. When designing Group Policy, also keep in mind delegation of authority. Specific users and groups can be granted administrative responsibility over a GPO. The design team will need to determine who will be responsible for administering different GPOs and the type of privilege required.

When delegating control over a GPO to a user or group, you basically have three options to assign: creating, modifying, and linking. Here are some questions to keep in mind:

➤ Should the user or group have the ability to create new GPOs (specifying his or her own policy settings) for a container?

➤ Should the user or group have the ability to modify an existing GPO?

➤ Should the user or group have the ability to link a container to an existing GPO?

The option you choose will obviously determine the scope of administrative control a user or group has over a GPO. Remember to only assign the necessary permissions for a user or group to carry out his or her job.

Testing Group Policy

The last step (and one of the most important steps) in designing Group Policy is to test the plan that has been developed. Nothing could be more disastrous than to implement a Group Policy plan only to find out that it does not execute as intended. Keep the following points in mind when testing the Group Policy plan:

➤ Ideally you should test your plan in a controlled environment similar to the actual business environment.

➤ If you don't have access to a controlled environment, test the plan within the actual business environment.

➤ Just because your plan passes the first test does not mean that your Group Policy will work as expected in production. Be sure to test your plan in a variety of situations.

➤ Keep good documentation. This will make it easier to troubleshoot any problems that arise.

Following these general guidelines when testing the Group Policy plan will ensure that any undesired results are identified before the plan is actually implemented.

Practice Questions

Case Study: Allrisks Insurance

Allrisks Insurance is a large insurance company with offices throughout the United States. Allrisks is deploying Windows 2000 on servers and workstations in all its offices, starting with the home office in Chicago. Aside from the home office in Chicago, Allrisks has regional offices in San Francisco, Dallas, Orlando, and Boston. Agents for each of the major lines are located in each regional office as well as the home office.

LAN/Network Structure

Allrisks has a deployment plan in place to migrate from Windows NT 4.0 Server and Workstation to Windows 2000 Server and Professional. The deployment is approximately 50% complete.

Allrisks has implemented Active Directory in a single forest, with a root domain of **allrisks.com** and child domains for each of its major lines of insurance, namely, **propcas.allrisks.com**, **health.allrisks.com**, and **life.allrisks.com**.

Ethernet and Fast Ethernet connections are used throughout the company.

Proposed LAN/Network Structure

The migration is scheduled to be completed within 12 months. No further changes are planned at this time.

WAN Connectivity

The regional offices are connected to the home office via full 1.5Mbps T1 circuits. Sites have been created for each of the regional offices as well as the home office. No changes are planned at this time.

Directory Design Commentary

Director, Corporate Information Services: We are concerned with the high cost of supporting PCs with different configurations in each office. The Allrisks help desk staff is constantly troubleshooting problems that occur when new software is deployed and conflicts arise between the new programs and the existing software on the computer. An excessive amount of time is spent researching problems because there is no way of enforcing software standards, and many computers have configurations with minor, but troublesome, differences.

Vice President, Large Group Insurance: Allrisks has instituted a new program of installing kiosk computers at certain corporate clients. These kiosks are linked to Allrisks' data center by dial-up connections. The kiosk computers run a single application that helps employees of the corporate clients select insurance coverage. The kiosk computers should run only this application and not be available for Web browsing or any other applications.

Internet Positioning

Allrisks has a Web site (**www.allrisks.com**) that is primarily used for public relations. All Allrisks employees have email with an allrisks.com domain.

No changes to the Internet positioning are planned for the next 12 months.

Question 1

> Allrisks wishes to use Group Policy to distribute certain small applications specific to a given line of insurance. In particular, it has developed a life insurance underwriting program that should be available to all Allrisks life insurance agents. The IT department has created a Group Policy Object to distribute this life insurance software. What container should this GPO be linked to?
>
> ○ a. The domain allrisks.com
>
> ○ b. The domain life.allrisks.com
>
> ○ c. The Chicago site
>
> ○ d. The Organizational Unit Agents within the domain life.allrisks.com

The correct answer is d. The GPO to distribute software should be linked to the Agents OU within the life insurance division's domain. Answer a is incorrect because agents are located in regional offices, not in the home office. Answer b is incorrect because distributing software at the domain level means that all employees of the life insurance division would get a copy of the software. Answer c is incorrect because it would give the software to all employees in Chicago, including agents based in the home office, but not to agents located in the regional offices.

Question 2

> A small group of life insurance agents-in-training should not receive the life underwriting software until their training program is completed. How can Allrisks' IT staff ensure that these agents do not have the software installed prematurely?
>
> ○ a. Move the agents-in-training to the home office domain allrisks.com.
>
> ○ b. Create a security group for agents-in-training and configure a filter for the GPO to deny the Apply Group Policy permission for this security group.
>
> ○ c. Create a child Organizational Unit off the Agents OU called "In Training," move all agents-in-training into this new OU, and block policy inheritance for the In Training OU.
>
> ○ d. Place the accounts for the agents-in-training in the Users container.

The correct answer is b. The filter will prevent application of the GPO that distributes software but will not affect any other Group Policies that may be in force. Answer a is incorrect. It is not possible to move users between domains without special migration utilities. If all domains are in native mode, users cannot be moved under any circumstances. Answer c is incorrect because blocking policy inheritance may prevent application of other GPOs that are required. Likewise, answer d also may affect more policies than necessary. Therefore, answer d is incorrect as well.

Question 3

> In what order is Group Policy applied? Select all appropriate answers from the following list and arrange them in the proper order.
>
> Site
>
> Organizational Unit
>
> Domain
>
> Local computer
>
> Container
>
> Forest

The correct answer is:

Local computer

Site

Domain

Organizational Unit

Note that neither containers (such as Users or Computers) nor forests can have Group Policy Objects linked to them.

Question 4

A consultant retained by Allrisks has recommended creating a single Group Policy Object with generic corporate settings and linking this GPO to the root domain. He says that the Group Policy will be enforced for the root domain, and any child domains off of the root. Is the consultant's recommendation valid?

○ a. Yes

○ b. No

The correct answer is b. Domain Group Policy settings do not affect child domains. Domains are security boundaries, and no permissions or GPO settings can cross between domains.

Question 5

The CEO of Allrisks has mandated that the "Run" command should not appear on the Start menu for any personal computers. How can the IT manager ensure that this policy is always enforced? [Check all correct answers]

❏ a. Create a Group Policy Object that removes the Run command and link it to the root domain. Then check the No Override option.

❏ b. Create a GPO in each domain that removes the Run command and link it to all the top-level Organizational Units in the domain. Then check the No Override option.

❏ c. Create a GPO that removes the Run command and link it to all domains. Then check the No Override option.

❏ d. Create a GPO in each domain that removes the Run command and link it to the domain. Then check the No Override option.

❏ e. Create a GPO in the root domain that removes the Run command and link it to every site. Then check the Block Policy Inheritance option.

Answers b and d are correct. A GPO must be created in each domain, unless a site-level policy is to be applied. Answers a and c are incorrect because GPOs cannot be referenced across domain boundaries. Answer e is incorrect because the Block Policy Inheritance option is inappropriate here.

Question 6   .

The vice-president of the Life Insurance division wants to distribute additional applications using Group Policy. She has asked you to describe the differences between application publishing and application assignment. Which of the following statements are true regarding application assignment and publishing? [Check all correct answers]

❏ a. Assigning an application to a user means that the app is automatically installed the next time the user restarts his or her computer.

❏ b. Published applications are available from the Add/Remove Programs Control Panel applet.

❏ c. Published or assigned applications may be installed through document invocation by clicking a file that has been associated to the application.

❏ d. Applications that are assigned to a computer cannot be uninstalled by the user.

❏ e. Assigned applications cannot be upgraded without uninstalling them first.

Answers b, c, and d are correct. Published applications are typically installed from the Add/Remove Programs applet or through document invocation. Applications that are assigned to a computer can only be uninstalled by administrators, not ordinary users. Answer a is incorrect because applications assigned to a computer are installed at startup, not applications assigned to a user. Answer e is incorrect because upgrades can be configured to uninstall the older version, or not.

Question 7

An Organizational Unit has three Group Policy Objects linked to it, as shown in Figure 6.11. In what order will the GPOs be processed?

○ a. Software Distribution, Base Agent Desktop, Standard Corporate Desktop

○ b. Standard Corporate Desktop, Base Agent Desktop, Software Distribution

○ c. All settings will be merged into one policy and processed together, with conflicts discarded.

○ d. To determine the proper order, you must look at the property sheets for each policy and compare the values in the Policy Weight field to determine processing order

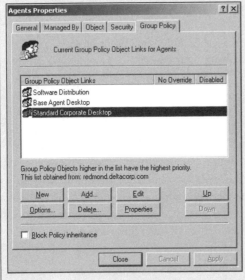

Figure 6.11   Group Policy Objects linked to the Agents Organizational Unit.

Answer b is correct. Policies listed on the Group Policy tab are processed from bottom to top. The last policy processed—Software Distribution in this case—will override any conflicting settings from previously processed policies. Answer a is incorrect because it lists the policies in the order shown, not processed. Answer c is incorrect because GPOs are never merged, and conflicts are resolved in favor of the last policy processed. Answer d is incorrect because there is no such field as Policy Weight for Group Policy Objects.

Question 8

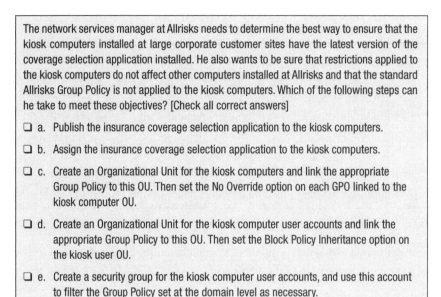

The network services manager at Allrisks needs to determine the best way to ensure that the kiosk computers installed at large corporate customer sites have the latest version of the coverage selection application installed. He also wants to be sure that restrictions applied to the kiosk computers do not affect other computers installed at Allrisks and that the standard Allrisks Group Policy is not applied to the kiosk computers. Which of the following steps can he take to meet these objectives? [Check all correct answers]

❑ a. Publish the insurance coverage selection application to the kiosk computers.

❑ b. Assign the insurance coverage selection application to the kiosk computers.

❑ c. Create an Organizational Unit for the kiosk computers and link the appropriate Group Policy to this OU. Then set the No Override option on each GPO linked to the kiosk computer OU.

❑ d. Create an Organizational Unit for the kiosk computer user accounts and link the appropriate Group Policy to this OU. Then set the Block Policy Inheritance option on the kiosk user OU.

❑ e. Create a security group for the kiosk computer user accounts, and use this account to filter the Group Policy set at the domain level as necessary.

Answers b, d, and e are correct. Assigning the special application to the kiosk computers can ensure that the latest version of the application is always installed. Creating an OU for the kiosk users and blocking policy inheritance for that OU will prevent the normal Allrisks Group Policy from affecting the kiosk users. Also, should any domain-level GPO have the No Override option selected, it will be necessary to filter out that GPO for the kiosk users. Setting the permissions on the GPO to Deny for the kiosk users will prevent the standard domain policy from executing at the kiosk computers. Answer a is incorrect because you cannot publish software to a computer. Answer c is incorrect because it would not be appropriate to use the No Override option in this case.

Question 9

> The CIO is concerned that someone can set the No Override option on a Group Policy Object linked to an Organizational Unit, thus overriding a No Override option set at the domain level. Which of the following statements correctly describes the processing of No Override?
>
> ○ a. No Override set at the site or domain level will take precedence over No Override set at a lower level.
>
> ○ b. Only one No Override can be handled in GPO processing. If a second No Override is encountered, the GPO is not processed.
>
> ○ c. Because Organizational Unit GPOs are processed after domain GPOs, there is nothing that can be done to prevent the Domain GPO from being overridden.
>
> ○ d. A Registry key can be set to ignore No Override at the Organizational Unit level.

Answer a is correct. Although normal GPO processing will have OU policy override domain or site policy, the No Override option is handled differently. The highest No Override will take precedence over a lower No Override. Answer b is incorrect because multiple No Override options can be processed successfully, although they are very difficult to troubleshoot. Answer c is incorrect because the No Override order is different from the normal GPO processing order. Answer d is incorrect because there is no such Registry key.

Question 10

Here are two lists, one of container objects where Group Policy may be linked, and a second of GPOs and their functions. Based on the requirements stated for Allrisks, link the GPO and function to the appropriate site, domain, or Organizational Unit. Not all Group Policy Objects may be used, and some may be used more than once.

Container objects to which Group Policy may be linked:

The Chicago site

The life insurance domain

The Agents Organizational Unit

The Kiosk Computers Organizational Unit

Group Policy Objects and functions:

Agent Software GPO—Distributes software to agents only

Standard Corp Desk GPO—Sets the standard corporate desktop for all users

Large Application GPO—Distributes large applications that should not cross WANs

Special Life Desk GPO—Modifies the corporate desktop for the life insurance division

Kiosk Application GPO—Installs applications at kiosk computers

Security Settings GPO—Sets security rules

Agent Desk GPO—Adds special options to desktops for agents

HR Applications GPO—Publishes applications for HR users

The correct answer is:

The Chicago site

> Large Application GPO

The life insurance domain

> Standard Corp Desk GPO

> Special Life Desk GPO

> Security Settings GPO

Agents OU

> Agent Software GPO

> Agent Desk GPO

Kiosk Computers OU

    Kiosk Application GPO

The Large Application GPO is most appropriate at the site level because the installation of these apps should not run across WAN links. Remember that Allrisks domains are structured by line of business, not geography, so it would not be a good idea to link this GPO to a geographically dispersed domain. The Standard Corp Desk GPO is most appropriate at the domain level. Each domain should have a copy of this GPO. The Special Life Desk GPO is intended for all life insurance division employees, so it is also best linked to the domain. Because security policy must be set at the domain level, the Security Settings GPO should also be linked to the domain.

The Agent Software and Agent Desk GPOs are intended for insurance agents, so it makes sense to link them to the Agents OU. The Kiosk Computers OU is the logical place to link the Kiosk Application GPO.

There is no appropriate place to link the HR Applications GPO in this example.

Need to Know More?

 The *Microsoft Windows 2000 Server Resource Kit* contains in-depth information about Group Policy.

 Try searching the TechNet CD or use Microsoft's online version at **www.microsoft.com**. Search for keywords such as *delegation*, *delegation of control*, and *inheritance*.

Designing a Domain

Terms you'll need to understand:

✓ Domain local group

✓ Global group

✓ Universal group

✓ Local group

✓ Security group

✓ Native mode

✓ Mixed mode

Techniques you'll need to master:

✓ Analyzing the administrative and security requirements of a business

✓ Choosing an appropriate name for the first Active Directory domain

✓ Identifying the three main types of security groups and their characteristics

✓ Implementing nesting of security groups to ease administration

✓ Designing an Organizational Unit (OU) structure to meet the administrative requirements

✓ Tailoring the OU structure for the application of Group Policies

One of the main goals when designing an Active Directory domain is to ensure that the needs of the business are met. It is crucial to have a thorough understanding of how objects can be organized within domains and OUs in order to create a structure that will meet the administrative needs of the business. The strategy that you use to organize objects into domains and OUs should reflect the structure of the business.

The following topics will be covered throughout this chapter and will assist you in designing an Active Directory domain:

➤ Determining business needs

➤ Creating the first domain in Active Directory

➤ Planning security groups

➤ Planning Organizational Unit design

Also, keep in mind the terms and techniques listed on the previous page when working through the chapter.

Determining Business Needs

As you've probably already noticed, assessing the needs of the business is crucial in all aspects of designing an Active Directory infrastructure. The needs of the business should also be the first thing considered when designing a domain. The domain design created by the design team should reflect the current structure of the business. When assessing the business, you need to detail the administrative requirements as well as the security requirements. Both of these requirements are going to have a major impact on the domain and OU structure planned for the business.

Administrative and Security Requirements

When designing a domain, the first thing that should be documented (or reviewed if it has already been determined) is the administrative strategy that the business has implemented. The type of administrative structure that a business has in place will determine the creation and organization of domains within the Active Directory. Does the business implement a centralized or decentralized strategy for administration? Knowing how the administrative tasks are distributed throughout the business will help to determine the model for administration that will best meet the needs of the business. The administration model that is implemented should allow the business to distribute administrative tasks in a way that meets its administrative requirements. The administration model will also determine the organization of domains and OUs in the Active Directory hierarchy.

If you recall from Chapter 5, there are basically four models for administration that can be implemented: geographical (location), organizational (business unit), functional (role), and hybrid models. Table 7.1 summarizes the characteristics of each model (refer back to Chapter 5 for a more in-depth review).

Once you've determined the administrative requirements of the business, the security requirements will need to be assessed (security within a business is usually crucial, so be sure the assessment is thorough). When assessing the security requirements, you'll need to determine who is responsible for administration within the business (delegation of authority). Documenting this information will ensure that the proper individuals are assigned the proper permissions. Use the following questions as a guide when performing the assessment:

➤ Who in the business requires administrative privileges?

➤ What are they responsible for?

➤ What type of administrative privileges do they require to do their jobs?

➤ What is the scope of their responsibilities?

➤ Will their privileges apply at the site, domain, or OU level?

Once the administrative and security requirements of the business have been determined, you should have a good understanding of the domain structure that will best meet the business's needs. Your next step will be to plan the creation of the first domain within the Active Directory structure.

Table 7.1 Summary of the common models for administration.	
Model	**Characteristics**
Geographical (location)	The Active Directory structure is organized around the different geographical locations within a business.
Organizational (business unit)	The organization of the Active Directory structure is based on the different departments or business units within a business.
Functional (role)	This type of model is based on the different job roles within a business.
Hybrid	This type of model implements a combination of the preceding models. Two common hybrids are "location then organization" and "organization then location."

Creating the First Domain in Active Directory

The first domain created within Active Directory becomes the forest root domain. This is the domain that will represent the entire business. It is important to plan which domain will become the forest root domain, because once it is established it cannot be renamed or deleted.

Note: If you recall from Chapter 2, the forest root domain stores common information that is shared between all domains within the forest. Shared information includes the following:

➤ *Schema*

➤ *Configuration container*

➤ *Schema Admin*

➤ *Enterprise Admin*

For a more in-depth discussion of forests, refer back to Chapter 2.

Careful planning is required when choosing a name for the forest root domain. The first thing to note is that the forest root domain cannot be renamed. If it's decided after the fact that the name chosen is no longer suitable, be ready to spend a lot of time and effort re-creating the Active Directory structure. Second, choosing an appropriate name for the forest root domain is also important because all other domains created under the forest root (child domains) will derive a portion of their namespace from it.

When deciding what to name the first domain in Active Directory, keep the following points in mind:

➤ Choose a name that will not be changing in the near future; a name that is static. Changing the name of the forest root domain is not easy, so choose a name that will not be changing in the next three to five years.

➤ Choose a name that is meaningful to the business, its employees, and its clients. When naming the forest root, consider using the name of the business.

➤ Make sure the name is available for use on the Internet. Even if the business has no intention of using its name on the Internet, make sure the name is registered in case the business changes its mind in the future.

When creating the forest root domain, the design team may determine that the business's name would be an appropriate choice (as long as the business has no intention of changing the company name in the near future). The name would provide a general representation of the business and an appropriate namespace for child domains within the forest. The company name would be meaningful to employees and clients and would make the domain easily identifiable. For example, the XYZ Corporation shown in Figure 7.1 uses xyz.corp as its forest root domain. The root domain namespace has been passed on to the training and consulting child domains.

Planning Security Groups

In Windows NT 4.0, the recommended strategy for assigning permissions to resources was to assign permissions to groups and add specific users to the appropriate groups. Windows 2000 maintains a similar strategy but allows for much more flexibility; different types of security groups can be created at different levels in the Active Directory hierarchy. Windows 2000 uses these different security groups to logically organize users and computers to assign permissions. By placing users into security groups, permissions to access resources can be easily assigned to a large number of users. When planning security groups, consider the following topics, which will be covered in this section:

➤ Types of security groups

➤ Nesting security groups.

Types of Security Groups

When you are planning security groups, you must determine what type of security group to use. You can choose from basically three security group types:

➤ Global group

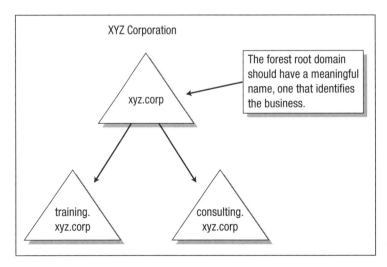

Figure 7.1 The first domain created is the forest root domain. Its namespace is inherited by all child domains and should therefore be a good representation of the business.

➤ Domain local group

➤ Universal group

Note: There is also a fourth type of group called a local group. Local groups are found on computers running Windows 2000 Professional and those running Windows 2000 Server configured as member servers. Local groups can only contain user accounts on the local computer. They are used to assign a group of users permissions to resources on the computer where the group is created. The difference between a local group and a domain local group is that domain local groups can be used to grant users permissions to resources throughout a domain. On the other hand, local groups only provide access to resources on a local computer.

You will select the type of group, as shown in Figure 7.2, when creating a new group using the Active Directory Users and Computers MMC snap-in. You may also change the group type for existing groups using the same interface.

Global Group

The first type of security group is the *global group*. Global groups are used to logically group users within a domain who have common needs to assign them permissions to network resources. When deciding whether to use global groups, keep the following characteristics in mind:

➤ Global groups can only contain other global groups or user accounts from the domain in which the group was created. Referring back to Figure 7.1, if a

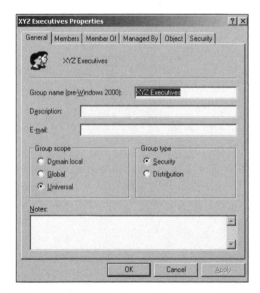

Figure 7.2   The different security groups available in Windows 2000.

global group is created in the training.xyz.corp domain, it could only contain user accounts from within this domain. User accounts from the Consulting domain could not be added to the group.

➤ Once the group is created, it can be assigned permissions to resources throughout the forest. The group name will appear in the Global Catalog so that trusted domains can assign the group permissions to their resources (refer back to Chapter 2 for a review of Global Catalog Server).

Therefore, the global group that was created in the Training domain could be assigned permissions to resources within the Consulting domain.

➤ If network traffic is a concern, consider using global groups. Because only the name of the group is replicated to the Global Catalog Server, not the actual membership, network traffic is less than for universal groups (discussed later).

Note: Group membership will still be replicated within the domain but not to other domains.

Domain Local Group

Domain local groups are also used to assign permissions to resources on the network. They do not have the same characteristics as global groups. This type of group is used to group users throughout the forest to assign them permissions to resources in the local domain. Here are some points to keep in mind concerning domain local groups:

➤ Domain local groups can contain global groups and user accounts from any domain in the forest. Referring once again to Figure 7.1, if a domain local group is created in the Training domain, any user accounts within the forest can be added to the group (this is opposite of global groups).

➤ The domain local group can only be used to assign permissions to resources within the domain where the group is created.

The domain local group created in the Training domain can be used to grant users throughout the forest access to resources only in the Training domain. To grant users throughout the forest permissions to a resource located in the Consulting domain, a domain local group would have to be specifically created in that domain.

 Unlike a global group, a domain local group is not replicated to Global Catalog Servers within the forest because other domains cannot use it. The group name and membership is still replicated throughout the domain.

Universal Groups

The third type of security group that can be used is the universal group. This type of group is used to assign a group of users from different domains permission to network resources throughout the forest. Here are some points to keep in mind concerning universal groups:

➤ Universal groups can contain other universal groups (nesting), global groups, and also user accounts from any domain.

➤ A universal group can be assigned permissions to resources throughout the forest.

 When determining whether to use universal groups, keep in mind that they are only available in native mode, so they can only be used when all the domain controllers have been upgraded to Windows 2000.

Any universal groups created will be replicated to all Global Catalog Servers in the forest, as well as their membership, so be sure to keep membership static and to a minimum. This will help to reduce replication traffic. It is good practice to restrict universal group membership to global groups only. This will minimize the number and frequency of changes, thus reducing Global Catalog replication traffic.

Now that you've become familiar with the different types of security groups available in Windows 2000, let's take a look at group nesting.

Nesting Security Groups

Nesting is the process of adding groups to groups or creating a hierarchy of groups. Recall the discussion of OUs and how they can be nested within each other; the same thing can be done with security groups. Nesting security groups can greatly simplify the process of assigning permissions and can also reduce network traffic.

Note: Group nesting is only available in native mode. If a domain is still in mixed mode, groups cannot be nested, as was the case with Windows NT.

For example, within the XYZ Corporation, specific groups could be created for each group of executives within the different geographical locations. These groups could then be nested into one group that would represent all executives from each location (see Figure 7.3). In cases where all the executives required access to network resources, permissions need only be assigned once to the XYZ Executives group.

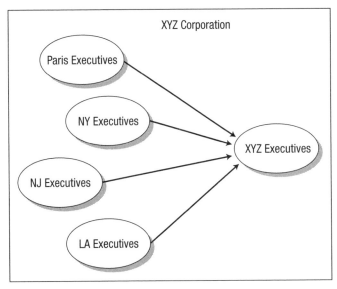

Figure 7.3 By nesting the four groups created for the executives into another group (XYZ Executives), permissions only need to be set once to give all executives access to network resources.

Here are a couple of guidelines to follow when you are nesting security groups:

➤ Less is usually best, so try to minimize the level of nesting implemented. The deeper the hierarchy of nested security groups, the harder it will be to track permissions and troubleshoot permission problems.

➤ A good design team maintains good documentation. Be sure to document group membership, nested groups, and permissions that have been assigned. This will reduce the chance of errors when establishing group membership and permissions, and troubleshooting problems will be easier when there is documentation to refer back to.

If you recall from Windows NT 4.0, the acronym for creating groups and assigning permissions was AGLP (assign user Accounts to Global groups, assign global groups to Local groups, and assign Permissions to the local group). Windows 2000 maintains a similar version of this strategy. When creating security groups, use the recommended AGDLP (assign user Accounts to Global groups, assign global groups to Domain Local groups, and assign Permissions to the local group) model, which will ensure some form of consistency within a business when creating security groups:

1. Place the user accounts into global groups.

2. Add global groups to domain local groups.

3. Assign permissions to the domain local groups.

Mixed Mode Vs. Native Mode

Windows 2000 domains can operate in either mixed mode or native mode. Mixed mode is used to provide backward compatibility with Windows NT domain controllers during a migration from NT to Windows 2000.

When you're upgrading a domain to Windows 2000, the first server to be converted should be the primary domain controller (PDC). When the upgrade is complete, this server will be a Windows 2000 domain controller and also hold all appropriate Operations Master roles. Operations Master roles are discussed in detail in Chapter 9. The critical Operations Master role in a mixed mode domain is the PDC Emulator. The Windows 2000 domain controller with this role acts as a Windows NT PDC to all the down-level (NT) backup domain controllers (BDCs) in the domain, thus providing notification of updates and sending updates when requested by the BDCs.

While in mixed mode, universal groups are not available, nor can group nesting be performed. Also, it is important to monitor the size of Active Directory for domains operating in mixed mode. Domain size should be limited to 40,000 objects as long as there are Windows NT BDCs still active.

Once there are no more Windows NT domain controllers in the domain, the conversion to native mode is easily accomplished from the Active Directory Domains and Trusts MMC snap-in. Simply right-click the domain to be upgraded, select Properties from the drop-down list, and click the button labeled Change Mode on the General tab of the Properties page.

Once in native mode, all the new security group features of Windows 2000 are available. The domain controller with the PDC Emulator role no longer advertises itself as an NT PDC and can no longer provide SAM updates to down-level NT BDCs.

The conversion from mixed mode to native mode is one-way and cannot be reversed.

Planning Organizational Unit Design

The OU structure that is designed should reflect the administrative needs of the business. The structure is irrelevant to the regular users within the business. The OU structure is created for the purpose of administration. The design should allow administrators to easily delegate control over groups of objects to the appropriate user or group. The OU hierarchy should also allow for the linking of Group Policies. The following topics will be covered in this section:

➤ Starting with administrative requirements

➤ Tailoring for group policy application

Starting with Administrative Requirements

Remember when you are creating an OU structure that it must meet the needs of administration (this cannot be emphasized enough). The structure you design should be based on the administrative model that the business implements. If you recall from Chapter 5, the administrative model defines who is responsible for administration of the users and network resources within a business. Therefore, the structure designed should allow the business to continue to delegate authority and distribute administrative tasks in a way that meets its needs.

When designing the OU structure, keep in mind that the upper layers of the hierarchy will be based on the model for administration. If the design team determines that a model for administration based on geographic location is needed, the upper layers of the OU hierarchy will reflect this model.

Chapter 5 discussed some of the models for administration that can be implemented. Be sure to base the structure of the upper layers of the OU hierarchy on something that will remain static (geographic location as opposed to department or business unit). This will help to avoid a reorganization of the Active Directory hierarchy in the future.

If the design team determines that a model for administration based on location would be best suited for the XYZ Corporation, the OU structure may be similar to the diagram shown in Figure 7.4. One domain could be created for the entire business and upper level OUs created based on location. Remember that when planning domains, it is always best to use the single domain model. The next chapter will discuss implementing a multiple domain model.

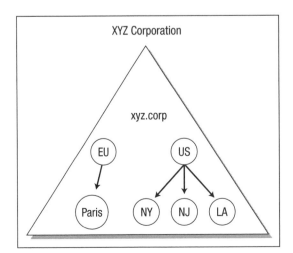

Figure 7.4   The upper layer of the OU structure should represent the administrative model of the business.

This type of OU structure would be ideal for the XYZ Corporation if there are users or groups in each location who are assigned administrative authority over objects within their respective locations.

The lower levels within the OU hierarchy should be created with specific administrative tasks in mind; in other words, what types of objects will users and groups be responsible for administering? How can these objects be grouped to allow for this administration? For example, if a group is to be responsible for printer administration within its location, an OU could be created for printer objects and delegation of authority assigned to the group. By nesting OUs within one another, you can create an OU structure that will meet the specific administrative requirements of the business.

 Although nesting of OUs is a good thing, it can get difficult to administer and troubleshoot if the hierarchy is too deep.

Once it is determined that the administrative requirements have been met by the OU structure, you will also need to determine how it will be affected by the application of Group Policies.

Tailoring for Group Policy

Group Policy is used to administer the computing environment of users and computers within a business, as was discussed in Chapter 6. Group Policy objects can be linked to different levels within the Active Directory hierarchy, and the level at which it is linked will determine the scope of the policy. Group Policies are most commonly linked to the OU level because this provides administrators with the most control over the computing environment and also allows for delegation of authority to users and groups, thus eliminating the need to give them administrative privileges at the domain level.

The lower levels of the OU hierarchy should allow administrators to apply specific Group Policies to the necessary objects. For example, if a Group Policy needs to be applied to a group of specific users, a lower-level OU could be created for this group and linked to the appropriate Group Policy.

Using the XYZ Corporation as an example, if a Group Policy needs to be applied to its users within the Paris location without affecting its clients, an OU structure similar to the one shown in Figure 7.5 could be created.

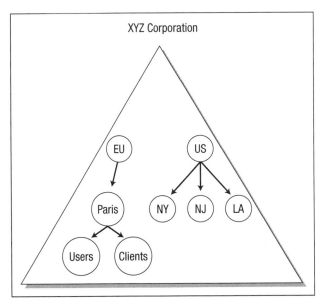

Figure 7.5 An OU structure such as this would allow the XYZ Corporation to apply a Group Policy Object (GPO) to its users while not affecting its clients.

 Remember that GPOs are applied from the top level down, and if the OU structure is too deep with GPOs at different levels, it may result in poor network performance. However, it is the number of GPOs, not the OU depth, that affects logon times.

Practice Questions

Case Study: Velocipede Tours

Velocipede Tours is a bicycle tour operator with three offices in the United States. The main office is in Manchester, Vermont, and the other two offices are in Hilton Head, South Carolina and Maui, Hawaii. Velocipede Tours is deploying Windows 2000 on servers and workstations in all its offices, starting with the Vermont office.

Velocipede Tours has recently merged with two other specialty tour operators. Wet World Excursions conducts diving tours in the Florida Keys from its Key Largo, Florida location. Alpine Adventures organizes hiking and mountain climbing expeditions from its offices in San Francisco and Salzburg, Austria.

LAN and Network Structure

Velocipede Tours has a deployment plan in place to migrate from Windows NT 4.0 Server and Workstation to Windows 2000 Server and Professional. The deployment plan is complete, and the actual rollout is scheduled to begin shortly.

Velocipede Tours was originally to implement a single-domain Active Directory design. However, with the recent merger and decision to maintain each company's identity, Velocipede will now create a separate domain for each.

Alpine Adventures is currently running Windows NT 4.0 Server with Windows 98 at the desktop. Wet World has a Novell NetWare 3.12 network, with three Windows 95 client computers.

Ethernet and Fast Ethernet connections are used throughout the Velocipede and Alpine Adventures offices. Wet World uses thin coax Ethernet.

Proposed LAN and Network Structure

All companies are scheduled to be upgraded to Windows 2000 within 12 months.

Wet World's thin Ethernet infrastructure will be replaced with twisted-pair as part of a complete hardware upgrade.

WAN Connectivity

The South Carolina and Hawaii offices are connected to the home office using a virtual private network (VPN) and 384Kbps SDLC circuits. These circuits are more than adequate for current and forecast traffic.

Alpine Adventures has 56Kbps Frame Relay connections to each office.

Proposed WAN Connectivity

The Wet World office in Key Largo and the Alpine Adventures office in San Francisco will upgrade to the same type of SDLC circuits as used by Velocipede. The Salzburg, Austria office will remain on Frame Relay because the cost of upgrading that link is prohibitive.

Directory Design Commentary

President, Velocipede: We are a small company, so our employees wear many hats. We need the flexibility to allow employees to change roles at a moment's notice. Now, with the merger, my colleagues at the other two companies will need to have the same access to company data that I do.

Manager, IT: With a staff of three here in the Vermont office supporting 100 employees, we need to delegate as many administrative tasks as possible, especially in the Hawaii office. We also need to be able to control the desktop better so that we are not constantly troubleshooting user self-inflicted wounds. Because employees change jobs so frequently, we need to be able to automatically install new software as the employees move from one job responsibility to another. Now with the merger, we have even less time available.

Office Manager, Maui: Currently, it takes over a day to process security updates, password changes, and most other administrative tasks. We need to be able to do some of the administration locally, because our employees are always changing responsibilities and we can't wait for Vermont to make the changes.

President, Alpine Adventures: We will keep our company name and Internet presence. It would not make much sense for a company called Velocipede to offer mountain climbing adventures. People recognize our company by name, and we don't want to change that. We will retain much of our autonomy, anyway.

Internet Positioning

Velocipede Tours has a registered Internet domain name of **velocipede.com**. Velocipede has a Web site hosted in the Vermont office, and all employees have velocipede.com email addresses.

Alpine Adventures' registered name is **alpine-adv.com**. They, likewise, have a Web site, which is currently hosted by an ISP.

Proposed Internet Positioning

Velocipede has just registered the domain name **wetworlddives.com** for the Wet World operation and is planning a Web site as well as email addresses for all employees.

Question 1

> Will the Velocipede forest consist of a contiguous or a disjoint namespace?
>
> ○ a. Contiguous
>
> ○ b. Disjoint
>
> ○ c. From the information given in the example, it is impossible to determine the type of namespace
>
> ○ d. Neither

The correct answer is b. Because the business requirements dictate retention of the Alpine Adventures domain name (alpine-adv.com), the forest will contain at least two domain trees. Answer a is incorrect because a contiguous namespace would require Alpine Adventures to become a child domain off the Velocipede root (for example, **alpine-adv.velocipede.com**). Answer c is incorrect because the business requirements have been clearly stated in the scenario. Answer d is incorrect because there are only two types of DNS namespaces in Active Directory: contiguous and disjoint.

Question 2

> Two tour planners in the Vermont office have been moved temporarily to the finance department and need to be granted access to a finance application. What steps are needed to allow the employees to use the application? [Check all correct answers]
>
> ❏ a. Move the employee user objects from the TourPlanner Organizational Unit to the Finance OU.
>
> ❏ b. Delete the employee user objects from the TourPlanner Organizational Unit and re-create them in the Finance OU.
>
> ❏ c. Add the employees to the FinanceUsers global group.
>
> ❏ d. Link the FinanceSoftware GPO to the TourPlanner global group.

The correct answers are a and c. By moving the employees to the Finance OU, finance software that is distributed through Group Policy will be automatically installed on the users' desktops. Adding the employees to the FinanceUsers global group will allow access to the finance files. Answer b is incorrect because deleting a user object will destroy all current security settings, as was the case with Windows NT. When a new user is created, even though the username is the same, a new SID will be generated and group memberships will need to be rebuilt. Answer d is incorrect because GPOs are linked to sites, domains, and Organizational Units, not security groups.

Question 3

After reading a technical journal article on Windows 2000, the IT manager has decided to implement universal groups to help manage user access to resources in all three offices. However, when he attempted to create a universal group, the option was grayed out, and he could not perform the operation. Why?

- O a. The manager was not logged on as an Enterprise Admin, and only Enterprise Admins can create universal groups.
- O b. The Global Catalog Server was down.
- O c. The domain in which he wanted to create the universal group was still in mixed mode.
- O d. A trust relationship existed between the domain where the universal group was to be created and a Windows NT 4.0 domain.

The correct answer is c. Universal groups cannot be created while a domain is in mixed mode. When operating in mixed mode, the PDC Emulator operations master must act like a Windows NT PDC, and universal groups are not available under NT.

Question 4

The CEO of Velocipede Tours has mandated that the Run command should not appear on the Start menu for any clerical employees. How can the IT manager ensure that this policy is always enforced? [Check all correct answers]

- ❑ a. Create a Group Policy Object that removes the Run command and link it to the domain. Then check the No Override option.
- ❑ b. Create a GPO that removes the Run command and link it to all the top-level Organizational Units in the domain. Then check the No Override option.
- ❑ c. Create a GPO that removes the Run command and link it to any OU that contains clerical employees. Use security group filtering and allow the Apply Group Policy permission only to members of the Clerks global group.
- ❑ d. Create a GPO that removes the Run command and link it to OUs created especially for clerical employees.
- ❑ e. Create a GPO that removes the Run command and link it to every site.

The correct answers are c and d. You may either link the GPO to an OU or domain and use security group filtering to limit the application of the policy to the clerical employees or set up special Organizational Units for the clerks and link the GPO to those OUs. Answers a, b, and e are incorrect because they will remove the Run command from all employee desktops.

Question 5

A portion of the proposed Velocipede Organizational Unit structure is shown in Figure 7.6. Four Group Policy Objects have been created to configure the desktop and distribute software to the employees. The GPOs have the following function:

Maui Desktop—Configures desktop and offline folders

Finance Applications—Installs standard finance apps

Clerk Restrictions—Provides a more-restrictive environment for clerical employees

Manager Desktop—Adds applications and creates a less-restrictive desktop

Drag the GPO name to the Organizational Unit to which the GPO should be linked. A GPO may be used more than once.

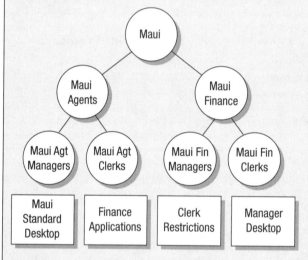

Figure 7.6　Drag the GPO to the Organizational Unit(s) to which it should be linked.

The correct answer is shown in Figure 7.7.

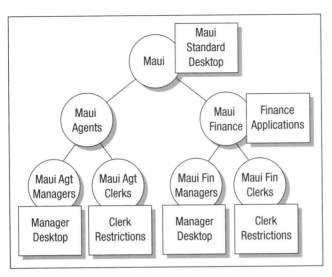

Figure 7.7   The correct answer for Question 5.

Question 6

The presidents of all three merged companies have agreed that the top-level executives in each company should have full access to all companies' financial information and business plans. The IT manager has been asked to "make it so." How can the IT manager grant access to the requested data? [Check all correct answers]

❏ a. Create a global group in the velocipede.com domain and make the Executives global groups from all the other companies' domains members of this new global group. Make the new global group a member of all necessary domain local groups to give the executives access to the merged corporate resources.

❏ b. Create a universal group and make the Executives global groups from all the other companies' domains members of this new global group. Make the new universal group a member of all necessary domain local groups to give the executives access to the merged corporate resources.

❏ c. Make the Executives global groups from all three companies members of all necessary domain local groups to give the executives access to the merged corporate resources.

❏ d. Create a global group in the velocipede.com domain and make the executive user accounts from all companies members of this new global group. Make the new global group a member of all necessary domain local groups to give the executives access to the merged corporate resources.

The correct answers are b and c. Answer b uses universal groups to accomplish the same task as answer c. The advantage to using universal groups is that it is easier to assign access to all the executives by specifying one universal group rather than one global group from each domain. Answer a is incorrect because global groups have a domain scope. You cannot nest a global group from one domain in a global group in another domain. Answer d is incorrect because global groups can only contain user accounts from the same domain.

Question 7

How many domains will be required in the Alpine Adventures domain tree? [Check the best answer]

- O a. One domain.
- O b. Three domains—a root domain and one geographical child domain for each location.
- O c. Alpine Adventures will be a single domain off the Velocipede domain tree.
- O d. Two domains—a root domain and a domain for the employees of the San Francisco and Salzburg offices.

The correct answer is b. The slow WAN links to the Salzburg office will prevent successful Sysvol replication as well as Active Directory replication via RPC. Answer a is incorrect because the domain naming context cannot be successfully replicated. Answer c is incorrect because the business requirements call for a distinct corporate identity and Internet domain name. Answer d is incorrect, again, because of replication issues.

A two-domain solution would work successfully if the San Francisco office was in the root domain and the Salzburg office were a child off the parent.

Question 8

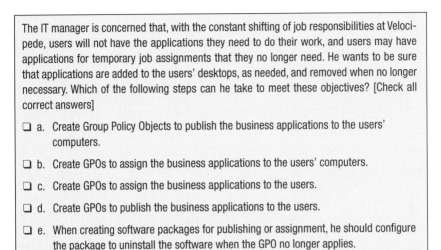

The IT manager is concerned that, with the constant shifting of job responsibilities at Veloci-pede, users will not have the applications they need to do their work, and users may have applications for temporary job assignments that they no longer need. He wants to be sure that applications are added to the users' desktops, as needed, and removed when no longer necessary. Which of the following steps can he take to meet these objectives? [Check all correct answers]

❑ a. Create Group Policy Objects to publish the business applications to the users' computers.

❑ b. Create GPOs to assign the business applications to the users' computers.

❑ c. Create GPOs to assign the business applications to the users.

❑ d. Create GPOs to publish the business applications to the users.

❑ e. When creating software packages for publishing or assignment, he should configure the package to uninstall the software when the GPO no longer applies.

Answers c and e are correct. The manager should assign the business applications to users. Then, the applications will be automatically installed when the users are given temporary job duties in a different area of the company, and their user accounts are moved to a different OU. When the user is moved back to the original OU, the software from the temporary assignment will be removed automatically at the next logon. Answers a and b are incorrect because the software should be assigned to users, not computers. Also, software cannot be published to a computer. Answer d is incorrect because published software is typically installed from the Add/Remove Programs Control Panel applet, although it could also be installed by document invocation, if that option was selected when the software package was created.

Question 9

While familiarizing himself with the Windows 2000 Administration Tools, the IT manager accidentally converted the velocipede.com domain from mixed mode to native mode at one of the Windows 2000 domain controllers. There are still two Windows NT 4.0 BDCs in the domain. How can the manager convert the domain back to mixed mode?

○ a. From the Active Directory Domains and Trusts MMC snap-in, select the properties page for the domain, select the Advanced tab, and click the Convert to Mixed Mode button.

○ b. Run the dcpromo utility to convert the affected domain controller to a member server. Then run dcpromo again to make it a domain controller.

○ c. He cannot convert back to mixed mode. The BDCs will have to be upgraded to Windows 2000 as soon as possible.

○ d. Using the Registry Editor, change the value of HKLM\Software\Windows\ Domain\Mode from 1 back to 0.

Answer c is correct. Once converted to native mode, a domain cannot be switched back to mixed mode. Answer a is incorrect because no such option exists. Answer b is incorrect because conversion to native mode affects the entire domain, not a specific domain controller. Answer d is incorrect because there is no such Registry value.

Question 10

For the Velocipede Active Directory forest, drag the appropriate Active Directory objects from the second list under the container in the first list where the object should be found. Not all objects may be used, and some may be used more than once.

Active Directory containers:

velocipede.com domain

alpine-adv.com domain

Maui Finance Organizational Unit

Manchester Office Organizational Unit

Active Directory objects:

Schema Admins group

Manchester Finance Organizational Unit

salzburg.alpine-adv.com domain

Domain Admins group

Maui Fin Manager Organizational Unit

AlpineAdv Standard Desktop GPO

MauiFin printer

Enterprise Admins group

Finance Applications GPO

Hilton Head Office Organizational Unit

The correct answer is:

velocipede.com domain

> Schema Admins group
>
> Domain Admins group
>
> Enterprise Admins group
>
> Hilton Head Office Organizational Unit

alpine-adv.com domain

> Domain Admins group
>
> AlpineAdv Standard Desktop GPO

Maui Finance Organizational Unit

Maui Fin Manager Organizational Unit

MauiFin printer

Finance Applications GPO

Manchester Office Organizational Unit

Manchester Finance Organizational Unit

Remember that parent domains are not containers for child domains, so the salzburg.alpine-adv.com domain cannot be placed within the alpine-adv.com domain.

Need to Know More?

 Microsoft Press. *Windows 2000 Active Directory Services.* Microsoft Corporation, Redmond, WA, 2000. ISBN 0735609993. There is a chapter in this book that provides some general information about security groups.

 The *Microsoft Windows 2000 Server Resource Kit* contains in-depth information about designing an Active Directory domain.

 Try searching the TechNet CD or use Microsoft's online version at **www.microsoft.com**. Search for keywords such as *domains, forest root,* and *security groups.*

Designing a Domain Tree

Terms you'll need to understand:

✓ Transitive trust

✓ External trust

✓ Shortcut trust

✓ Kerberos

✓ Key Distribution Center (KDC)

Techniques you'll need to master:

✓ Determining the business requirements for creating a multiple-domain structure

✓ Identifying the three types of trust relationships within Active Directory

✓ Describing the process of authentication between domains

✓ Determining the business requirements for a multiple-tree structure

✓ Determining the business requirements for a multiple-forest environment

The previous chapter discussed the single-domain model, which is the recommended model when designing an Active Directory infrastructure. There will be instances where a single-domain model will not meet the requirements that a business has. In cases such as this, a multiple-domain structure will be necessary. Before designing a multiple-domain structure, it is important that you understand how an Active Directory structure with more than one domain will function. The following topics will be covered throughout this chapter to assist you in designing this type of structure:

➤ Determining business needs

➤ Planning domain trees

➤ Domain design issues

➤ Multiple-tree forests

➤ Multiple forests.

Also refer to the previous page for a list of key terms and concepts that are important for this chapter.

Determining Business Needs

Several elements make up an Active Directory infrastructure. When you're planning for each element, different aspects of the business need to be assessed to ensure that each element is implemented in a way that will meet these business requirements. When you're designing a domain tree, one of the first things that needs to be done is an assessment of the business. When designing a domain structure, always keep in mind that a single model is simpler to implement and easier to administer. There will definitely be times when a single model will not be suitable for a business, but only a thorough assessment of the business will determine whether a multiple-domain structure is necessary.

Requirements for Multiple Domains

Use the points discussed in the following subsections as a guideline when performing an assessment. For a business that requires one or more of the following, a multiple domain structure may be necessary.

Decentralized Administration

Does the business want to maintain decentralized administration among its business units or geographical locations? If the business requires each division or geographical location to be responsible for its own administration, multiple domains may need to be created.

Distinct Administrative Boundaries

Is there a need to maintain a distinct administrative boundary between different areas within the business? If so, multiple domains should be considered. If you recall from Chapter 2, domains determine both the security and administrative boundaries within an Active Directory hierarchy. When multiple domains are created in a forest, the Domain Admins group within each domain only has privileges within its own domain (unless permissions to another domain are explicitly granted).

Separate Security Policies

Does the business require multiple security policies? Remember that in an Active Directory hierarchy, the domain is the security boundary. In some cases a single security policy will be able to meet the security needs of an entire business. In cases where a business needs to create multiple security policies for different areas within the business, a multiple-domain structure will be needed.

Business Partnerships

Does the business have subsidiaries that need to maintain separate and distinct namespaces? For those businesses that have established partnerships and need to be included in the Active Directory structure, a multiple-domain structure will be necessary, especially if a separate namespace is required. For example, if the XYZ Corporation has established a partnership with the ABC Corporation, in order for the two businesses to maintain their own administration and independent namespaces, two separate domains need to be created, as shown in Figure 8.1.

Slow Links

Does the physical structure of the current network present a need for multiple domains?

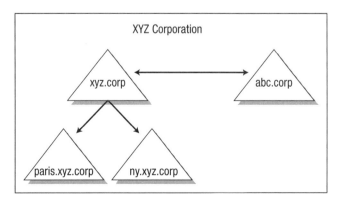

Figure 8.1   If a business has established partnerships, it may be necessary to create a multiple-domain structure in order for the businesses to maintain its independence.

Replication within a domain occurs between all domain controllers. If there are locations within a business that are connected by physical links that are slow or unreliable, multiple domains can be created to optimize replication.

Planning Domain Trees

In order to create a domain structure that will meet the business requirements, it is crucial that you first have a thorough understanding of how certain operations occur between domains (certain operations that occur within a domain may occur differently between domains). When you're planning domain trees, an understanding of the following topics is necessary:

➤ Accessing resources between domains

➤ Authentication across domains

➤ Types of trust relationships

➤ Creating an empty root domain

Accessing Resources between Domains

A new security feature in Windows 2000 is its support for the Kerberos version 5 protocol (an industry-supported authentication protocol), which is responsible for the authentication of users across domains. One of the features of the Kerberos version 5 protocol is transitive trusts (the Kerberos protocol will be discussed in more detail in the next section). If you recall from Chapter 2, in a multiple-domain structure, two-way transitive trusts are automatically configured between parent domains and child domains within a forest. This allows users to be granted permissions to resources throughout the forest.

When a user attempts to access a resource located within another domain in the forest, the transitive trust path is followed. For example, in Figure 8.2, if a user from the Paris domain attempts to access a resource located in the NY domain, the trust path must be followed. The user will first receive authorization from the **xyz.corp** domain (because Paris has a transitive trust with this domain) and then the user will receive authorization from the NY domain.

Authentication across Domains

Authentication is the process of confirming the identity of a user attempting to gain access to network resources. Before a user in one domain can access resources in another domain within the forest, he or she must be authenticated. As already mentioned, the Kerberos version 5 protocol is responsible for authentication across domains. By support being included for this industry-standard security protocol, users need only provide a single username and password at logon to gain access to resources throughout the forest.

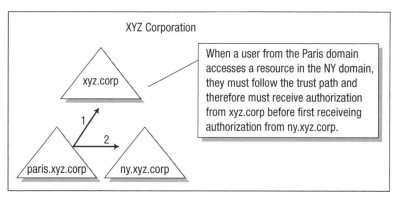

Figure 8.2   When resources are accessed in another domain within the forest, the trust path must be followed.

Before a user is granted access to resources in another domain, the Key Distribution Center (KDC) from each domain in the trust path must first authenticate the user.

Note: The Key Distribution Center has two roles: It is responsible for authenticating users and it is also responsible for issuing "session tickets" to users so they can identify themselves to other domains.

Referring back to Figure 8.2, when a user from the Paris domain attempts to access a resource located on a server in the NY domain, the following authentication process will occur:

Note: This authentication process is completely transparent to the user.

1. When the user attempts to access a resource in the NY domain, the Key Distribution Center within the user's own domain—in this case, Paris—will issue the user a session ticket. The session ticket will simply identify the user to other servers in the forest.

2. Following the trust path, the user will present his or her session ticket to the KDC in the **xyz.corp** domain.

3. The user is then issued another session ticket from the KDC in the **xyz.corp** domain that will identify the user to the next domain in the trust path.

4. The user presents the session ticket to the KDC in the NY domain and is issued a session ticket for the server that contains the resource.

5. Once the user presents his or her session ticket to the server with the desired resource, he or she will be granted the appropriate access to that resource.

Types of Trust Relationships

Basically, three different types of trust relationships can be implemented in Windows 2000 to allow users to gain access to resources located in other domains: transitive, shortcut, and external trusts. Transitive trusts are automatically established, whereas shortcut and external trusts must be explicitly defined.

Transitive Trusts

Transitive trusts are two-way trusts that are automatically created between parent domains and child domains, as well as between the root domain of a forest and any new trees. The trust path created from transitive trusts makes resources throughout the forest accessible to all users. Figure 8.3 shows the default transitive trusts created for the XYZ Corporation's forest.

Shortcut Trusts

As already mentioned, when a user attempts to access a resource in another domain within the forest, the trust path must be followed. Depending on the structure of the Active Directory hierarchy, the trust path between two separate domains can be long.

In cases such as this, creating a shortcut trust can actually shorten the trust path. A shortcut trust is basically a transitive trust (a two-way trust); the difference is that it must be explicitly defined or created. Creating a shortcut trust between two separate domains within a forest can improve the authentication process discussed in the previous section.

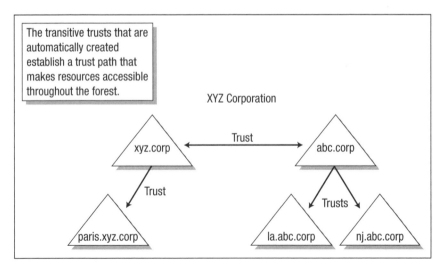

The transitive trusts that are automatically created establish a trust path that makes resources accessible throughout the forest.

XYZ Corporation

Figure 8.3 Transitive trusts are established between all parent domains and child domains. Transitive trusts are also created between the forest root and any new trees.

For example, the trust path that is automatically created between the domains and trees within the XYZ Corporation would require that a user from the Paris domain be authenticated by at least three KDCs from three separate domains before being able to access a resource in the NJ domain. To optimize the authentication process between these two domains, a shortcut trust can be defined between them, as shown in Figure 8.4.

External Trusts

The third type of trust that can be implemented is an *external trust*. External trusts are similar to the trusts set up between Windows NT 4.0 domains. They are one-way trusts and must be manually created.

 External trusts can be created between Windows 2000 domains and Windows NT domains. They are also possible between Windows 2000 domains in different forests. External trusts are one-way and are not transitive. When created between Windows 2000 domains in different forests, the trust will link individual domains, not the forests.

Within a forest, two-way trusts are automatically established; however, by default no trusts are established between separate forests. If users need to access resources that are located within another forest, an external trust must be established. Remember that external trusts are one way, so if the need to share resources between two forests goes both ways, two external trusts will need to be created.

For example, if users within the NY domain need access to resources located in the Sales domain located within another forest, an external trust would need to be created.

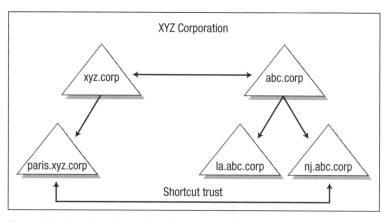

Figure 8.4   Creating a shortcut trust between two domains can shorten and therefore improve the authentication process.

One important point to keep in mind when creating external trusts: They only apply to the domains specified. Any other trusts that a domain has remain separate from the external trusts. In other words, if A and B share a transitive trust and an external trust is defined between B and C, there is still no trust between A and C.

In Figure 8.5, the one-way external trust is defined between the NY domain and the Sales domain to give NY users access to resources in Sales. The external trust, however, does not give users access to any other domains in the LMO Corporation.

Table 8.1 summarizes the three types of trusts that can be created.

Creating an Empty Root Domain

In an Active Directory hierarchy where there are multiple domains, the design team may choose to create an empty forest root domain. This domain would not contain any OUs, and the only users in this domain would be the members of the Enterprise Admins group. The empty forest root domain would establish the namespace that would be inherited by child domains.

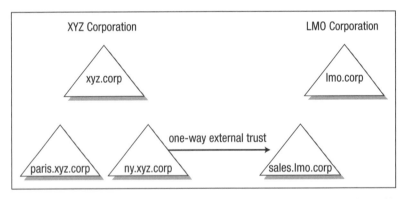

Figure 8.5   An external trust can be created to give users access to resources located in another forest.

Table 8.1	Types of trust relationships in Active Directory.
Trust	**Description**
Transitive	A two-way trust that is automatically established between parent domains and child domains as well as any trees in the forest.
Shortcut	A two-way transitive trust that must be manually created between two domains to shorten the trust path.
External	A one-way trust that must be manually created between domains in separate forests.

Creating an empty forest root domain would be appropriate for a business that wants to maintain a contiguous namespace throughout the organization while allowing for decentralized administration. For example, the XYZ Corporation wants to maintain decentralized administration for its two business divisions while maintaining a contiguous namespace that will identify each division as part of the corporation. To meet the business's requirements, an empty forest root domain can be created to establish the namespace. Separate domains can then be created for each business division under the forest root that will allow for decentralized administration of each division.

Now that you've familiarized yourself with how some of the operations occur within a multiple-domain structure, let's take a look at some of the guidelines that need to be considered when designing multiple domains.

Domain Design Issues

When planning a multiple-domain structure, keep the following design issues in mind:

➤ Security

➤ WAN or LAN bandwidth constraints

➤ Legal issues

➤ Domain-wide policies

Security

One of the reasons why a multiple-domain structure may be created is to meet the security requirements of a business. If the business implements decentralized administration and needs to maintain a distinct security boundary between its different business units, a multiple-domain structure will need to be established. Creating a separate domain within the forest for each business unit will allow each one to maintain its own administration.

If the different locations or departments within a business have different security needs (such as password requirements) or if a single security policy for the entire organization cannot be agreed upon, multiple domains may have to be created. This way, the administrators from each domain can establish security policies that meet their specific requirements.

 Also keep in mind that the more domains you create, the more Domain Admin groups there are to monitor. This adds administrative overhead and may become difficult to track (especially for security purposes).

WAN or LAN Constraints

If you recall from Chapter 2, replication is based on the multimaster replication model. All domain controllers within a domain are equal and all maintain an up-to-date working copy of the directory database. This means that there will be more replication traffic within a domain (as opposed to between domains) because any changes made to the directory will be replicated throughout the domain to all domain controllers.

 Also keep in mind that every attribute associated with an object is replicated throughout the domain, which adds to network traffic. On the other hand, only certain attributes are replicated to Global Catalog servers in other domains.

The point of this discussion is that if there are LAN or WAN links within the organization that are slow, unreliable, or already heavily used, they may not be able to support the amount of replication traffic that will be generated within a domain. In cases such as this, multiple domains will need to be created to optimize replication.

Note: Only a thorough assessment of the physical structure within the network will determine whether there are WAN or LAN constraints that will result in the need for multiple domains.

Let's take a look at an example. If the XYZ Corporation implements a single-domain model, all objects and their associated attributes will be replicated to every domain controller in every location. Every time a change is made to the directory, the change will be replicated throughout the domain. If the physical link between NY and Paris is slow, this may not be the best model to implement. In order to optimize replication, at least two separate domains should be created so that replication traffic can be reduced across the slow link.

Legal Issues

In today's world of enterprise networks that span different countries, there may be legal issues to consider when planning domains that may result in the implementation of a multiple-domain structure. For example, a business that has an international presence may be required to maintain separate domains for its overseas locations. An organization may need to keep employee information for its European subsidiaries separate from U.S. employees because the European Union has much more stringent confidentiality requirements than the U.S. In order to meet the security requirements of different countries, separate domains would have to be created.

Domain-Wide Policies

If there is a need within a business to create different security configurations for different groups of users and computers throughout the business, it may be necessary to create more than one domain. Only a thorough assessment of a business's security requirements will determine whether more than one domain will be needed.

The following are some security options set on a domain basis:

➤ *Password Policy*—Password policies determine the requirements for user passwords, such as a minimum password length.

➤ *Account Lockout Policy*—An account lockout policy determines the guideline for locking a user account out of the system.

➤ *Kerberos Policy*—A Kerberos policy will determine the settings pertaining to Kerberos security, such as session ticket expiration time.

If a business requires unique security policies to be applied to different groups of users within a business, more than one domain will be required because these settings are applied on a domain basis. For example, if the XYZ Corporation requires a separate, more secure password policy to be applied to its employees within the Paris location, a multiple-domain model would have to be implemented.

Note: Because security policies are applied at the domain level, they will have to be applied and managed at each domain, which increases administrative overhead.

Multiple-Tree Forests

Chapter 2 discussed the characteristics of forests and trees. A *forest* is established when the first Active Directory domain is created; this domain is known as the *forest root*. Within a forest, any domains that share a contiguous namespace form a *tree*. Once a tree has been established within a forest, any new domains added to an existing tree will inherit a portion of its namespace from its parent domain. Any domains added to the forest that maintain a unique namespace will form a new tree. It is, therefore, possible to have more than one tree within a single forest; there may be instances where multiple trees will be required in order to meet the needs of a business. This section looks at the business requirements for creating multiple trees as well as the trust relationship between trees within a forest.

Business Requirements

Remember: When you're planning a domain structure, simplicity is always best. If a business does not require multiple trees, don't make things more difficult by creating an elaborate multiple-tree structure. There will, however, be instances where multiple trees are required. Again, only a thorough assessment of the business will determine whether this is necessary. When considering a multiple-tree structure, keep the requirements discussed in the following subsections in mind. If a business requires any one of the following, you may need to design a multiple-tree structure after all.

DNS Names

If a business is comprised of different subsidiaries or has partnered with other businesses that need to maintain their distinct public identities as well as separate (noncontiguous) DNS names, multiple trees may have to be created within a single forest.

 If an organization has subsidiaries with unique DNS domain names, the organization can create a domain tree for each namespace, maintaining the subsidiaries' individual DNS identification.

If the XYZ Corporation has a subsidiary, the ABC Corporation, that needs to have a public identity separate from the main organization as well as maintain its registered DNS name, a separate tree within the forest could be created to meet the business's requirements, as shown in Figure 8.6.

Central Directory Information

All trees within a single forest share the same schema, configuration container, and Global Catalog. If an organization wants to have centralized administration of these and maintain a single schema, configuration container, and Global

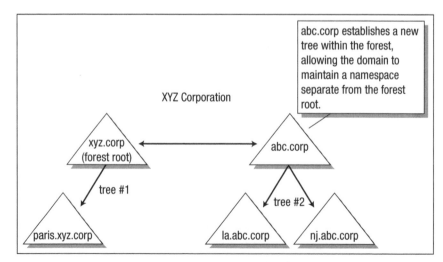

Figure 8.6 A single forest that maintains two separate trees, each with its own namespace.

Catalog for the entire organization and all its business units, a single forest with multiple trees can be implemented.

 One of the nice features of being able to create a distinction between business units while keeping them within the same forest is that users within different trees can still easily search for objects forest-wide because they all share a common Global Catalog.

Trusts between Trees

When a new tree is established within a forest, a two-way transitive trust is automatically established between the two root domains. This two-way trust creates a trust path that allows users from one tree to be able to access resources located within another tree in the same forest (the really nice thing about this is that a path is created throughout the Active Directory hierarchy without any administrative effort).

Looking at the example in Figure 8.6, once abc.corp is established as a new tree within the forest, a transitive trust is automatically set up between **abc.corp** and **xyz.corp**. This makes resources within the forest accessible to all users.

Note: Keep in mind when you're designing multiple domains and multiple tress that the more domains you have, the more trust links you need within the forest, and these trust links can become a point of failure. Users must be authenticated, and if the physical link is not available, the users cannot gain access to resources.

Now let's take a look at one more option when designing a multiple-domain structure: creating multiple forests.

Multiple Forests

In some instances it will be necessary to consider a multiple-forest environment in order to meet the requirements of a business. This type of model is one of the most difficult to design and administer, so when you're considering a model such as this, keep the following topics in mind:

➤ Business reasons

➤ Trust relationships

➤ Schema issues

Business Reasons

Before going ahead and designing an elaborate structure that includes multiple forests, be sure to assess the business to determine whether there is an actual need for more than one forest. Consider a multiple-forest structure if a business has any of the requirements discussed in the following subsections.

Limited Trusts

Does the business maintain partnerships or have subsidiaries with which it needs to maintain a very limited partnership? One of the most common reasons why you would create a multiple-forest environment is to meet an organization's need to maintain a limited trust with another organization or its subsidiaries. Situations such as this may arise when a business establishes a limited partnership with another organization or when an organization includes subsidiaries gained through corporate acquisitions. Separate forests may need to be created for security purposes, and when multiple forests are established, the scope of the trust relationship can be limited and closely monitored.

Separate Global Directories

Does the business need multiple Global directories? The Global directory maintains a listing of all objects within the forest as well as certain attributes pertaining to each one, and all domains within a forest will have access to a common Global directory. If a business does not want one global directory for its entire organization, a multiple-forest structure will need to be implemented.

Separate Schema

The schema maintains a list for the entire forest of all objects that can be stored within Active Directory as well as the attributes associated with each object. (A default schema policy comes with Windows 2000, but it can be modified if it does not meet your business's requirements.) If an organization requires different schema policies for its different business units or if the administrators from the different business units cannot agree on a schema policy, multiple forests will need to be created.

Trust Relationships

By default, trusts are not automatically established between separate forests. Any intercommunication between two forests can only occur if a trust is explicitly defined.

To allow users from one forest to access resources in another forest, a one-way external trust must be created. If interaction between two forests is going to go both ways, two external trusts will need to be defined. When you're planning for trusts between forests, also keep in mind that external trusts are not forest-wide—they only pertain to the domains specified. Referring back to Figure 8.5, a one-way external trust is created between the NY domain from one forest and the Sales domain from another forest. It is a one-way trust that only allows users from the NY domain access to the resources in the Sales domain. If the NY users need access to resources located within another domain in the forest, a second external trust would need to be created.

Schema Issues

Schema policies are applied at the forest level, so all domains within a forest will be affected by the same schema policy. If a business plans on making changes to the default schema policy but does not want its entire organization to be affected by changes, a multiple-forest structure will need to be considered. An appropriate schema policy can then be implemented for each forest.

Because schema policies are not replicated between forests, schema changes in one forest will not affect another forest.

Practice Questions

Case Study: Neptune Watercraft

Neptune Watercraft is a boat builder based in Boston, Massachusetts. Over the past 10 years, Neptune has acquired a number of boat and nautical gear manufacturers and today has 5 subsidiary companies: Trident Power Boats, Seven Seas Yachts, Competition Sailcraft, Neptune Outboards, and Long Lake Boats. The subsidiaries are run as independent businesses, with very limited control from Neptune upper management. Most of the subsidiaries are based in the Boston area, except for Trident Power Boats, which is located in Toms River, NJ, and Long Lake Boats, which is headquartered in Glens Falls, NY.

Recently, Neptune entered into a joint venture with Allegro Fashions, a New York apparel manufacturer, to create a line of boating-related clothing. The resulting company, NA Boatwear, is run independently of both Neptune and Allegro but is located in the Neptune office complex in Boston.

LAN/Network Structure

Neptune has a mix of Unix, Windows NT, and Novell NetWare servers in its home office and subsidiaries. Although most of the network infrastructure is sound—consisting of 10 and 100Mbps switched Ethernet—the mix of network operating systems has caused interoperability problems in the past.

The NA Boatwear network is currently being set up. The Neptune IT staff is using the joint venture as a pilot for an eventual corporate rollout of Windows 2000.

Proposed LAN/Network Structure

All companies are scheduled to be upgraded to Windows 2000 within the next two years.

WAN Connectivity

T1 circuits connect the Boston offices of Neptune and the Boston-based subsidiaries. These circuits are used for both voice and data traffic, with 512Kbps devoted to data, and are more than adequate for current and forecasted traffic.

Long Lake Boats has a 56Kbps Frame Relay connection to Neptune's headquarters. This circuit is adequate today for the limited data traffic requirements. Trident Power Boats uses a T1 configured for 384Kbps data.

Directory Design Commentary

Vice President, Neptune IT: We are having trouble maintaining our diverse computing environment. Hopefully, Windows 2000 will help us become a bit more homogeneous and thus save us some money. We will need to retain our Unix DNS and Web servers for some time, however, because we do not have the resources to migrate these to another platform right now.

General Manager, NA Boatwear: We are an independent company and will be going our own way with only limited input from our two corporate parents. I like our role as a technology innovator and want to be on the leading edge when new advances occur. We don't want to be held back because of issues with the parent companies.

HR Manager, Trident Power Boats: We need to have a more uniform Human Resources system with the other Neptune companies. When job openings come up, we often have no idea if someone from one of the other companies is interested or would fit.

Internet Positioning

Neptune has a corporate Web site and a registered DNS domain name of **neptuneboats.com**. All Neptune headquarters employees have neptuneboats.com email addresses.

All the subsidiaries, except Long Lake Boats, also have registered domains.

The NA Boatwear joint venture has just registered na-boatwear.com as its domain name.

Question 1

Based on the information given, how many forests should be created for Neptune Watercraft?

- O a. 1
- O b. 2
- O c. 5
- O d. 6

The correct answer is b. The business requirements of NA Boatwear suggest that a separate forest would be the most appropriate for the joint venture company. Answer a is incorrect because having the company in the same forest would require the schema-modification policy to be coordinated with the Neptune companies.

Answers c and d are incorrect because creating an excessive number of forests will greatly complicate administration.

Question 2

Neptune management requires access to financial information from NA Boatwear. How can the managers be granted access to NA Boatwear data without compromising security at Neptune?

- ○ a. Create a two-way Kerberos trust between the Neptune forest and the NA Boatwear forest.
- ○ b. Create a two-way Kerberos trust between the Neptune domain and the NA Boatwear domain.
- ○ c. Create a one-way trust between the Neptune forest and the NA Boatwear forest.
- ○ d. Create a one-way trust between the Neptune domain and the NA Boatwear domain.

The correct answer is d. It is only possible to create an NT-style, one-way, nontransitive trust between two domains in different forests. Therefore, answers a, b, and c are incorrect.

Question 3

Place the domains shown in the second list into the appropriate forest from the first list.

Forests:

    Neptune Watercraft

    NA Boatwear

Domains:

    neptuneboats.com

    na-boatwear.com

    tridentboat.com

    comp-sail.com

    sevenseas-yachts.com

    neptune-ob.com

The correct answer is:

Neptune Watercraft

    neptuneboats.com

    tridentboat.com

comp-sail.com

sevenseas-yachts.com

neptune-ob.com

NA Boatwear

na-boatwear.com

Question 4

> The CEO at Competition Sailcraft is concerned about security in the Research and Development (R & D) area of the company. He would like to see more stringent password security applied as well as greater use of IPSec. How can additional security be set up for the R & D unit without affecting the rest of the company?
>
> ○ a. Create an Organizational Unit for R & D and apply a more stringent security policy to the OU.
>
> ○ b. Create an R & D domain and modify the domain password policy.
>
> ○ c. Create a universal group for employees in the R & D department and configure a tighter security policy for that universal group.
>
> ○ d. Move the R & D operation to a separate forest and create a special forest security policy.

The correct answer is b. Password policies are set at the domain level, so to enforce more stringent requirements, a separate domain must be created. Otherwise, the tighter policy will apply to all employees. Answer a is incorrect because password security parameters cannot be set at the OU level. Answer c is incorrect because Group Policy cannot be applied to members of a security group. Answer d is incorrect because, again, security policy is set at the domain level. Although it would be possible to do this in a separate forest, the administration issues raised by such an approach make it unrealistic.

Question 5

> What steps must still be taken before Windows 2000 can be deployed at Neptune Watercraft? [Check two answers]
>
> ❑ a. Obtain a registered domain name for Long Lake Boats.
>
> ❑ b. Upgrade the WAN link from headquarters to Trident Power Boats.
>
> ❑ c. Upgrade the WAN link from headquarters to Long Lake Boats.
>
> ❑ d. Determine a DNS strategy regarding the existing Unix-based DNS servers.

The correct answers are a and d. Even if Long Lake Boats has no plans for an Internet presence, it is important to register the name, which will be used in Active Directory, just in case Internet connectivity becomes an important issue. Neptune also needs to determine what should be done with the existing DNS infrastructure, since there are no plans for migration or upgrade at the present time.

Answer b is incorrect because a 384Kbps link is more than adequate for Active Directory. Likewise, answer c is incorrect. Because all Neptune subsidiaries are run fairly independently of the home office, Long Lake Boats will have its own domain. Therefore, SMTP replication can be used over the 56Kbps circuit.

Question 6

> By default, where is the Schema Operations Master located? [Check all correct answers]
>
> ❑ a. neptune-ob.com
>
> ❑ b. tridentboats.com
>
> ❑ c. na-boatwear.com
>
> ❑ d. neptuneboats.com
>
> ❑ e. na-neptune.com

Answers c and d are correct. Both are the forest root domains in their respective Active Directory forests. Answers a and b are incorrect because they are not the parent company for Neptune Watercraft and therefore should not be the forest root. Answer e is incorrect because it is not a domain in either forest.

Question 7

> Because NA Boatwear is physically located in the Neptune Watercraft headquarters, the IT Director has asked whether the two domains should be placed in the same site. Can both companies share the same site?
>
> ○ a. Yes
>
> ○ b. No

The correct answer is b. The domains are in different forests. A forest defines the boundaries of an Active Directory implementation, and sites are defined within a single Active Directory. Therefore, it is impossible for the two domains to share a single site. Also, because there is no replication between forests, there is no need to use sites to manage interforest replication.

Question 8

> Competition Sailcraft and Seven Seas Yachts share offices in a northern suburb of Boston. Because of their proximity, they have been placed in the same Active Directory site. Users at both companies need access to a special sail design application. How can this application be distributed to users at both companies? [Check all correct answers]
>
> ❑ a. Create a Group Policy Object (GPO) to publish the software to users in either domain and link it to the shared site.
>
> ❑ b. Create a GPO in the comp-sail.com domain to publish the software to users and link it to the Sailmaker OU.
>
> ❑ c. Create a GPO in the comp-sail.com domain to publish the software to users and link it to both the comp-sail.com domain and the sevenseas-yachts.com domain.
>
> ❑ d. Create GPOs to publish the software to users in both the comp-sail.com domain and the sevenseas-yachts.com domain.
>
> ❑ e. Create a GPO in the forest root domain, neptuneboats.com, and use universal group filtering to prevent application to anyone outside of the comp-sail.com and the sevenseas-yachts.com domains.

Answers a, c, and d are correct. Answer a takes advantage of the fact that both companies share the same site. The disadvantage to this approach is that the administrators in the domain where the GPO was not created have no control over the GPO. The same drawback holds true for answer c. Answer d gives the administrators of both domains control over the software-distribution process, but there is a possibility of inconsistent deployment because two separate GPOs are created.

Answer b is incorrect because the application will not be distributed to Seven Seas Yachts. Answer e is incorrect because domains are security boundaries, and creating a GPO in the forest root domain has no effect on the other domains in the forest.

Question 9

What steps must be taken so that users in the tridentboat.com domain access resources in the neptune-ob.com domain?

- O a. A two-way, transitive Kerberos trust must be created between the domains.
- O b. Two one-way NT-style trusts must be created between the domains.
- O c. Nothing needs to be done.
- O d. A shortcut trust should be created between the two domains.

The correct answer is c. Two-way, transitive Kerberos trusts are automatically created between parent and child domains as well as between the root domains in a multiple-tree forest. Answers a and d are incorrect because a trust already exists between the two domains. There would be no benefit to creating another one. Answer b is likewise incorrect. Because there is already a two-way, transitive trust in place, there is no reason to create an NT-style trust as well.

Question 10

For the Neptune enterprise, drag the appropriate Active Directory object from the second list to the domain in the first list where the object should be found. Not all objects may be used, and some may be used more than once.

Domains:

neptuneboats.com domain

r-d.comp-sail.com domain

na-boatwear.com domain

Active Directory objects:

Schema Admins group

Domain Admins group

Enterprise Admins group

Users container

Domain Controllers OU

The correct answer is:

neptuneboats.com domain

      Schema Admins group

      Domain Admins group

      Enterprise Admins group

      Users container

      Domain Controllers OU

r-d.comp-sail.com domain

      Domain Admins group

      Domain Controllers OU

      Users container

na-boatwear.com domain

      Schema Admins group

      Domain Admins group

      Enterprise Admins group

      Users container

      Domain Controllers OU

Need to Know More?

 Microsoft Press. *Windows 2000 Active Directory Services*. Microsoft Corporation, , Redmond, WA, 2000. ISBN 0735609993. Some sections in this book provide general information about trees, domains, and trust relationships.

 The *Microsoft Windows 2000 Server Resource Kit* contains in-depth information about designing Active Directory domains.

 Try searching the TechNet CD or use Microsoft's online version at **www.microsoft.com**.

Designing a Physical Active Directory Topology

Terms you'll need to understand:

✓ Bridgehead servers
✓ DNS servers
✓ Domain controllers
✓ Global Catalog Server
✓ Intersite replication
✓ Intrasite replication
✓ Operations Masters
✓ Site
✓ Site link
✓ Site link bridge
✓ Transport

Techniques you'll need to master:

✓ Describing how sites can be used to control replication within an Active Directory infrastructure
✓ Determining how to configure sites within a network to take advantage of the physical topology
✓ Designing connectivity between sites
✓ Determining the need for site link bridges
✓ Planning the placement of servers within sites
✓ Selecting an intersite transport

The previous chapters in this book have focused on designing Active Directory elements around the needs of the business, with little attention given to the actual physical structure of the network. During this phase of designing an Active Directory infrastructure, the design teams will now focus on assessing the physical structure of the network. The information gathered will assist the design team in creating an Active Directory topology that optimizes replication across the physical links within the network.

The following main topics will be covered throughout the chapter:

➤ Assessing network topology

➤ Replication basics

➤ Planning site boundaries

➤ Planning site links

➤ Locating domain controllers

➤ Selecting an intersite transport

Keep in mind that knowledge and understanding of each topic are essential in designing a topology that will enhance the replication of information throughout the organization.

Assessing Network Topology

As with the design phases discussed in the previous chapters, your first step in designing an Active Directory topology will be to perform a thorough assessment of the business. Your focus during the assessment should now be on the physical topology of the current network—more specifically the type of WAN links connecting the different business locations and the amount of bandwidth available for each one. Gathering this information will later help in determining which areas to organize into Active Directory sites. Not performing an assessment at this time could later result in heavy replication traffic occurring over a link that cannot support it.

WAN Links and Available Bandwidth

When assessing the WAN links connecting different business locations, keep the points discussed in the following subsections in mind (the links that will be able to support regular replication traffic are those considered to be fast, cheap, and reliable).

What Is the Speed of the WAN Links Connecting the Different Business Locations?

You will need to know the speed of the links to determine whether they are fast enough to support a large amount of replication traffic. Normal RPC-based replication can be performed successfully across a 128Kbps link, although a faster circuit would be preferable.

What Is the Utilization of the Link?

A WAN link that is fast but completely congested is far worse than a slow but unused circuit. Available bandwidth is far more important than total bandwidth.

What Is the Current Status of the Link?

If the link is considered to be unreliable in the past, you will not want to have a large amount of replication traffic occurring across the link.

When you are performing the assessment of WAN links and available bandwidth, it is recommended that you begin by drawing a basic diagram representing the current network topology. As you assess the different aspects of the physical topology, you can continue to add information to the diagram. Having a complete diagram will help you later in determining which areas to combine into sites. It may also be easier for administrators within the business to understand your recommendations when there is a detailed diagram to support them.

Once the characteristics of the WAN links within the business have been assessed, you will also need to assess the amount of bandwidth available over each link. This will determine whether there is enough bandwidth available to support replication traffic. For example, two business locations may be connected by a high-speed link, but if the link is already heavily used, it may not be able to support regular replication traffic. Consider the following additional traffic-generating events over each link when assessing the amount of available bandwidth:

➤ How many users within each location are logging on to the network?

➤ When do most of the logons occur?

➤ Are group policies being applied? (Downloading group policies will take up bandwidth.)

➤ How often are users required to change their passwords?

➤ Are there a large number of DNS queries performed throughout the day?

Replication Basics

In order to design an Active Directory topology that will optimize the replication of information within a business, you need to understand a couple of replication basics first. This section discusses some of the concepts behind Active Directory replication, including the following:

➤ Sites

➤ Site links

➤ Replication schedules and compression

Sites

Chapter 2 briefly introduced you to the concept of Active Directory sites. If you recall, an *Active Directory site* is basically a collection of well-connected IP subnets. The links between the subnets within a site are generally fast enough to support replication, available (not saturated), and very reliable.

Note: Because the creation of sites is based on the physical topology, a site can contain IP subnets from multiple domains.

Active Directory sites are designed to optimize replication. Replication within a site occurs differently than it does between two separate sites. Intrasite replication is designed to take advantage of the fact that the IP subnets within a site are connected by fast, reliable links. Replication between sites (intersite replication) is designed to occur differently because it is assumed that the links connecting two sites are slow and unreliable.

Table 9.1 compares replication as it occurs within a site and between sites.

Table 9.1 A comparison of intersite and intrasite replication.	
Intrasite Replication	**Intersite Replication**
Information replicated within a site is uncompressed.	Information replicated between sites is compressed to optimize bandwidth.
Domain controllers within a site notify each other when a change occurs, which reduces the time for changes to appear throughout a site.	To optimize bandwidth, there is no notification process between sites, which means information on domain controllers may not always be up to date.
Domain controllers within a site poll each other for changes on a regular basis.	Domain controllers between sites poll each other at a preconfigured interval during scheduled times.
Intrasite replication can occur between multiple domain controllers.	Replication between sites only occurs between specific domain controllers.

The following traffic-generating events are controlled and optimized by the creation of sites:

➤ *User authentication*—When a user attempts to log on to a workstation, a domain controller within the same site is contacted to authenticate the user. This means the logon process will be more efficient (the user does not have to log on over a slow, unreliable link).

➤ *Controlled replication*—Creating multiple sites allows replication across slow, unreliable links to be controlled by specifying a schedule, frequency, and cost (these options will be covered later in the chapter).

➤ *Site-aware applications*—Applications that are site-aware, such as the Distributed File System (DFS), can take advantage of the site topology by attempting to connect to a domain controller within the same site before attempting to connect to a domain controller in another site.

One important point to note is that site creation is easy, and changing a site is as simple as adding or deleting a subnet. Therefore, if any erroneous assumptions were made in designing a site hierarchy, correcting the design is very straightforward.

Once the Active Directory sites have been defined and the IP subnets added to the appropriate site, site links will need to be established. Before doing so, it is important that you understand the function of site links.

Site Links

Site links are similar in concept to trust relationships. A *trust* is the link between two domains; a *site link* is the connection between two Active Directory sites. The site link that is established between two sites is used to control replication across the physical link.

Site links are transitive by default. This means that if a site is defined between sites A and B, and another is defined between sites B and C, it is automatically assumed that sites A and C can communicate. These transitive site links basically establish a replication path so information can be replicated throughout the organization.

 Remember that site links are transitive, unless the default settings have been modified. To change from transitive to nontransitive site links, the Bridge All Site Links checkbox must be deselected for a given site protocol.

For example, if the site structure created for the XYZ Corporation were based on geographical locations, it would look similar to what's shown in Figure 9.1. If site links were established between LA and NJ and also between NJ and NY, a replication path would be created between LA and NY due to the transitiveness of

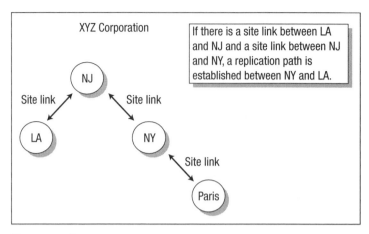

Figure 9.1 Site links within Active Directory are transitive in nature. This allows a replication path to be created within an organization.

the site links. A site link created between Paris and NY would establish a replication path that would allow for the replication of information throughout the business.

When you're defining a site link, certain options are used to control replication over the link. A site link is basically defined by the following characteristics, each of which will be discussed in detail later in the chapter:

➤ *Transport*—This is the method used to transfer data between two sites. You can use one of two methods: RPCs or SMTP.

➤ *Schedule*—The schedule defined for a site link specifies the times when replication can occur over the link.

➤ *Cost*—The value assigned to the site link. If there are multiple site links, the one with the lowest cost is tried first.

➤ *Interval*—This specifies how often during the scheduled times the site link can be used to check for updates within another site (this process is referred to as *polling*).

 You can only select a transport protocol for intersite replication. All intra-site replication occurs using RPC.

Replication Schedules and Compression

One of the main differences between intersite and intrasite replication is that replication between sites can be scheduled by an administrator to only occur at certain times. Intrasite replication is based on a notification process. Anytime a change occurs, other domain controllers within the site will be notified. As already mentioned, sites are designed to optimize bandwidth usage; therefore, there is not a notification process between sites. Instead, a schedule is defined specifying when the link is available for intersite replication. This allows an administrator to possibly schedule the site link to only be available during off-hours.

For example, if the site link shown previously in Figure 9.1 between Paris and NY is heavily used during the morning hours, an administrator may choose to schedule that site link to be available during the afternoon or evening hours when the link is not being used as much.

Another feature of intersite replication that optimizes throughput is *data compression*. Any replication cycle where more than 50K worth of updates has been generated will automatically be compressed to save bandwidth. Replication compression is extremely efficient, reducing the data transferred by approximately 90 percent. Compression does require additional CPU and RAM resources, however.

Conversely, because it is assumed the links within a site have plenty of bandwidth, replication within a site remains uncompressed. This also reduces the processor load on domain controllers within a site.

Now let's take a look at some considerations to keep in mind when you're determining how many sites to establish and which IP subnets to place into which sites.

Planning Site Boundaries

Creating site boundaries gives an administrator the ability to control workstation logons and replication throughout a business. When planning and defining the site boundaries, your main focus will be on the physical topology of the network. At this point it would be a good idea to refer to the diagram you created when performing an assessment of WAN links and available bandwidth.

When planning site boundaries, use the following guidelines:

➤ Create a site for each group of IP subnets connected by fast, available, and reliable links.

➤ For a network compromised of a single LAN, a single site is usually sufficient.

➤ Create a separate site for those IP subnets connected by slow, unreliable, and heavily used links.

➤ For any sites that do not have a domain controller located within them, consider merging them with another nearby site.

These are just some basic guidelines to follow when determining how many sites to create. As you'll see in the next section, in order to manage replication, there may be instances when following these guidelines will not be appropriate.

Managing Replication

Even though it is suggested that IP subnets be grouped into one site, there may be instances when you'll need to do just the opposite to manage replication.

Within a site, a process called the Knowledge Consistency Checker (KCC) is responsible for generating a replication topology. The KCC ensures that there are always two replication paths between domain controllers within a site (this way, if one link is unavailable, the other can be used). The KCC also creates extra connections between domain controllers so that updates between them are never more than three hops away.

With this in mind, you can imagine how many replication paths would exist in a single site with a large number of domain controllers. For example, if an organization maintains a central headquarters, there may be 20 to 30 domain controllers within a single site. Even though the entire network is well connected, and your first instinct might be to create one site, the intrasite replication topology becomes very complicated, and more replication traffic is generated. Remember, within a site, enough connections are automatically created to ensure that two domain controllers are never three hops away. In a situation like this, in order to create a more manageable replication topology, the headquarters could be divided into smaller sites.

Sometimes there will be instances when the rule may be broken the other way in order to manage replication. If a company has one large office along with two satellite offices linked by a 1.5Mbps T1 line, you would normally create three separate sites. However, there may be business reasons why there should only be one site created, such as faster replication. If it is critical that all three offices have up-to-date Active Directory information, the three offices can be grouped into one site. You might even try this with lines as slow as 256Kbps, although this is not recommended.

Planning Site Links

When you're planning the site links between multiple sites, you are basically defining a replication topology for an organization. It is important to understand the different components associated with a site link and how they are used to control and optimize intersite replication. Consider the following issues when planning for site links, each of which are discussed in this section:

➤ Link costs

➤ Link schedules

➤ Determining the need for site link bridges

➤ Selecting bridgehead servers

Link Costs

One of the advantages of using site links is that they can be assigned a site cost. A *site cost* is basically a number that is assigned by an administrator to a site link. By assigning costs to site links, an administrator can basically define a preferred route for replication when multiple routes exist.

When assigning costs to site links, keep in mind that a site link with a lower value is seen as the preferred route over a site link with a higher value. For example, if multiple replication routes are available between the LA site and the NJ site, a site cost can be assigned to each of the links to define a preferred route. If the preferred route is not available, the other will be used, as shown in Figure 9.2.

Note: Link costs should be assigned based on link speed, availability, and reliability, with a low cost designating a fast, available, and reliable link.

Link Schedules

One of the options an administrator has to control replication between sites is to schedule when site links are available. Intersite replication does not use the process of notification. If changes occur within one site, the other sites are not notified. Instead, a domain controller in one site will periodically check for changes by contacting a domain controller in another site.

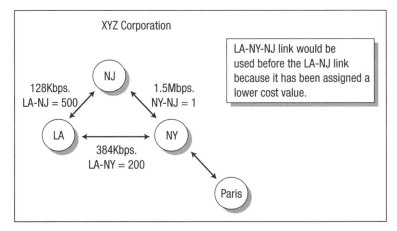

Figure 9.2   Assigning a cost value to site links allows an administrator to specify a preferred route when multiple site links exist.

In order to optimize this process, an administrator can schedule certain times when the site link can be used for intersite replication. This will ensure that replication does not occur when the link is already heavily used. For example, the XYZ Corporation may choose to schedule the site link between LA and NJ to only be available during nonworking hours so that the already heavily used link is not tied up with replication traffic, as shown in Figure 9.3.

One of the drawbacks of placing a schedule on a site link is that it can increase replication latency. *Replication latency* is the time it takes for changes made on one domain controller to appear on another domain controller. Obviously, placing a schedule on a link means that information between sites may not always be up to date.

However, if a link used for RPC replication is saturated when a replication cycle begins, the replication may fail with an RPC timeout. Therefore, although latency can be a problem in a multiple-master environment such as Active Directory, setting site link schedules may actually improve replication performance.

Determining the Need for Site Link Bridges

In a fully routed IP network, all site links are transitive (or *bridged*). The transitiveness of the site links establishes a replication route throughout a network with little administrative effort. Administrators do not have to define site links between every site; in other words, if two sites have links with a common site, a replication route does not have to be explicitly defined between them.

However, there may be situations where networks are not fully routed. If, for example, two subnets are connected at a multihomed server, but that server does

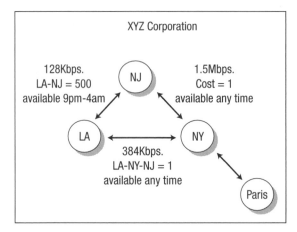

Figure 9.3 Placing a schedule on the site link between LA and NJ allows an administrator to control when intersite replication can occur over the link.

not route or routes only very specific traffic, the network is not fully routed. Dial-on-demand routers, one-way dialup connections, firewalls, and a number of other configurations can create a network that is not fully routed.

In cases where the network is not fully routed, the transitiveness of site links can be turned off and site link bridges can be created to establish a replication path. Once the transitiveness of site links is turned off, a replication path will not exist between sites A and C if there are site links between sites A and B and sites B and C. In order to allow information from site A to be replicated to C, a site link bridge will need to be defined. Sites that do not have an explicit site link between them can be linked using multiple site links to establish site link bridges.

For example, if the ABC Corporation does not have a fully routed network, the transitiveness of the site links can be turned off and an administrator can create site link bridges to establish a replication topology that models the routing operation of the network. If three sites have been configured within an organization and two site links exist, a site link bridge can be defined to establish a replication path, as shown in Figure 9.4.

 The cost of the site link bridge is calculated by adding the cost of each of the site links included in the bridge. Therefore, the cost of sending information from site A to C would be 5 (that is, the cost of site link AB plus the cost of site link BC).

Selecting Bridgehead Servers

If you refer back to Table 9.1 (which compares intrasite and intersite replication), you'll see that to replicate information within a site, multiple connections

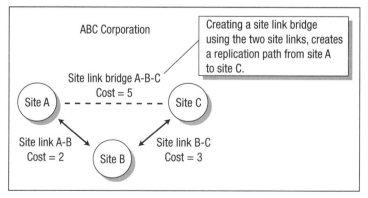

Figure 9.4   A site link bridge establishes a replication path between sites that do not have an explicit site link between them. Establishing site link bridges reduces the administrative overhead associated with a replication topology because explicit site links do not have to be defined between every site.

between domain controllers are automatically established. Between sites, connections are established between dedicated computers called *bridgehead servers.*

Bridgehead servers are those computers that have been designated the responsibility of intersite replication. The bridgehead servers within a site are responsible for receiving updates from other sites. This obviously means that these computers must be able to handle a large amount of replication traffic—much more than other servers within the site. Once a bridgehead server receives updates from another site, that information will then be replicated to other domain controllers within its own site. This is much more efficient than having multiple connections with multiple domain controllers established over a slow link to replicate information from one site to another.

For example, within the different sites in the XYZ Corporation, there would be at least one bridgehead server per site responsible for receiving updates from other sites and replicating them throughout its local site, as shown in Figure 9.5.

When planning for bridgehead servers, keep in mind that a bridgehead server is needed for each naming context within a site. If a site contains IP subnets from more than one domain, multiple bridgehead servers will be needed in the site. The reason for this is that domain controllers can only replicate data to other domain controllers within their own domains. Therefore, in order for replication to occur between sites, a bridgehead server for one domain must be able to connect to a bridgehead server from the same domain in the remote site.

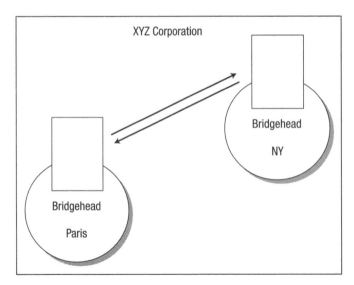

Figure 9.5 The bridgehead servers in each site are responsible for intersite replication.

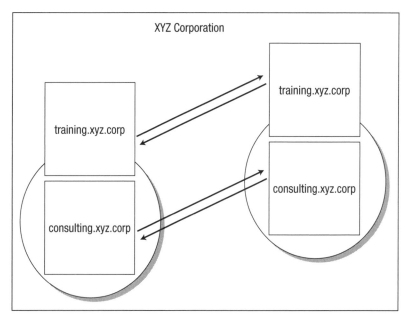

Figure 9.6   If there are IP subnets from multiple domains within the sites, a bridgehead must be designated for each naming context within each site in order for intersite replication to occur.

For example, if the Paris and NY sites contain IP subnets from the Training domain and the Consulting domain, multiple bridgehead servers must be designated within each site, one for each naming context, as shown in Figure 9.6.

The designation of bridgehead servers within a site can be done automatically or manually. When it's done automatically, the KCC will designate a computer as the bridgehead server—usually the first domain controller within each site. If the server designated as the bridgehead is unavailable, the KCC will designate another server to take its place. If you opt to designate the bridgehead server for a site manually, the KCC only uses this server and will not designate another to take its place if it is unavailable. If you are going to manually designate a bridgehead server, it is a good idea to configure more than one for a site; if the bridgehead server is unavailable, the KCC will attempt to use one of the others.

Data compression is a processor- and memory-intensive task. Servers designated as bridgehead servers should be configured with extra CPU and RAM in order to adequately handle the compression and decompression workload.

Locating Domain Controllers

Once the sites and site links have been determined, your next step will be to determine the location of domain controllers within the sites. For each site within the Active Directory infrastructure, you'll need to determine the domain controllers required as well as the number (some sites may require more domain controllers than others).

When you're assessing the need for servers, you'll need to determine the placement of domain controllers, Global Catalog Servers, Operations Masters, and DNS servers throughout the site topology. Table 9.2 summarizes the different server roles within sites, each of which will be covered in this section.

Domain controllers are responsible for authenticating user logon requests and controlling access to network resources. When you're planning the placement of domain controllers, keep in mind that in order for users to be authenticated, a domain controller for their domain must be available.

Where domain controllers are placed within the site topology will have a major impact on server response time for users. For example, if there is no domain controller within a site, users will have to locate a domain controller within another site. Response time obviously is slow because users will have to be authenticated across a WAN link (depending on the reliability of the link, there may be no response at all).

When you're determining where to place domain controllers, a good rule of thumb to follow is to place at least one domain controller within each site that contains users and workstations. In this way, users can take advantage of the high-speed links within a site as opposed to having to be authenticated across a slow, unreliable WAN link.

Table 9.2	The different server roles within an Active Directory Standard Domain Controller site.
Server	**Role**
Domain controller	A computer running Windows 2000 that is responsible for logon authentication and controlling access to network resources.
Global Catalog Server	A server that maintains a copy of the Global Catalog for the entire forest. The Global Catalog contains a subset of the properties for every object in every domain.
Operations Masters	Servers that have been assigned specific roles, such as Schema Master and Domain Naming Master. These roles are exceptions to the multimaster design of Windows 2000.
DNS servers	Servers that are responsible for resolving domain names to IP addresses.

The only time you may choose not to put a domain controller in a site is if there's a very small number of users within a site. In cases such as this, it may be more cost effective—both in terms of bandwidth and dollar amounts—to have users access a domain controller within another site.

The first time a user logs on to a Windows 2000 network using a Windows 2000 client, any domain controller for that domain may be returned by DNS. Client computers are not site-aware, so they have no way of asking for a domain controller in the site.

The authenticating domain controller will compare the IP address of the client against the Active Directory site and subnet information to make sure that it should be validating the logons for this particular computer. If it is determined that another domain controller would be a better choice, the initial domain controller will validate the logon request and then pass a referral back to the client computer that suggests a closer domain controller. The client will then attempt to contact the closer domain controller and will cache the location for future use.

The referral processes is important because access to network resources is now controlled through Kerberos and the Key Distribution Center (KDC). Every Windows 2000 domain controller runs both Kerberos authentication and KDC services. Whenever a user wants to access a network resource, a Kerberos session ticket must be issued. Obviously, tickets will be issued more efficiently if a local server is contacted, rather than one across wide-area links.

Once the placement of domain controllers has been determined, you'll also have to determine the number of domain controllers required within each site. Consider placing at least two domain controllers within each site for load balancing. This way, one server isn't solely responsible for servicing client requests within the site. You'll obviously need to assess the number of client requests within a site to determine whether another is needed for load balancing.

If users must log on to a domain controller across a WAN link, consider configuration of a backup link—perhaps a dial-on-demand router—to ensure access to network resources.

Global Catalog Servers

A *Global Catalog Server* stores certain information pertaining to every object within an Active Directory forest. When a user is searching for objects within the forest, a Global Catalog Server can be queried to determine the location of the object. This eliminates the need for users to perform an extensive search of all domains when trying to locate an object within the forest.

Because access to a Global Catalog Server is required for successful logon, it is important to have at least one Global Catalog Server per site. The Global Catalog Server is needed to enumerate universal group membership, and the logon process will fail if a Global Catalog Server cannot be reached.

Note: The Global Catalog Server is critical because a user could be a member of a universal group that has No Access permission to a particular resource. Remember that No Access overrides all other security settings. As a result, the user could gain access to a critical or confidential resource if the universal group membership could not be determined from the Global Catalog.

Once you have determined which sites will contain Global Catalog Servers, you'll also need to determine how many will be required within each site. Generally, a single server should suffice for all but the largest of sites. Servers hosting a Global Catalog have additional Performance Monitor counters available to assist in determining whether additional Global Catalog Servers are needed.

Operations Masters

As discussed in previous chapters, Windows 2000 implements a multimaster replication model, where all domain controllers are equal and all maintain an up-to-date working copy of the directory. In some instances, though, it does not make sense to have certain information replicated using this model. Specific servers can be designated as an Operations Master, meaning these servers will be responsible for those updates that cannot be replicated using the multimaster model.

There are five Operations Master roles: Schema Master, Domain Naming Master, Primary Domain Controller Emulator, Relative Identifier (RID) Master, and Infrastructure Master. Table 9.3 summarizes the role of each Operations Master.

Table 9.3 The Operations Masters within Active Directory.	
Operations Master	**Role**
Schema Master	The master copy of the schema is stored on this server. All schema modifications will update the Schema Master first and then be replicated to the other domain controllers in the forest.
	There is only one Schema Master per forest.
Domain Naming Master	This Operations Master is responsible for the addition or removal of domains. When a new domain is added, it verifies that the domain name does not already exist.
	Only one Domain Naming Master exists in a forest.

(continued)

Table 9.3   The Operations Masters within Active Directory (continued).

Operations Master	Role
Primary Domain Controller Emulator	This is the server that acts as a Windows NT 4.0 PDC to remain backward-compatible with any Windows NT BDCs on the network. In addition, password changes made to any domain controller in the domain are "pushed" to the PDC Emulator. During logon, if a password mismatch occurs, the PDC Emulator is checked to determine whether a password change has occurred that has not replicated to all other domain controllers yet. Finally, the PDC Emulator is the default server used by the Group Policy Editor MMC snap-in.
	There can only be one PDC Emulator per domain.
Relative Identifier Master	The RID Master is responsible for assigning series of numbers known as *relative IDs* to the domain controllers within its domain (the relative ID is used to create SID numbers). The RID Master role is critical because, unlike in Windows NT, new security accounts can be created on any domain controller in a domain. By assigning a pool of RIDs to every domain controller, unique SIDs can be guaranteed.
	There is one RID master per domain.
Infrastructure Master	The Infrastructure Master is responsible for updating security information across domains any time a change is made to a security group. Without an Infrastructure Master, domain local groups, for example, might not show correct information for global group members from other domains.
	There can only be one Infrastructure Master per domain. Note that this role must not reside on a server that also hosts the Global Catalog.

Keep the following points in mind when planning Operations Master roles:

➤ The first domain controller in a forest is assigned all five roles. These roles can be moved as needed.

➤ The Schema Master should be moved to a DC that is physically closer to the users responsible for schema administration.

➤ The three domain roles (PDC Emulator, RID Master, and Infrastructure Master) should be located "centrally" in a domain to minimize router hops. If you have a domain spread over three sites, put them where the most number of users and DCs can get to them with as few hops as possible.

➤ A server should be designated as a "Backup Operations Master." This will eliminate some confusion if an existing Operations Master fails and the role must be transferred to another server. There is no special Windows 2000 artifact to identify a Backup Operations Master; a small hand-lettered sign will do.

 Be sure to understand the functions of each Operations Master role, and to know which Operations Masters are forest-wide versus domain-wide in scope.

DNS Servers

As you already know, Windows 2000 has adopted the DNS naming convention for naming objects within Active Directory. This means that in order for users to resolve information pertaining to DNS names, there has to be a DNS server available at all times.

Ideally you should plan to place at least one DNS server within each Active Directory site because they are required by users to locate domain controllers. This will improve the query response time for users because they will not have to query a DNS server from another site to locate servers within their own site.

Selecting an Intersite Transport

One of the last things to consider when designing a physical Active Directory topology is the transport that will be used to replicate information between sites. You basically have your choice of using Remote Procedure Calls (RPC) or Simple Mail Transfer Protocol (SMTP).

RPC

The default transport that can be used for intersite replication is RPC over TCP/IP. This transport can be used for intersite as well as intrasite replication. RPC uses synchronous transfer, meaning there has to be a direct connection with the destination server before any information will be replicated. This poses a problem for WAN links that are unreliable because if a connection cannot be established, replication will not occur. Also, if the WAN link is slow or congested, RPC timeouts can occur, causing replication to fail. RPC is inadvisable for link speeds under 128Kbps. RPC timeouts and replication failures can also occur when using VPN connections, even at 128Kbps or higher. The reason for the timeouts is the unpredictable latency of VPN circuits, which depend on the Internet to transmit data from one location to another.

One of the main advantages of using RPC over TCP/IP is that it can support intersite replication traffic between all servers, including domain controllers from the same domain. RPC is also more efficient as an intersite transport.

Table 9.4	The features of the RPC transport for intersite replication.
Advantage	**Disadvantage**
Faster than SMTP	Must have a direct connection with a destination server to send information
Can be used for intersite replication between DCs in the same domain	Can only be used within a TCP/IP-based network
Uses the schedules set on the site links	Can only have one outstanding connection at one time

Table 9.4 summarizes some of the advantages and disadvantages of using RPC over TCP/IP.

SMTP

SMTP basically sends information to be replicated between sites as email messages. Unlike RPC, it provides asynchronous data transfer, meaning that a direct connection with the remote server is not required. It also uses the store-and-forward method of sending information, meaning that if the destination host is not available, the message can be stored. This transport is an ideal choice if the link between two sites is unreliable. For example, when the link is not available, the message can be stored and sent when the destination server is available. Note, however, that the schedules set on a site link by an administrator are ignored when the SMTP protocol is used.

Note: Even though this is an intersite transport, it cannot be used to replicate information between domain controllers in the same domain. In cases such as this, RPC would have to be used. The primary reason is that Sysvol replication, which is required to replicate part of a Group Policy Object, must use RPC. Even if no GPOs are configured, Windows 2000 will not replicate the Domain naming context via SMTP.

Table 9.5 outlines some of the advantages and disadvantages associated with this transport.

Table 9.5	The advantages and disadvantages of using SMTP as an intersite transport.
Advantages	**Disadvantages**
Uses store-and-forward messaging.	Generally slower than RPC
Multiple messages can be sent at one time.	The format of messages increases network traffic
Because the information is in the form of an email message, it can be routed.	Can only be used for intersite replication

Comparing the Protocols

When evaluating a site link to determine the proper protocol to use, consider the following points:

➤ RPC requires a relatively fast, reliable WAN link. If links are slow (less than 128Kbps), unreliable, or congested, SMTP is a better choice.

➤ If a domain spans sites, any links between these sites must use RPC.

➤ SMTP replication uses the SMTP component of Internet Information Server (IIS) to communicate with other domain controllers.

➤ SMTP replication ignores site link schedules.

➤ SMTP replication generates slightly more network traffic than RPC—typically about 5 to 10 percent more.

Practice Questions

Case Study: Global Delivery

Global Delivery is a worldwide freight-shipping company headquartered in Baltimore, Maryland. With offices on every continent, except Antarctica, Global has an extensive wide-area network infrastructure.

Administratively, Global is divided into three regions: Americas, Europe/Africa, and Asia/Australia. The Americas regional headquarters is in Dallas, Texas, the Europe/Africa region is headquartered in Zurich, Switzerland, and the Asia/Australia headquarters is in Sydney, Australia.

There are hundreds of local offices; these offices report to the appropriate regional headquarters.

LAN/Network Structure

Global is predominantly a Unix shop, although a number of Windows NT Servers have been deployed over the past three years. Currently, four master account domains exist—one at each regional headquarters and one at the corporate offices in Baltimore. These four domains are linked in a complete trust model.

The local offices typically run Unix applications using either VT100-style terminals or personal computers with VT100-emulation software installed. Few local offices have a server.

Existing Unix Web and DNS servers will not be replaced. These servers are located at the Baltimore headquarters. The DNS servers are running BIND 4.9.7.

Proposed LAN/Network Structure

Global is committed to replacing the bulk of its older Unix applications with *n*-tier client/server applications using Web interfaces. These replacement applications are already under development. Windows 2000 will be deployed at all locations over the next several months to support the new apps.

WAN Connectivity

Corporate headquarters is connected to the Europe/Africa and Asia/Australia regions with 64Kbps circuits. These circuits are very heavily used during overlapping business hours.

The Dallas office has a full T1 connection to Baltimore. This circuit is underutilized, except from 10 A.M. until 1 P.M. and from 2 P.M. until 5 P.M. Baltimore time.

The local offices typically use dial-up connections to either the regional office or to an ISP to access corporate systems. These connections can be as slow as 9600bps.

Proposed WAN Connectivity

Although the 64Kbps lines are slow and sometimes saturated, there are no immediate plans to upgrade them.

As part of the Windows 2000 and client/server application deployment, the local offices will use local dial access and VPN technologies to access the corporate applications.

Directory Design Commentary

Director, Corporate Telecommunications: We cannot afford to upgrade our WAN links at this time. We will be working to cut communications costs using VPNs at our local offices, but the transatlantic and transpacific circuits will have to stay "as is."

Security Administrator: Our current Windows NT domain model is poorly designed. We need a better way to control access to our corporate resources, especially with the migration of many of our applications to a Windows 2000 platform.

DNS Administrator: Our current DNS servers work just fine, and I am not going to replace them with something new and unproven. Our Web and DNS servers are mission-critical to our business.

Director, Information Technology: Our new client/server applications mean that we do not have to put servers out in the local offices. This takes a tremendous load off of my mind because there were numerous tricky support issues.

Internet Positioning

Global has an extensive Web presence that allows customers to request pickups, track shipments, and display billing information online. Global's registered domain name is **global-deliver.com**.

Question 1

> What types of replication can occur over the 64Kbps lines from Baltimore to Sydney and Zurich?
>
> ○ a. RPC over IP only.
>
> ○ b. SMTP only.
>
> ○ c. RPC and SMTP.
>
> ○ d. None. The line speed is too slow to support replication.

The correct answer is b. For low-speed WAN links, SMTP is much more reliable. RPC over IP is extremely unreliable at such low line speeds, especially with saturation during certain times of the day. Therefore, answers a and c are incorrect. Answer d is also incorrect because 64Kbps is certainly capable of supporting SMTP traffic.

Question 2

> How many sites should be created for Global Delivery?
>
> ○ a. One
>
> ○ b. Two
>
> ○ c. Four
>
> ○ d. Four, plus one for every local office

The correct answer is c. A site should be created for each regional office and the headquarters office. Answers a and b are incorrect because separate sites are necessary for locations on the other side of slow (64Kbps) WAN links. Answer d is incorrect because servers will not be deployed at the local offices.

Question 3

Place the Operations Masters shown in the second list into the appropriate domains from the first list.

Domain:

global-deliver.com

americas.global-deliver.com

asia-australia.global-deliver.com

europe-africa.global-deliver.com

Operations Masters:

Schema Master

PDC Emulator

RID Master

Infrastructure Master

Domain Naming Mater

The correct answer is:

global-deliver.com

> Schema Master
>
> PDC Emulator
>
> RID Master
>
> Infrastructure Master
>
> Domain Naming Mater

americas.global-deliver.com

> PDC Emulator
>
> RID Master
>
> Infrastructure Master

asia-australia.global-deliver.com

> PDC Emulator
>
> RID Master
>
> Infrastructure Master

europe-africa.global-deliver.com

    PDC Emulator

    RID Master

    Infrastructure Master

Question 4

To provide a measure of fault tolerance, Global Delivery has decided to create backup connections to Sydney and Zurich. For each of the site links shown in Figure 9.7, drag an appropriate cost from the boxes on the left to the circuit. You may use a cost more than once. The backup site links should be used only if the main links fail.

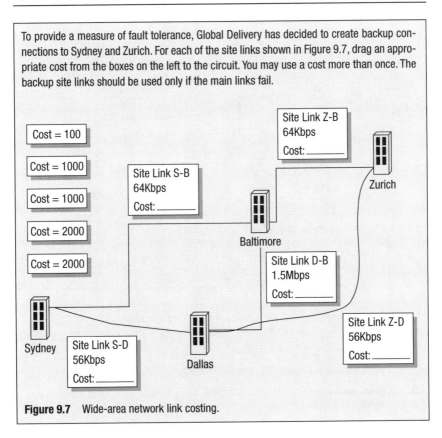

Figure 9.7 Wide-area network link costing.

Refer to Figure 9.8 for the correct answers.

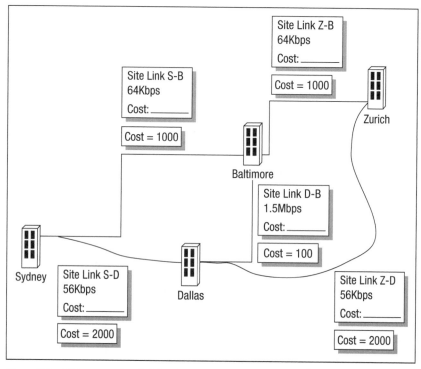

Figure 9.8 Wide-area network links with costs applied.

Question 5

The WAN link between Baltimore and Dallas is at full capacity at certain times of the day. What can be done to make sure that RPC replication does not occur when the T1 line is typically saturated? [Check two answers]

❏ a. Create a site link schedule and prevent replication during peak hours.

❏ b. Configure a link monitor agent to determine when the link is saturated and set it to stop replication when this occurs.

❏ c. Use an SMTP site link rather than an RPC link.

❏ d. Set the Replication Governor Registry value to reduce the impact of replication traffic on the link.

❏ e. Set the replication frequency to once every 240 minutes.

The correct answers are a and c. A site link schedule will set times when replication cannot occur over the site link. Another option is to use SMTP for replication. If the link is saturated, the SMTP server will time out waiting for a connection with the server on the other side, effectively delaying replication until the link is less busy.

Answer b is incorrect because there is no such thing as a link monitor agent in Windows 2000. Answer d is incorrect because there is no Replication Governor Registry value in Windows 2000. That parameter was used to configure replication in Windows NT. Finally, answer e is incorrect because changing the replication frequency will not prevent replication from occurring during peak periods.

Question 6

The server holding the role of PDC Emulator for the **global-deliver.com** domain has failed and will be unavailable for at least a day. What can be done to fill this Operations Master role? [Check all correct answers]

❏ a. Use dcpromo to create a new domain controller. Run a restore from the latest backup of the failed server to update the new domain controller. Then place the new PDC emulator online.

❏ b. From another domain controller in the same domain, run the Active Directory Users and Computers MMC snap-in. Right-click the **global-deliver.com** domain and select Operations Masters from the drop-down list. Select the PDC tab in the Operations Masters dialog box and click the Change button.

❏ c. Use the NTDSUTIL command-line utility to seize the role of PDC Emulator.

❏ d. Do nothing. A new PDC Emulator will automatically be chosen within 15 minutes of the failure of the original PDC Emulator.

❏ e. Do nothing. The PDC Emulator is not needed once a domain is in native mode.

Answers b and c are correct. Either the Active Directory Users and Computers MMC snap-in or the NTDSUTIL command-line utility can be used to transfer the PDC Emulator role to another domain controller. Answer a is incorrect because it will create duplicate computer SIDs on the network, among other things, when the old PDC Emulator is brought back online. Answer d is incorrect because a new PDC Emulator must be manually selected. Answer e is incorrect because the PDC Emulator still has roles in native mode for password changes and as the source of Group Policy updates, to name just two.

Question 7

> For intrasite replication, how many minutes will elapse before all domain controllers are updated with a change to Active Directory?
>
> ○ a. 5
>
> ○ b. 15
>
> ○ c. 30
>
> ○ d. 180

The correct answer is b. The intrasite replication topology creates connection objects so that no server is more than three hops away from any other server in the site. With the standard five-minute delay after a change is detected, no more than 15 minutes will elapse before a change has been replicated to all domain controllers. Therefore, answers a, c, and d are incorrect.

Question 8

> The Director of Information Technology is wondering whether it would be better to put the Baltimore and Dallas locations into a single site. From the second list, place the advantages of each type of replication under the Intrasite or Intersite headings in the first list.
>
> Type of replication:
>
> Intrasite
>
> Intersite
>
> Advantages:
>
> Replication traffic is compressed.
>
> A choice of protocols is available for replication.
>
> Domain controllers are updated more quickly.
>
> Replication can be scheduled to avoid peak traffic periods.
>
> Replication occurs as soon as a change is made.
>
> The replication topology is always self-repairing if a domain controller is down.

The correct answers are:

Intrasite replication:

  Domain controllers are updated more quickly.

  Replication occurs as soon as a change is made.

The replication topology is always self-repairing if a domain controller is down.

Intersite replication:

Replication traffic is compressed.

A choice of protocols is available for replication.

Replication can be scheduled to avoid peak traffic periods.

Question 9

Which two naming contexts share a replication topology?

○ a. Domain and Schema

○ b. Global Catalog and Domain

○ c. Schema and Configuration

○ d. Global Catalog and Schema

○ e. Global Catalog and Configuration

The correct answer is c. The Schema and Configuration naming contexts replicate to all domain controllers in a forest and use the same replication topology. Answer a is incorrect because the Domain naming context replicates to only domain controllers in a single domain. Answers b, d, and e are incorrect because only Global Catalog Servers use the Global Catalog replication topology.

Question 10

The domain controller in Baltimore that acts as the bridgehead server has gone down. How can a new bridgehead server be brought online?

○ a. Using the Active Directory Sites and Services MMC snap-in at the server that will be the new bridgehead server, select the affected site and right-click it. Select Bridgehead Servers from the drop-down list and click the Change button.

○ b. Run the NTDSUTIL command-line utility and seize the role of Bridgehead Server.

○ c. Do nothing. A new bridgehead server will be selected automatically as soon as the KCC detects that the current server is not available.

○ d. Using the Active Directory Sites and Services MMC snap-in, right-click any site link in the affected site. Select Properties from the drop-down list and select the Bridgehead Servers tab from the Properties page. Select a new bridgehead server from the list of available domain controllers.

The correct answer is c. A new bridgehead server is selected automatically. Answers a, b, and d are incorrect because there is no way of selecting a bridgehead server from either NTDSUTIL or the Sites and Services MMC snap-in.

Need to Know More?

 Microsoft Corporation. *Optimizing Network Traffic (Notes from the Field).* Microsoft Press. Redmond, WA, 1999. ISBN 0-7356-0648-X. The last two chapters of this book contain excellent articles written by Andreas Luther on Active Directory database sizing and replication traffic.

 Microsoft Corporation. *The Microsoft Windows 2000 Server Resource Kit.* Microsoft Press. Redmond, WA, 2000. ISBN 1-5723-1805-8. Contains in-depth information about the design elements within Active Directory.

 Try searching the TechNet CD or use Microsoft's online version at **www.microsoft.com**. Search for keywords such as *sites*, *site links*, and *replication*.

Sample Test

Case Study 1

Golden Sun Mining Company

Golden Sun Mining Company operates several mineral mines around the world. With headquarters in Alberta, Canada and regional offices in Lima, Peru and Johannesburg, South Africa, Golden Sun also has six field offices located in the mining areas: two in Canada, two in South Africa, one in Zaire, and one in Chile.

LAN/Network Structure

Golden Sun is currently running Windows NT 4 servers in the headquarters and regional offices. Using a single-domain model, a PDC and two BDCs are located in the Alberta office, and the Lima and Johannesburg offices each house a BDC. The Alberta home office has 2,000 employees, whereas Lima and Johannesburg have 250 and 375 employees, respectively. The field offices each have from 25 to 100 employees. Client computers run a mix of Windows NT Workstation and Windows 98. A few of the field office computers are running Windows 95.

The headquarters and regional offices use 10Mbps Ethernet, with Category 5 cabling throughout. This network infrastructure is considered adequate for current and future needs.

The field offices are a mixed bag of technologies. Some have only a small peer network; the larger ones have a BDC and a server-based network. In most cases, there is no dedicated person to support the computers in the field offices, and support comes from one of the regional offices or headquarters.

Proposed LAN/Network Structure

Golden Sun wants to upgrade to Windows 2000 throughout the organization. Specifically, it sees the connectivity and security features of Windows 2000 as critical to the company, especially for connecting field offices to the larger offices.

WAN Connectivity

The regional offices are connected to headquarters by means of 512Mbps fractional T1 circuits. The circuits are not generally heavily used.

Field offices are connected using 56K Frame Relay. The links at two of the larger field offices are heavily saturated during business hours.

Proposed WAN Connectivity

No changes are anticipated for the T1 connections between the regional offices and headquarters.

The field offices will be upgraded to 256Kbps VPN connections prior to the Windows 2000 deployment. Golden Sun is looking for Windows 2000 to provide IPSec over the connections to improve security and to safeguard the transmission of sensitive company information.

Directory Design Commentary

CEO: Our company management has always been based here in Alberta. We don't want anyone in the regional offices making changes without our approval, and we need to keep tight control of our resources.

Director of Information Technology: Our field offices require far too much support from the headquarters staff. We want to allow them to reset passwords and change certain user fields, though, so that they do not constantly call us for these trivial issues. We also need to make sure that sensitive mining data transmitted from the field offices is secure.

Director, Human Resources: We need to allow the regional office personnel the ability to add users to the network. We will be installing a new HR application after the Windows 2000 implementation that will use information in the Windows 2000 directory, so this capability is important.

Internet Positioning

Golden Sun Mining has a registered Internet name of **goldsunmine.ca**. It currently runs a small Web site with basic company information and operates an Exchange email server from the Alberta headquarters. DNS services are currently handled by the ISP.

Future Internet Positioning

No changes in Internet strategy are forecast.

Question 1.1

Which of the following design issues are critical to meeting the business requirements of Golden Sun Mining? [Check two answers]

❑ a. The 56Kbps connections out to the field offices

❑ b. The need to delegate administration

❑ c. Use of Group Policy to manage desktops

❑ d. Schema-modification policy

Question 1.2

How will the proposed upgrade of WAN links out to the field offices affect the Active Directory design for Golden Sun?

○ a. There will be no effect.

○ b. The site design will be affected.

○ c. The domain design will be affected.

○ d. Fewer cross-link trust relationships will be needed.

Question 1.3

How many sites should be created?

○ a. 1

○ b. 3

○ c. 6

○ d. 9

Question 1.4

Here are two lists. The first list shows four Golden Sun locations, and the second contains Windows 2000 Server roles. Under each location, place the appropriate server roles for that location. You may use a role more than once.

Locations

Alberta corporate headquarters

Johannesburg regional office

Lima regional office

Chile field office

Server roles

Domain controller

DNS server

Schema Operations Master

PDC Emulator

Global Catalog Server

Question 1.5

Figure 10.1 shows a portion of the proposed Golden Sun Active Directory design.

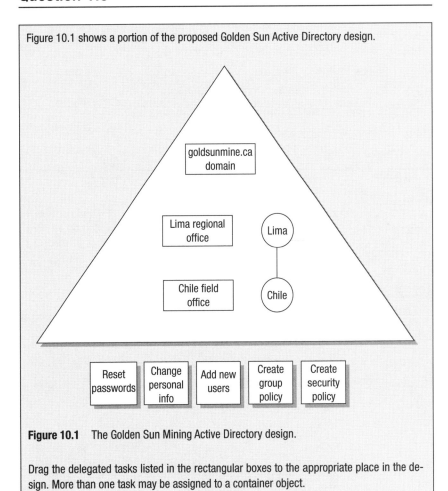

Figure 10.1 The Golden Sun Mining Active Directory design.

Drag the delegated tasks listed in the rectangular boxes to the appropriate place in the design. More than one task may be assigned to a container object.

Question 1.6

What kind of Active Directory design is shown in Figure 10.1?

○ a. Geographical

○ b. Organizational

○ c. Functional

○ d. Hybrid (geographical then organizational)

Question 1.7

External DNS will still be handled by Golden Sun's ISP. Internal DNS will use the Windows 2000 DNS service. Which tasks should be performed to ensure that the internal DNS functions properly? [Check two answers]

❑ a. Manually add the IP address of the Golden Sun Web server.

❑ b. Change the character set option to allow UTF-8 encoding.

❑ c. Turn on Dynamic Update.

❑ d. Change the internal zone to Active Directory integrated.

Question 1.8

Figure 10.2 shows a site link's Properties page. For two sites connected by DEFAULTIPSITELINK, how often will replication occur?

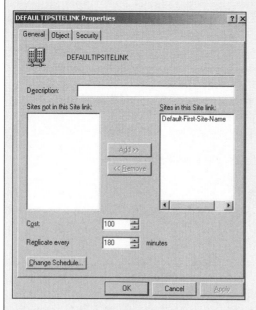

Figure 10.2   The Properties page for the DEFAULTIPSITELINK site link.

○ a. 5 minutes.

○ b. 100 minutes.

○ c. 180 minutes.

○ d. The replication frequency cannot be determined from this page.

Case Study 2

Madeleine Confectioners

Madeleine Confectioners is a small, closely held bakery supply company based in Jacksonville, Florida, with facilities in the Southeastern United States. Until recently a very small company, Madeleine has suddenly experienced rapid growth. It just acquired Lone Star Sugars, a sugar refiner based in Houston, Texas.

LAN/Network Structure

Madeleine Confectioners is currently running a Novell 3.12 network using 10Mbps Ethernet coaxial cabling in its main office in Jacksonville. Most of the client computers at Madeleine are running Windows 95.

The sales offices, in six major cities in the Southeast, typically have just one or two computers that use dial-up connections to access local ISPs. Data sharing is done through email and file attachments. Because of the rapid growth of the company, these arrangements have become totally inadequate.

Lone Star Sugars uses a Windows NT 4.0 Server-based network in its Houston office. 10BaseT Ethernet cabling connects the Windows 98 and 95 workstations to the two servers. These two servers act as PDC and BDC and host Exchange email and a SQL Server 6.5 database server as well.

Proposed LAN/Network Structure

Madeleine management recognizes that its current LAN is seriously outdated and has committed the necessary budget to upgrade all its computers and its network infrastructure. With the Lone Star Sugars merger now complete, management is also looking to link the Jacksonville and Houston offices.

Madeleine plans to move the combined companies to Windows 2000 Server as quickly as possible and upgrade client computers to Windows 2000 Professional over a two-year time schedule.

WAN Connectivity

Currently, there is little connectivity between sales offices, outside of dial-up connections, and none between the Madeleine and Lone Star offices.

Proposed WAN Connectivity

The Jacksonville and Houston offices will be connected by T1, using half the bandwidth for data and the other half for voice connections.

The sales offices require a more robust connection, especially in light of the need to dramatically expand the computing power available at each location. An SDSL solution, using VPN connections to the Jacksonville office, will be implemented prior to the Windows 2000 rollout.

Directory Design Commentary

Owner: We used to be a small company, but we have grown so much in the past year that it's difficult to keep up with the changes. Our network is completely outdated. I want every employee in every office to have access to all important company data.

IS Manager: With the new company we just bought, we now have to connect two very different operations. Administration is a headache, and we do not have the staff to keep up with the changes. We need help with user account administration.

Sales Manager: Our sales force is trying to get its work done, but it is getting nearly impossible to work with the sales office computers. We can't get fast updates to any of our product sheets, and we can't communicate orders to the home office easily.

Internet Positioning

Madeleine has no Internet presence at this time. Lone Star Sugars has a registered domain name of **lonestarsugar.com** but only uses it for email at this time.

Future Internet Positioning

Madeleine has just registered the domain name **madeleine.com** and is planning to install an email server and establish a Web presence in the next 12 months. For now, Lone Star will maintain its email address, and there is a possibility of a Web site as well.

Question 2.1

What should be the root domain name for Madeleine Confectioners' new Active Directory structure? [Check the best answer]

○ a. **madeleine.com**

○ b. **lonestarsugar.com**

○ c. **confectioners.com**

○ d. **madeleineconfectioners.com**

Question 2.2

Within Active Directory, what should the domain name be for Lone Star Sugars? [Check the best answer]

○ a. **madeleine.lonestarsugar.com**

○ b. **lonestarsugar.madeleine.com**

○ c. **lonestarsugar.com**

○ d. **madeleine.com**

Question 2.3

How should Active Directory be structured for Madeleine Confectioners?

○ a. Two forests

○ b. One forest, two domain trees

○ c. One forest, one domain

○ d. One forest, one domain tree

Question 2.4

Place the appropriate Operations Masters from the second list under the correct domain name in the first list. You may use an Operations Master more than once.

Domain names:

lonestarsugar.com

madeleine.com

Operations Masters:

PDC Emulator

Schema Master

RID Master

Domain Naming Master

Infrastructure Master

Question 2.5

Once the proposed WAN upgrades have been completed, how many Global Catalog Servers should be configured for the Madeleine Confectioners forest?

○ a. 1

○ b. 3

○ c. 8

○ d. 9

Question 2.6

Madeleine management plans to delegate the administration of passwords to the managers of each sales office as well as the ability to update basic employee information and printer configuration. Managers will also be able to delegate these administrative tasks to their administrative assistants for the office staff and to the sales supervisor for the office staff.

Create the Organizational Unit structure shown in Figure 10.3 using the Orlando, Florida sales office as a model. Drag the OU name onto the appropriate OU for the delegation described previously.

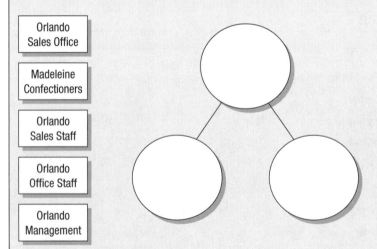

Orlando
Sales Office

Madeleine
Confectioners

Orlando
Sales Staff

Orlando
Office Staff

Orlando
Management

Figure 10.3   Create the OU structure for the Orlando sales office.

Question 2.7

A consultant has recommended placing the printers for the sales offices in a separate Organizational Unit for ease of delegation. Can printers be placed in an Organizational Unit?

○ a. Yes

○ b. No

Question 2.8

If a site is created for each Madeleine Confectioners sales office, and a domain controller is placed in each sales office as well, what server roles should be assigned to these domain controllers? [Check all correct answers]

❑ a. Global Catalog Server

❑ b. RID Operations Master

❑ c. PDC Emulator

❑ d. DNS server

❑ e. Infrastructure Master

Case Study 3

Gramm Records

Gramm Records operates a chain of retail stores in North America, with a limited number of outlets in Europe, South America, and Australia. The business is run from a home office in San Francisco, which is housed in two separate buildings a block away from each other. Gramm has six distribution centers located in Chicago, Dallas, New York City, London, Buenos Aires, and Sydney. There are approximately 250 retail locations in North America, and 10 to 20 stores on each of the other continents.

LAN/Network Structure

Gramm runs Windows NT 4.0 servers at all locations. The PDC for the master accounts domain is located in the San Francisco home office, and there are six resource domains with PDCs located at each of the distribution centers. BDCs for the accounts domain are situated in San Francisco and each distribution center.

The only exceptions to the Windows NT 4 environment are the Gramm Web and DNS servers, which are all Unix-based. Gramm does not intend to migrate either the Web server or the DNS servers. The DNS servers currently run BIND version 8.2.2.

The retail stores each have a single NT 4.0 member server.

Workstations are a mix of Windows NT 4.0 Workstation and Windows 98 SE.

The home office recently upgraded to 100Mbps Ethernet, whereas distribution centers and retail stores use 10Mbps twisted-pair Ethernet. This network infrastructure is considered adequate for current and future needs.

Proposed LAN/Network Structure

No major changes are planned to the network infrastructure. Gramm Records is planning to migrate to Windows 2000, replacing any client or server computers that cannot run on the new platform.

WAN Connectivity

The two San Francisco headquarters buildings are connected by a full 1.5Mbps T1 line.

The distribution centers are connected to headquarters by means of a Frame Relay cloud. These 56Kbps circuits are frequently saturated, especially during peak periods of the day.

Retail locations connect to the nearest distribution center using an analog dial-up connection, which is initiated at the start of the business day and closed when the store is closed.

Proposed WAN Connectivity

Gramm is investigating DSL as a way to ease WAN congestion and reduce costs for communications between the home office and the distribution centers, as well as between the distribution centers and the retail stores. However, there is neither a timetable nor a budget for this upgrade.

Directory Design Commentary

Chief Technologist: We need to get bandwidth out to each of our retail stores fast. The recorded music industry is changing so quickly, and we need to keep ahead of those changes. We need to be able to deliver music to the stores on demand and to get the technology in place to deliver custom recorded music to our customers.

Network Services Manager: We are getting swamped with requests for new user accounts, password changes, printer configuration changes, and the like. I have a staff of trained technology experts who are doing nothing but routine, mind-numbing tasks.

Store Manager: Whenever I hire a new employee, I need to fill out three pages of paperwork, fax it to the home office, and then hope that someone looks at it and sets up a user account before the employee finds a new job elsewhere. If someone forgets a password, it seems that it takes forever to get it fixed.

Internet Positioning

Gramm Records has an extensive Web site where customers can buy recorded music, paraphernalia, and accessories. Its registered Internet domain name is **Grammrecords.com**. All Gramm employees also have an email account on the corporate Exchange server.

Future Internet Positioning

Gramm recently created a subsidiary company called Gramm On Demand Music and registered the domain name **Grammod.com**. Gramm On Demand will compile custom music CDs based on customer requests. Management believes that the new venture will become a major portion of Gramm's business over the next three years.

Question 3.1

Can Gramm Records use the existing BIND 8.2.2 DNS servers for Windows 2000 Active Directory? [Check the best answer]

○ a. No, Windows 2000 requires Windows 2000 DNS to operate properly.

○ b. Yes, but only if SRV records are added manually, because BIND 8.2.2 does not support Dynamic Update.

○ c. No, the BIND server must be upgraded to BIND 10.1.3 to support SRV records.

○ d. Yes, BIND 8.2.2 is completely compatible with Windows 2000 and Active Directory.

Question 3.2

Based on the current wide area network connectivity, how many sites should be created at Gramm Records?

○ a. One site for the entire company

○ b. Eight sites, one for each home office building and one for each distribution center

○ c. Four sites, one for North America, and one each for London, Buenos Aires, and Sydney

○ d. Seven sites, one for the home office and one for each distribution center

Question 3.3

The Gramm network services manager is designing the replication topology for the company's Active Directory implementation. What is the best way to manage replication traffic between San Francisco and the distribution centers?

○ a. Configure a site link using RPC over IP and allow replication to occur at any time.

○ b. Configure a site link using RPC over IP and set a site link schedule to allow replication only during evening hours.

○ c. Configure a site link using SMTP.

○ d. Configure a site link using SMTP and set a site link schedule to allow replication only during evening hours.

Question 3.4

Gramm management has decided to delegate some user management functions to the managers of the retail stores. Select the steps that must be performed from the following list and arrange them in the proper order. Some steps in the list may not be needed.

Add the store manager global group to the Store Administration domain local group membership.

Create an OU for all retail store managers.

Move all retail store employees into the appropriate OU.

Create a global group for the managers at each retail store and add the manager user accounts to these global groups.

Create an OU for each retail store.

Create a universal group for all store managers.

Create a domain local group for each store and delegate approved administrative tasks to the members of the domain local group.

Question 3.5

There are four domain controllers situated in one of Gramm Records' San Francisco locations, as shown in Figure 10.4. Select a server role from the boxes on the left and place it on the most appropriate server in the diagram.

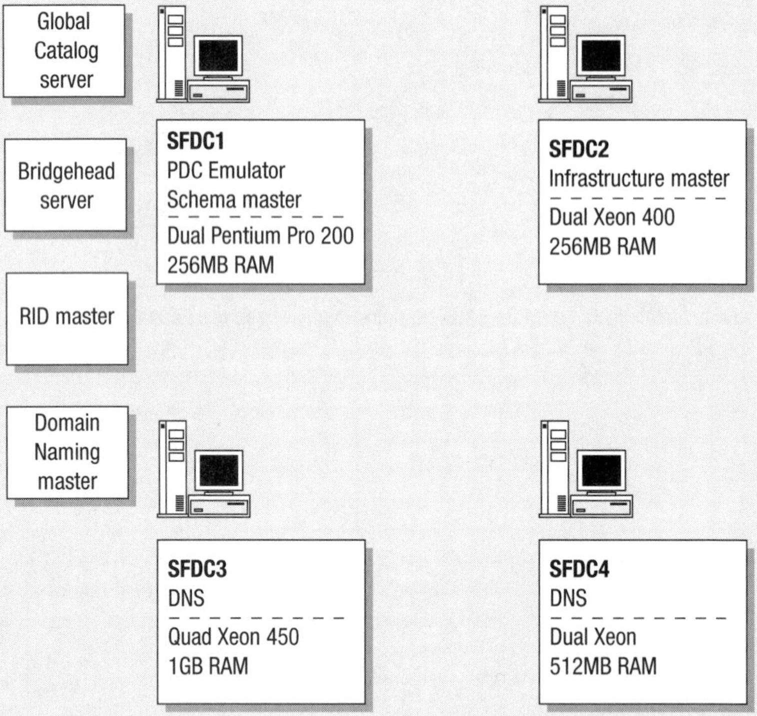

Global
Catalog
server

Bridgehead
server

RID master

Domain
Naming
master

SFDC1
PDC Emulator
Schema master
- - - - - - - -
Dual Pentium Pro 200
256MB RAM

SFDC2
Infrastructure master
- - - - - - - - -
Dual Xeon 400
256MB RAM

SFDC3
DNS
- - - - - - - -
Quad Xeon 450
1GB RAM

SFDC4
DNS
- - - - - - - -
Dual Xeon
512MB RAM

Figure 10.4   Select and place the appropriate server role on the server.

Question 3.6

The Help Desk supervisor in the Chicago distribution center updates the Last Name attribute for a user in the **chicago.grammrecords.com** domain. When will this change be replicated to the other domain controller in Chicago?

○ a. In five minutes.

○ b. In three hours.

○ c. This depends on the replication schedule.

○ d. This depends on the site link schedule.

Question 3.7

The Gramm Music On Demand operation is installing several applications that will require extensive schema modifications. Gramm management does not want these schema modifications to affect the corporate headquarters or the distribution centers. What is the best way to isolate Gramm Records from the schema changes required at Gramm Music On Demand?

- ○ a. Make **grammod.com** a child domain of grammrecords.com and block inheritance at the domain level.
- ○ b. Make **grammod.com** a separate tree in the Gramm Records forest.
- ○ c. Create a new forest for **grammod.com**.
- ○ d. Install a second Schema Operations Master server in the Gramm Records forest.

Question 3.8

To ensure availability of network resources, which of the following actions should be taken? [Check all correct answers]

- ❑ a. Place a Global Catalog Server at each site.
- ❑ b. Place a DNS server at each site.
- ❑ c. Install a PDC Emulator at each site.
- ❑ d. Provide at least two domain controllers for every domain.
- ❑ e. Configure multiple site links for every site.

Question 3.9

Can Gramm Records place a Windows 2000 domain controller at each retail store?

- ○ a. Yes
- ○ b. No

Question 3.10

Retail store managers require access to company-wide sales information that is compiled at the headquarters office. Currently, a global group exists for each store that contains the user accounts for the managers of the store. What options does Gramm have to provide the store managers access to sales information? [Check two answers]

❑ a. Make each store manager global group a member of the domain local group that has access to the sales data.

❑ b. Create a global group in the home office domain and make each store manager global group a member. Then make the new global group a member of the domain local group that has access to the sales data.

❑ c. Create a universal group and make each store manager global group a member. Then make the universal group a member of the domain local group that has access to the sales data.

❑ d. Change all the store manager global groups to universal groups and make each universal group a member of the domain local group that has access to the sales data.

Case Study 4

Digital Information Services

Digital Information Services is an international computer consultancy, with offices throughout the world. Headquartered in New Orleans, Digital is divided regionally into North America, South America, Europe/Middle East, Africa, Asia, and South Pacific. Each region is given total autonomy and is run almost as a separate business. Digital employs about 120,000 people, with 5,000 in the smallest region, Africa, and 40,000 in the largest, North America.

Although each region enjoys autonomy, the branch offices are generally tightly controlled from the regional office, with little local authority.

LAN/Network Structure

Each region is running Windows NT servers of varying vintages. The Asia region, for example, is still running NT 3.51 on the majority of its servers, whereas Europe and Africa are entirely on NT 4.0 with the latest service packs applied.

Digital has six master accounts domains, one for each region. Each branch office within a region has a BDC from the appropriate accounts domain and houses a resource domain of its own.

Proposed LAN/Network Structure

Digital is in the process of upgrading to Windows 2000 throughout the organization. The root domain has already been created in the New Orleans home office.

WAN Connectivity

The regional offices are connected to headquarters by means of full 1.5Mbps T1 circuits. The T1 circuits are not generally heavily used.

Branch offices are connected to the regional offices using a variety of methods, primarily ISDN or fractional T1.

Proposed WAN Connectivity

No changes are anticipated for the T1 connections between the regional offices and headquarters.

Digital is looking for Windows 2000 to reduce communications costs for the branch offices. By replacing ISDN and T1 circuits with DSL and using VPN technology, management believes it can cut telco expenses by 50 percent. By using IPSec or PPTP over the VPN connections, security can be improved as the sensitive company information is safeguarded.

Directory Design Commentary

CEO: We may have decentralized our operations a bit too much. There is no central control over our computing environment at all, and it is costing us when we move personnel from one office to another.

General Manager, Asia region: We need better control over the branch offices. Support is difficult because each office is configured differently.

Help Desk Manager, South Pacific region: The telephones ring nonstop. We cover eight different time zones, and someone is always calling and asking for us to set up a new user, change a password, or something. There has to be a better way.

Internet Positioning

Digital has a registered Internet name of **digital-is.com**. Its extensive Web site contains numerous white papers and success stories, along with special areas for each region. All Digital consultants have an email account, hosted on one of six Exchange servers, and there is an extensive intranet for consultants to use as well.

Future Internet Positioning

No changes in Internet strategy are forecast.

Question 4.1

Would a single Active Directory domain be appropriate based on Digital's business model? [Check the best answer]

○ a. Yes, because Active Directory supports millions of objects in a single domain, there is no reason to use more than one domain.

○ b. No, the decentralized management style of Digital and the strong regional autonomy suggest multiple domains.

○ c. No, sysvol replication cannot take place over a 1.5Mbps T1 connection.

○ d. Yes, but only if Organizational Unit depth does not exceed three levels.

Question 4.2

Digital's Asia region consists of a headquarters office in Hong Kong and branch offices in Tokyo, Beijing, Singapore, Seoul, and Bangkok. The Asian branches are tightly controlled by Hong Kong. The WAN links are currently 128Kbps ISDN circuits. Currently, each branch office is a Windows NT resource domain. How should the Asia region approach migration to Windows 2000?

○ a. Create an **asia.digital-is.com** domain as a child of the root **digital-is.com** domain. Turn the current branch office resource domains into Organizational Units within the Asia domain.

○ b. Create an **asia.digital-is.com** domain as a child of the root **digital-is.com** domain. Turn the current branch office resource domains into child domains off the Asia domain (for example, **tokyo.asia.digital-is.com**).

○ c. Create an **asia.digital-is.com** domain as a child of the root **digital-is.com** domain. Turn the current branch office resource domains into child domains off the root domain (for example, **tokyo. digital-is.com**).

○ d. Create an **asia.digital-is.com** domain as a child of the root **digital-is.com** domain. Create a child **branches.asia.digital-is.com** domain and convert the current branch office resource domains into OUs within the **branches.asia.digital-is.com** domain.

○ e. Create an OU structure in the **digital-is.com** domain for the Asia region and branches. Convert all Asia domains to OUs within the root domain.

Question 4.3

The Organizational Unit structure for the North America domain was designed for delegation of administration. A top-level OU has been created for each branch, and second-level OUs exist for the three major organizational departments: consulting, sales, and administration. However, this structure is not granular enough for managing the desktop and software distribution through Group Policy.

For example, managers in the administration area require certain applications and desktop features, but clerks should not have either.

What technique can Digital employ to solve this problem?

○ a. Use filtering by security group to control the application of Group Policy.

○ b. Domains must be created for each branch to provide this level of granularity.

○ c. Change the OU structure to segregate users by title rather than department.

○ d. Place all the clerks in the Users container.

Question 4.4

The Panama City branch office reports to the North America regional office. However, the WAN links travel from the Miami branch, through Bogota, Columbia to Panama City, so site links have been created to mirror the physical network. What options does the network services staff have to ensure that domain controllers in the Panama City office are updated? [Check all correct answers]

❑ a. Place a domain controller for North America in the Bogota office. Replication cannot cross a site where no domain controller exists for the domain.

❑ b. Create a site link bridge for the Miami-Bogota-Panama City links.

❑ c. Configure offline replication and email the adupdat.csv file to the branch. Use this file as input to the LDIF utility to update one of the Panama City domain controllers.

❑ d. The network services staff does not need to do anything.

Question 4.5

Can trust relationships be established between the Windows NT 3.51 servers in Asia and Windows 2000 servers in other domains?

○ a. Yes

○ b. No

Question 4.6

A portion of the North America Active Directory structure is shown in Figure 10.5. Based on this diagram, arrange the list of AD objects in the order in which Group Policy will be applied.

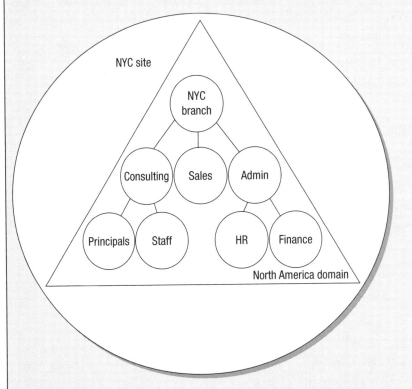

Figure 10.5   The New York Branch portion of the Digital North America domain.

AD objects:

New York branch OU

New York site

HR OU

North America domain

Admin OU

Question 4.7

Using Figure 10.5 again, the Director of Consulting Services has been given the ability to change passwords and update user information in the Consulting OU. Assuming default inheritance rules have not been modified, in which OUs can he change passwords?

○ a. Consulting

○ b. Consulting, Sales, and Admin

○ c. Consulting, Principals, and Staff

○ d. Consulting and NYC Branch

Question 4.8

Place the server roles shown in the second list under the appropriate sites from the first list. You may use a role more than once.

Sites:

New Orleans (world headquarters)

New York City (branch)

Buenos Aires (regional headquarters)

Casablanca (branch)

Server roles:

Schema Master

DNS server

Domain controller

Global Catalog Server

RID Master

PDC Emulator

Domain Naming Master

Case Study 5

Traviano Publishing

Traviano Publishing is the parent company for five different publishing houses. Each publishing house maintains its identity and, typically, a unique Web presence as well. Each publishing house reports to Traviano management, so the unique identity of each is for marketing purposes more than management. The Traviano companies, locations, and Internet domain names are summarized in Table 10.1.

LAN/Network Structure

Traviano and the subsidiary publishers all run Windows NT 4.0 networks, with NT at the desktop level as well. The only exception is for the sales force, which uses laptops running Windows 98.

The five subsidiaries operate independent NT 4 single-domain environments, as does Traviano. Currently, users needing access to more than one company must have a user account for each domain.

All offices use 10Mbps twisted-pair Ethernet, and this network infrastructure is considered adequate for current and future needs.

Proposed LAN/Network Structure

Traviano will upgrade the backbone in its corporate office to 100Mbps within the next six months. More importantly, the company is looking to upgrade to Windows 2000 as a way to better manage the corporate computing environment.

WAN Connectivity

The subsidiary publishers each have a T1 circuit to the corporate parent. These circuits are used for both voice and data, configured typically for 768Kbps data.

Proposed WAN Connectivity

No changes are contemplated.

Table 10.1 The Traviano companies, locations, and Internet domain names.		
Company	**Main Location**	**Domain Name**
Traviano Publishing	New York, NY	**traviano.com**
Pisces Press	Boston, MA	**piscespress.com**
Bard and Co.	London, England	**bard.co.uk**
Finn Books	St. Louis, MO	**finnbooks.com**
The Quill and Well	New York, NY	**quillnwellbooks.com**
Artisan Press	Hong Kong	**artisan.hk**

Directory Design Commentary

CIO: Although our network hardware infrastructure is sound, we have a poorly designed domain model with NT 4.0. We need to be able to manage access to resources better and eliminate extra user accounts.

VP, Marketing: We need to keep a strong brand identity for each of our subsidiaries. It is critical that each keeps its own Web site.

Security Administrator: The number of user accounts is becoming unwieldy. I am concerned that we are going to sacrifice security because we keep our publishers' systems separate.

Internet Positioning

Traviano and each subsidiary have registered Internet domain names. Refer to Table 10.1 for the names of each. In addition to Web and FTP servers, each company maintains an Exchange email server.

Future Internet Positioning

No changes in Internet strategy are forecast.

Question 5.1

What is the most appropriate Active Directory design for Traviano?

○ a. Six forests

○ b. One forest, six domains, with a disjoint namespace

○ c. One forest, six domains, with a contiguous namespace

○ d. One forest, one domain

Question 5.2

Traviano Publishing and The Quill and Well are located in the same building in New York. A consultant called in to assist with physical topology planning has stated that separate sites must be created for the two companies, even if they share the same forest. His statement was, "Since they do not share the same domain namespace, we must create separate sites for the two domains." Is the consultant's statement correct?

○ a. Yes

○ b. No

Question 5.3

How many domain trees will be needed in the Traviano forest?

○ a. 1

○ b. 3

○ c. 6

○ d. 7

Question 5.4

Will all the companies share a common Global Catalog and schema?

○ a. Yes

○ b. No

Question 5.5

Bard and Company has acquired an Active Directory-enabled application. During the installation process, the setup program aborted with the error message "Cannot update schema."

What is the probable cause for the error?

○ a. The schema can only be updated at the console of the Schema Operations Master.

○ b. The user account of the person performing the installation at Bard was not a member of the Schema Admins group.

○ c. The schema at Bard and Company is corrupt and must be restored from a backup tape.

○ d. You must be an Enterprise Admin to make changes to the schema, and the user performing the installation was not an Enterprise Admin.

○ e. The schema-replication topology has not been configured for the bard.co.uk domain.

Question 5.6

Which of the following servers must be found in the artisan.hk domain? [Check all correct answers]

❏ a. Domain Naming Master

❏ b. DNS server

❏ c. PDC Emulator

❏ d. RID Master

❏ e. Schema Master

Question 5.7

Traviano has just opened a San Francisco office. It is connected to the corporate WAN through Finn Books in St. Louis by a 384Kbps fractional T1 circuit. How can the domain controllers in San Francisco replicate with the domain controllers in New York? [Check the best two answers]

❏ a. Create a site link from St. Louis to San Francisco (STL-SFO). Replication will automatically be configured to bridge the STL-SFO link to the existing link from New York to St. Louis.

❏ b. Create a site link from St. Louis to San Francisco (STL-SFO). Create a site link bridge for the STL-SFO link and the existing link from New York to St. Louis.

❏ c. Place the San Francisco office subnet in the same site as the New York office.

❏ d. Reconfigure the T1 circuit to run from New York to San Francisco.

Question 5.8

For each of the domains shown in the first list, list the automatically created security groups that will be found on domain controllers in the domain. You may use a security group more than once, and not all security groups may be used.

Domains

traviano.com

piscespress.com

bard.co.uk

Security groups

Backup Operators

Schema Admins

Server Operators

Domain Admins

Power Users

Enterprise Admins

Case Study 6

DuBois Forest Products

Atlanta, Georgia-based DuBois Forest Products sells lumber and wood cabinetry across the United States. DuBois consists of four divisions: Timber and Mills, Lumber, Finished Products, and Woodworking Tools. Each division operates independently of the other, but the DuBois headquarters exercises strong central control of the Administrative, Human Resources, and Information Technology areas.

Two of the divisions, Finished Products and Woodworking Tools, are located in the headquarters complex. Timber and Mills and Lumber are located in the facility in Portland, Oregon.

LAN/Network Structure

DuBois runs a fairly homogeneous Windows NT 4.0 Server environment, except for two applications in the Timber and Mills division, which run on a Unix server, and DNS, which is also Unix-based, running BIND version 4.9.7.

DuBois uses a single-master domain model, with resource domains for each of the divisions.

Workstations are a mix of Windows 95, 98, and a few Windows NT 4.0 Workstation computers.

Proposed LAN/Network Structure

DuBois wants to upgrade to Windows 2000 throughout the organization. However, it cannot migrate the Unix applications and does not want to upgrade DNS at this time.

WAN Connectivity

The Portland and Atlanta offices connect via a VPN connection over 384Kbps SDSL. Rarely does utilization exceed 50 percent on this circuit.

Proposed WAN Connectivity

No changes are anticipated.

Directory Design Commentary

Director, Lumber Division: We need to be able to share information between divisions better. It is sometimes difficult to gain access to the information we need if it comes from a different division. This causes problems, especially for the Lumber Division, because we use the products from one division and send much of what we make to another division.

Director, Woodworking Tools: We operate independently of the other divisions. Unlike the other DuBois divisions, we do not receive our marching orders from the corporate office, and we have a great deal of leeway in making management decisions. For example, we will be setting up our own Web site shortly.

Manager, Administration: It is too hard to deal with the network. My staff in Portland can never get anyone to help them after lunch. Often, if a problem comes up when they are printing an important job, they have to let it wait until morning. The people in Atlanta have it better, but they still need to call the Help Desk every time something goes wring with a print job, and that wastes everyone's time.

Internet Positioning

DuBois uses email and has a Web site for the Woodworking Tools division. DuBois's registered Internet domain name is **duboiswood.com,** and it has registered an additional name of **duboistools.com** for the Woodworking Tools division's Web site. The Web servers are located in the Atlanta headquarters.

Future Internet Positioning

No changes in Internet strategy are forecast.

Question 6.1

Place the domains for DuBois Wood Products in the appropriate site. If a domain spans sites, place it under both sites.

Sites

   Atlanta

   Portland

Domains

   duboiswood.com

   duboistools.com

   tim-mill.duboiswood.com

   lumber.duboiswood.com

   prod.duboiswood.com

   tools.duboiswood.com

Question 6.2

Currently, DuBois is running BIND 4.9.7 DNS servers. What options does DuBois have with the existing DNS servers? [Check all correct answers]

❑ a. Use the BIND servers for external name resolution only.

❑ b. Use the BIND servers for internal and external resolution. BIND 4.9.7 supports both SRV records and dynamic update.

❑ c. Use the BIND servers for internal and external resolution. Delegate the _msdcs, _sites, _tcp, and _udp zones to Windows 2000 DNS servers.

❑ d. Upgrade the BIND servers to version 8.2.2 and use them for internal and external name resolution.

Question 6.3

What kind of organizational model is most appropriate for DuBois?

○ a. Geographical

○ b. Organizational

○ c. Functional

○ d. Hybrid

Question 6.4

Figure 10.6 shows the DuBois forest. Select the name of each DuBois division and place it on the appropriate domain or Organizational Unit.

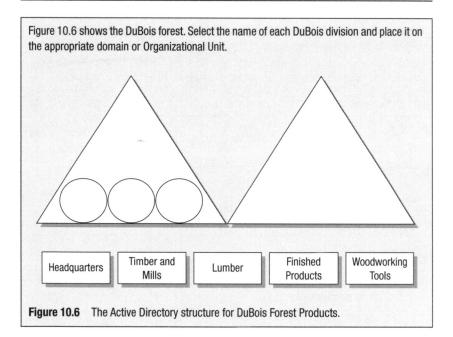

| Headquarters | Timber and Mills | Lumber | Finished Products | Woodworking Tools |

Figure 10.6   The Active Directory structure for DuBois Forest Products.

Question 6.5

How many PDC Emulator Operations Masters are located in the Atlanta site?

- ○ a. 0
- ○ b. 1
- ○ c. 2
- ○ d. 4

Question 6.6

The Telecommunications Manager has asked if it would be possible to use an SMTP Site Link between the Atlanta and Portland sites. Is this possible?

- ○ a. Yes
- ○ b. No

Question 6.7

The Director of Corporate IT would like a comparison of the various features of BIND to determine whether the existing Unix-based DNS servers should be upgraded, and he would also like to include Windows 2000 DNS in the comparison. Move the DNS features from the second list under each DNS server in the first list. You may use features more than once.

DNS servers

   BIND 4.8.3

   BIND 4.9.7

   BIND 8.2.2

   Windows 2000 DNS

DNS features

   SRV record support

   Dynamic update

   Secure dynamic update

   Active Directory integration

   Unicode hostnames

   Incremental zone transfers

Question 6.8

What Active Directory information will be replicated between domain controllers in the **duboiswood.com** and the **duboistools.com** domains? [Check all correct answers]

❑ a. Domain-naming context

❑ b. Schema-naming context

❑ c. Configuration-naming context

❑ d. Global Catalog

❑ e. Sysvol

Answer Key

For asterisked items, refer to the text in this chapter for the answer or completed diagram, as appropriate.

1.1	b, c	3.2	b	5.1	b
1.2	c	3.3	c	5.2	b
1.3	d	3.4	*	5.3	c
1.4	*	3.5	*	5.4	a
1.5	*	3.6	a	5.5	b
1.6	a	3.7	c	5.6	c, d
1.7	a, c	3.8	a, b, d, e	5.7	a, b
1.8	c	3.9	b	5.8	*
2.1	a	3.10	a, c	6.1	*
2.2	c	4.1	b	6.2	a, c
2.3	b	4.2	a	6.3	b
2.4	*	4.3	a	6.4	*
2.5	c	4.4	b, d	6.5	c
2.6	*	4.5	a	6.6	b
2.7	a	4.6	*	6.7	*
2.8	a, d	4.7	c	6.8	b, c, d
3.1	d	4.8	*		

Question 1.1

The correct answers are b and c. From the scenario, the need to delegate administration while retaining tight control over resources was expressed. Answer a is incorrect because it is a technical issue, not a business issue. Answer d is incorrect because the business users never discussed a schema-modification policy.

Question 1.2

The correct answer is c. Domain naming context replication requires RPC over IP, and it is not possible to reliably run RPC over a 56Kbps Frame Relay circuit. Without an upgrade, each field office would have to be a domain. Answer a is therefore incorrect. Answer b is incorrect because an upgrade of WAN connections to 256Kbps is not sufficient to change site boundaries. Answer d is incorrect because WAN link speeds have no impact on the number of cross-link trusts needed in a domain.

Question 1.3

The correct answer is d. Sites are areas of good network connectivity, and none of the WAN connections is robust enough to consider combining locations into one site. Therefore, answers a, b, and c are incorrect, because they would require combining one or more locations into a single site.

Question 1.4

The correct answer is as follows:

Alberta corporate headquarters

> Domain controller
>
> DNS server
>
> Schema Operations Master
>
> PDC Emulator
>
> Global Catalog Server

Johannesburg regional office

> Domain controller
>
> DNS server
>
> Global Catalog Server

Lima regional office

> Domain controller
>
> DNS server
>
> Global Catalog Server

Chile field office

> Domain controller
>
> DNS server
>
> Global Catalog Server

Note that the regional offices and the field offices are configured in a similar manner. Because the regional offices have more employees, there may be additional domain controllers deployed. Otherwise, the sound design practice of placing a DNS server and a Global Catalog Server at each site is maintained.

Question 1.5

The correct answer is shown in Figure 11.1.

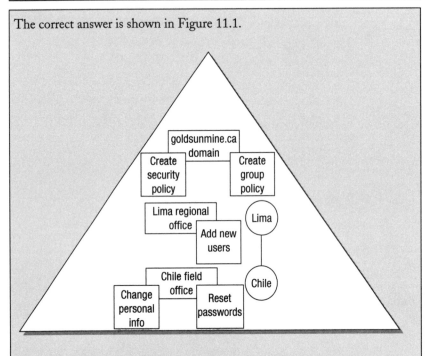

Figure 11.1 System administration tasks delegated.

Note that security tasks and Group Policy design are typically done at the domain level. The remainder of the tasks are assigned based on the scenario text.

Question 1.6

The correct answer is a. Golden Sun Mining has deployed Active Directory with two levels of geographical Organizational Units: regional offices and field offices. Therefore, answers b, c, and d cannot be correct.

Question 1.7

The correct answers are a and c. Because the external Web server needs to be accessed from the internal network, a host record needs to be added to the Windows 2000 DNS. Dynamic update should also be enabled, if only to simplify the task of adding additional domain controllers.

Answer b is incorrect because nothing in the business requirement calls for Unicode hostnames. It is better practice to permit only RFC-compliant hostnames.

Answer d is actually correct, but it is the "least correct" of the correct answers given. Sometimes, Microsoft will offer three answers that have varying degrees of "correctness," but ask for only two correct answers. In this case, you will need to select the most correct answers. Since Active Directory integration is the least important of the correct answers, it should not be selected.

Question 1.8

The correct answer is c. The Replicate Every variable, set to 180 minutes in the example, determines how often replication will occur. Answers a, b, and d are therefore incorrect.

Question 2.1

The correct answer is a. Madeleine Confectioners is the parent company, and its registered domain name is **madeleine.com**. Answer b is incorrect because Lone Star Sugars is the subsidiary company. Answers c and d are incorrect because neither are the registered domain name of Madeleine Confectioners.

Question 2.2

The correct answer is c. Lone Star Sugars will maintain its existing Internet identity, so the domain name of **lonestarsugar.com** will be retained. Answer a is completely incorrect because it would reflect a domain hierarchy where Lone Star is the parent company. Answer b is incorrect because it implies that Lone Star should be a child domain of the **madeleine.com** root, and that would run counter to the Active Directory design criteria specified. Answer d is incorrect because it is the domain name of Madeleine Confectioners. This answer would only be appropriate if Lone Star were to become an Organizational Unit within the Madeleine domain.

Question 2.3

The correct answer is b. The merged companies will share a single forest but maintain their individual DNS domain names, implying a disjoint namespace with two domain trees. Answer a is incorrect because two forests would make integration of the two companies' information more difficult. If Madeleine and Lone Star were to be operated completely independently of one another, two forests might be a better option, but this is not the case.

Answers c and d are incorrect because Madeleine and Lone Star will retain their domain names, thus requiring two trees in the forest.

Question 2.4

The correct answer is:

lonestarsugar.com

    PDC Emulator

    RID Master

    Infrastructure Master

madeleine.com

    PDC Emulator

    Schema Master

    RID Master

    Domain Naming Master

    Infrastructure Master

Note that the difference between the two domains is that the Madeleine domain is the forest root domain and therefore will be home to the forest-wide Operations Master servers.

Question 2.5

The correct answer is c. Using the rule of one Global Catalog Server per site, with Madeleine's Jacksonville home office, the Lone Star office and six sales offices, there will be eight sites. Therefore, answers a, b, and d are incorrect. Note that Madeleine is a small company, so there is little likelihood of needing an additional Global Catalog Server anywhere on the network.

Question 2.6

Refer to Figure 11.2 for the answer to Question 2.6.

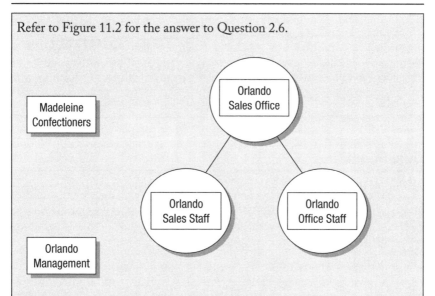

Figure 11.2   The OU structure for the Orlando sales office.

Note that the top-level OU is called Orlando Sales Office, not Orlando Management. Organizational Units should be structured as a hierarchy of objects to be managed, and within the Orlando sales office, only the sales staff and office staff require special handling.

Question 2.7

The correct answer is a. Printers are Active Directory objects that can be placed in an Organizational Unit for management purposes.

Question 2.8

The correct answers are a and d. Each site should have a Global Catalog Server and a DNS server. Answers b, c, and e are Domain Operations Masters, and only one will exist within a domain, regardless of the number of sites. Any of these Operations Masters could be moved to a sales office, but there is no reason to do so.

Question 3.1

The correct answer is d. BIND 8.2.2 works fine in a Windows 2000 environment, supporting both SRV records and dynamic update. Answer a is incorrect because there is no requirement for a specific vendor's DNS, just a feature set requirement. Answer b is incorrect because BIND 8.2.2 supports dynamic update, even from Windows 2000 client computers. Answer c is incorrect because, as of this writing, there is no BIND version 10.

Question 3.2

The correct answer is b. Sites are areas of good network connectivity, and the best site plan would create two sites for the home office (one for each building), and one site for each distribution center. Answer a is incorrect because 56Kbps Frame Relay is not adequate connectivity to create one site. Answer c is incorrect for the same reason. Finally, answer d is less correct than answer b. Although it would be possible to link the two San Francisco offices into one site, it would be better to split them at the T1 connection between buildings.

Question 3.3

The correct answer is c. Because SMTP is asynchronous, it ignores site link schedules, making answer d incorrect. Answers a and b are incorrect because RPC replication is extremely unreliable over 56Kbps connections.

Question 3.4

The correct answer is as follows:

Create an OU for each retail store.

Move all retail store employees into the appropriate OU.

Create a global group for the managers at each retail store and add the manager user accounts to these global groups.

Create a domain local group for each store and delegate approved administrative tasks to the members of the domain local group.

Add the store manager global group to the store administration domain local group membership.

Question 3.5

Refer to Figure 11.3 for the correct answer.

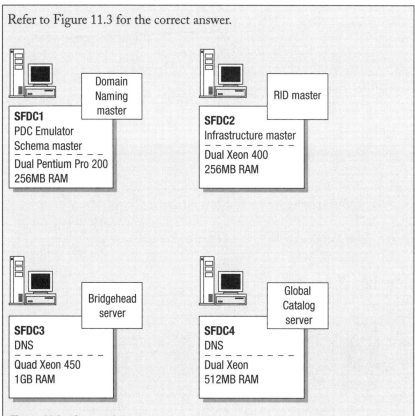

Figure 11.3 Server roles.

The Bridgehead Server role should always be placed on the server with the most processor and RAM, because it will be responsible for the compression and decompression of intersite replication traffic. Therefore, it was placed on SFDC3.

A Global Catalog Server cannot reside on the same computer as the Infrastructure Operations Master. A GC Server will require extra processor and RAM, so server SFDC4 was made Global Catalog Server.

The Domain Naming Master has possibly the lightest overhead of all operations masters, so the role was transferred to the oldest technology server, SFDC1.

The RID Master should be placed on a reliable server, so SFDC2 was the logical choice.

Question 3.6

The correct answer is a. Intrasite replication occurs within five minutes. Although this value can be changed by modifying the Registry, it is not wise to do so. Answer b is incorrect because 180 minutes is the default replication interval for intersite replication. Answers c and d are also incorrect because intrasite replication is not scheduled.

Question 3.7

The correct answer is c. There is no way currently to have separate schemas for two domains in the same forest. Answer a is incorrect because, additionally, there is no inheritance between domains. Answer b is incorrect because adding a domain tree to a forest does not create a separate schema. Answer d is incorrect because there can only be one Schema Operations Master in a forest.

Question 3.8

The correct answers are a, b, d, and e. Answers a, b, and d are standard domain planning practices. Answer e provides a backup in case of WAN link failure. Note that the KCC will use the least-cost route between sites, so a slower link with a higher cost can serve as a backup route.

Answer c is incorrect because there can be only one PDC emulator per domain.

Question 3.9

The correct answer is b. With an analog dial-up line, bandwidth is insufficient for the RPC replication of the domain naming context. Therefore, unless each retail store becomes a domain, which was not specified, it will not be possible to place a domain controller in each store.

Question 3.10

The correct answers are a and c. For answer a, domain local groups can contain global groups from any domain. Answer c will generate some additional Global Catalog replication traffic but will group store managers together in a single universal group, thus allowing for potentially easier administration.

Answer b is incorrect because global groups can only contain members from the same domain. Answer d is incorrect because although it would work to allow access to the sales data, it would generate a tremendous amount of Global Catalog replication traffic, which would be unacceptable over the slow 56Kbps Frame Relay circuits at Gramm.

Question 4.1

The correct answer is b. With Digital's decentralized management and strong regional office authority, regional domains are indicated. Answer a is incorrect because although it is technically possible to use a single-domain model, this solution is contraindicated by the business model. Answer c is incorrect because Sysvol replication uses RPC, which works fine over a full T1 connection. Finally, answer d is incorrect because it goes counter to the business requirements as well as contains false information about maximum OU level depth.

Question 4.2

The correct answer is a. Although the regional offices are autonomous, the branches are closely controlled. This implies regional domains and branch Organizational Units. Answers b, c, and d are incorrect because they all create one or more separate domains for the branch offices. Because domains are security boundaries, the ability to manage objects in another domain is very limited.

Finally, answer e is incorrect because it implies a single-domain model, which has already been rejected due to the autonomy of the regional offices.

Question 4.3

The correct answer is a. Filtering allows you to link multiple Group Policy Objects to a single OU but have only one execute for a given group of users. Answer b is therefore incorrect because there is no need to create additional domains. Answer c is incorrect because although it would work for Group Policy, it would ruin the administrative design. OUs should be structured for administration first and then for Group Policy. Finally, answer d does not really address the problem and would make it impossible to manage the clerks' desktops. The Users container cannot have Group Policy applied.

Question 4.4

The correct answers are b and d. Because site links are transitive by default, nothing needs to be done for replication to cross the two site links between Miami and Panama City. However, it is also possible to create a site link bridge, to give the KCC stronger "hints" about the path replication should take.

Answer a is incorrect, not because it would not work, but because of the reason. Replication can occur over multiple site links, even when an intermediate site has no domain controllers for the domain being replicated. Answer c is incorrect because there is currently no such thing as offline replication.

Question 4.5

The correct answer is a. The trust relationship will be an old-style NT one-way, nontransitive trust, however.

Question 4.6

The correct answer is:

> New York site
>
> North America domain
>
> New York branch OU
>
> Admin OU
>
> HR OU

Use the acronym SDOU (Site, Domain, Organizational Unit) to help you remember the order in which Group Policy is applied.

Question 4.7

The correct answer is c. The director can manage the OU where he was given permissions, and any child OUs, namely Principals and Staff. Answer a is incorrect because it does not account for inheritance. Answers b and d are incorrect because they specify OUs that are not children of the Consulting OU.

Question 4.8

The correct answer is:

New Orleans

Schema Master

DNS server

Domain controller

Global Catalog Server

RID Master

PDC Emulator

Domain Naming Master

New York City

DNS server

Domain controller

Global Catalog Server

Buenos Aires

DNS server

Domain controller

Global Catalog Server

RID Master

PDC Emulator

Casablanca

DNS server

Domain controller

Global Catalog Server

Question 5.1

The correct answer is b. Because Traviano and the subsidiaries all have distinct registered domain names but need to operate as a single company, the "single forest with disjoint namespace" strategy is best. Answer a is incorrect because six forests would be very difficult to manage. Answer c is incorrect because the subsidiary companies would lose their unique DNS domain names if a contiguous namespace were created off the **traviano.com** root. Answer d is incorrect for much the same reason, plus it ignores the business requirement of autonomy for the subsidiary publishers.

Question 5.2

The correct answer is b. Multiple domains can share the same site, just as a single domain can be spread over multiple sites.

Question 5.3

The correct answer is c. A separate domain tree will be created for each subsidiary, in addition to the Traviano domain tree. Note that all these domain trees will probably have only one domain, based on the business requirements stated in the scenario. Answers a, b, and d are incorrect for this reason.

Question 5.4

The correct answer is a. All domains in the same forest share a common Global Catalog and schema.

Question 5.5

The correct answer is b. A user must be a member of the Schema Admins group in order to update the schema. The Schema Admins group is defined only in the forest root domain, which in this case would be **traviano.com**.

Answer a is incorrect because updates can be performed from any computer in the network, as long as the security context is that of a Schema Admins user. Answer c is incorrect because there is no separate Bard and Company schema. Answer d is incorrect because Enterprise Admins membership will not allow an administrator to update the schema. Finally, answer e is incorrect because the schema-replication topology is configured automatically for the forest.

Question 5.6

The correct answers are c and d. A PDC Emulator and RID Master are mandatory Operations Masters for a domain, so they must always be present.

Answers a and e are incorrect because these are forest-wide Operations Master roles, which are typically found in the root domain of the forest.

Answer b is incorrect because a DNS server is not required in the domain, even though one would be highly recommended. The **artisan.hk** domain controllers could be pointed at DNS servers at another location, for example.

Question 5.7

The correct answers are a and b. Either approach will work correctly, although for answer a, make sure that the default setting for site link transitivity is still set.

Answer c is incorrect because even if the KCC could correctly calculate an intrasite replication topology, it is a very poor idea to create a single site across a 384Kbps WAN link. Answer d is incorrect as well. Although it would work, most companies would not appreciate the additional telecom expense, especially when the original approach works.

Question 5.8

The correct answer is as follows:

traviano.com

> Backup Operators
>
> Schema Admins
>
> Server Operators
>
> Domain Admins
>
> Enterprise Admins

piscespress.com

> Backup Operators
>
> Server Operators
>
> Domain Admins

bard.co.uk

> Backup Operators
>
> Server Operators
>
> Domain Admins

Question 6.1

The correct answer is as follows:

Atlanta

> **duboiswood.com**
>
> **duboistools.com**

Portland

> **duboiswood.com**

Note that no child domains are required in the DuBois forest.

Question 6.2

The correct answers are a and c. The existing BIND 4.9.7 servers can be used for external resolution only or can host the four Active Directory-specific zones but delegate them to Windows 2000 DNS servers (or any other DNS that supports dynamic update).

Answer b is incorrect because of the statement that BIND 4.9.7 supports dynamic update. Answer d is incorrect because the business requirements specifically state that DNS will not be upgraded at this time.

Question 6.3

The correct answer is b. DuBois clearly uses an organizational management structure. Therefore, answers a, c, and d are incorrect.

Question 6.4

The correct answer is shown in Figure 11.4.

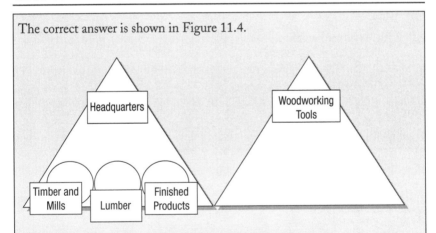

Figure 11.4   The Active Directory structure for DuBois Forest Products.

Because the Woodworking Tools division has a strong degree of autonomy, as well as its own registered DNS domain name, it belongs in a separate domain.

Question 6.5

The correct answer is c. Both the **duboiswood.com** and **duboistools.com** domains are in the Atlanta site, and the PDC Emulator Operations Master is a domain-wide role. Therefore, answers a, b, and d are incorrect.

Question 6.6

The correct answer is b. The **duboiswood.com** domain spans the Atlanta and Portland sites. The domain-naming context portion of Active Directory cannot replicate over SMTP. Sysvol replication also cannot be performed over an SMTP site link.

Question 6.7

The correct answer is as follows:

BIND 4.8.3

    No features

BIND 4.9.7

    SRV record support

BIND 8.2.2

    SRV record support

    Dynamic update

    Incremental zone transfer

Windows 2000 DNS

    SRV record support

    Dynamic update

    Secure dynamic update

    Active Directory integration

    Unicode hostnames

    Incremental zone transfers

Question 6.8

The correct answers are b, c, and d. The schema- and configuration-naming contexts are replicated to all domain controllers in a forest. The Global Catalog is replicated to all Global Catalog Servers in a forest. Answers a and e are incorrect because both the domain-naming context and Sysvol replication occur only between domain controllers in the same domain.

Glossary

administrative model

The administrative model implemented by a business basically determines who holds the decision-making authority and who is responsible for implementing decisions. The most common administrative models are centralized and decentralized.

blocking

Within Active Directory, blocking allows an administrator to modify the inheritance of a GPO so it is not passed on from parent container to child container.

bridgehead servers

The bridgehead servers are responsible for replicating information between sites. Once a bridgehead server receives updates, it is responsible for ensuring that changes are replicated to other domain controllers within the site. This optimizes interreplication because multiple connections do not have to be established across a slow link to send and receive updates.

contiguous namespace

The type of namespace created when a child object inherits a portion of its namespace from its parent domain.

delegation

The act of assigning administrative duties and responsibilities to other individuals and groups within a business. Delegation eliminates the need to have one user or group responsible for all network administration.

Delegation of Control Wizard

A wizard built into Windows 2000 that walks you through the process of assigning a user or group administrative privileges over a container in the Active Directory hierarchy.

disjoint namespace

The type of namespace created when a child object's namespace remains independent from that of its parent domain.

domain

A domain is the main administrative unit within Active Directory. It's a collection of computer, user, and group accounts that are maintained by the domain administrator and share a common directory database.

domain controllers

A computer running Windows 2000 Server that is responsible for authenticating user logons and managing access to resources on the network.

domain local group

A domain local group is used to assign users permissions to resources within the domain in which the group is created. This type of group can contain user accounts, universal groups, and global groups from any domain in the forest.

DNS servers

DNS servers are name servers responsible for a portion of the domain namespace. Client resolvers contact the DNS servers to map domain names to IP addresses (known as *name resolution*).

external trust

An external trust is a one-way explicit trust that can be established between two domains in different forests. This type of trust is one way, so if A trusts B, B does not trust A. Also, an external trust only applies to the domains specified.

filtering

Using filtering, an administrator can limit the scope of a GPO and exclude certain groups from being affected by the policy. Those groups specified will be exempt from the settings in the GPO.

forest

A forest is a group of Windows 2000 domains that share a common schema, configuration container, and Global Catalog. Two-way transitive trusts are automatically established between domains in the same forest.

Global Catalog Server

The Global Catalog Server is a Windows 2000 domain controller that maintains a copy of the Global Catalog for the entire forest. The Global Catalog contains a replica of every object within Active Directory and certain attributes pertaining to each one.

global group

A global group is used to assign users permission to resources throughout the forest. This type of group can contain user accounts from the domain in which the group is created.

Group Policy Object (GPO)

A GPO is simply a collection of Group Policy settings. It's basically a container for the policy settings specified in the Group Policy snap-in.

inheritance

With inheritance, permissions that have been set on a parent object can be passed onto any child objects. This makes administration simpler in that permissions may only need to be set once on the parent object.

inheritance modification
Inheritance modification allows an administrator to change how a GPO is inherited from parent to child. Modifying inheritance involves using either blocking or override.

intersite replication
The replication traffic that occurs between two or more Active Directory sites.

intrasite replication
The replication traffic that occurs within a single Active Directory site.

Kerberos
Kerberos version 5 is an industry-standard authentication protocol supported by Windows 2000. The Kerberos protocol is responsible for the authentication of users between domains within a forest

Key Distribution Center (KDC)
The KDC is a component of the Kerberos version 5 protocol. There is a KDC in each Active Directory domain responsible for authenticating users and for issuing "session tickets" so users can identify themselves to other KDCs in the forest.

local groups
Local groups are found on computers running Windows 2000 Professional and member servers. This type of group is used to assign permissions to resources on the local computer where the group resides.

Local Group Policy Object
Every computer running Windows 2000 has a local GPO that is stored on the local computer. This GPO is processed first, and nonlocal GPOs overwrite its settings.

mixed mode
During a migration to Windows 2000 from Windows NT, the Windows 2000 domain is initially created in mixed mode. While in mixed mode, the Windows 2000 domain controller with the PDC Emulator Operations Master role acts as a PDC for Windows NT BDCs. Certain features of Windows 2000 are not available in mixed mode, such as universal groups and group nesting. Also, Active Directory should not contain more than 40,000 objects if Windows NT BDCs still exist in the domain.

native mode
Once all domain controllers have been upgraded to Windows 2000, native mode can be enabled, which will allow businesses to take full advantage of Active Directory.

Organizational Unit (OU)
An Organizational Unit is a logical container object used to organize objects within a domain. OUs can contain users, groups, computers, printers, data, and other OUs.

Operation Masters
Operation Masters are those domain controllers that have been assigned responsibility over updates that cannot be replicated using a multimaster model. The Operation Masters' roles include PDC Emulator, Schema Master, Domain Naming

Master, Relative Identifier Master, and Infrastructure Master.

override

Setting the override option ensures that a GPO at a lower level in the hierarchy does not overwrite the settings of a GPO at a higher level in the hierarchy.

Remote Procedure Call (RPC)

RPC is the default transport used for intersite replication. It is synchronous, which means there must be a direct connection with the remote computer before any information is transferred. RPCs can be used for intersite and intrasite replication.

schema

The schema maintains a list of all object classes that can be stored within Active Directory and the attributes associated with each one. The schema also defines the required syntax for each attribute.

security group

Security groups in Windows 2000 are used to assign permissions to grant users access to network resources.

shortcut trust

A shortcut trust is a two-way transitive trust that must be explicitly created between two domains in the same forest. Shortcut trusts can be defined to shorten the trust path between two domains.

Simple Mail Transfer Protocol (SMTP)

SMTP can only be used for replication between sites; it cannot be used

for intrasite replication. It is asynchronous and ignores the schedules set by administrators on site links. Information is transferred in the form of email messages. If the remote server is not available, the information can be stored and forwarded when the server becomes available.

site

A site is a group of IP subnets connected by high-speed reliable links. Sites are created to control the replication process across slow links. Creating sites allows an administrator to take advantage of the physical network and optimize replication and Active Directory access.

site link

A site link is the logical connection between two sites that allows the replication of information to occur. Creating site links enables administrators to control when replication between the sites occurs by setting a schedule on the site link and specifying a time when the site link is available.

site link bridges

In a network that is not fully routable, site link bridges can be created to establish a replication path. Creating site link bridges eliminates the need to have site links defined between every site.

transitive trust

The logical link between domains within the same forest. Within an Active Directory forest, transitive trusts are automatically established between parent domains and child domains, as well as between forest root domains and any new trees within the forest. Transitive trusts are two-way and establish a trust path within an Active Directory forest.

transport

A transport defines the method that will be used to transfer information between sites. The two choices within Windows 2000 are SMTP and RPC.

trust

A trust is the logical link between two domains that allows for passthrough authentication. A user from a trusted domain is granted access to resources in the trusting domain.

universal group

This type of security group is used to grant users access to resources throughout the forest. Universal groups can contain user accounts, global groups, and universal groups from any domain within the forest.

Index